Prisons and Patriots

IN THE SERIES *Asian American History and Culture,*
edited by Sucheng Chan, David Palumbo-Liu, Michael Omi,
K. Scott Wong, and Linda Trinh Võ

ALSO IN THIS SERIES:

Prisons and Patriots

Japanese American Wartime Citizenship, Civil Disobedience, and Historical Memory

CHERSTIN M. LYON

TEMPLE UNIVERSITY PRESS
Philadelphia

TEMPLE UNIVERSITY PRESS
Philadelphia, Pennsylvania 19122
www.temple.edu/tempress

Library of Congress Cataloging-in-Publication Data

Lyon, Cherstin M., 1971– .
  Prisons and patriots : Japanese American wartime citizenship, civil disobedience, and
historical memory / Cherstin M. Lyon.
    p.   cm. — (Asian American history and culture)
  Includes bibliographical references and index.
  ISBN 978-1-4399-0186-1 (cloth : alk. paper)
  ISBN 978-1-4399-0187-8 (pbk. : alk. paper)
  ISBN 978-1-4399-0188-5 (e-book)
  1. Japanese Americans—Civil rights—History—20th century.   2. Japanese Americans—
Evacuation and relocation, 1942–1945.   3. Japanese Americans—Legal status, laws, etc.—
History—20th century.   4. World War, 1939–1945—Draft resisters—United States.
5. Civil disobedience—United States—History—20th century.   6. Prisoners—Arizona—
Tucson—Biography.   7. Hirabayashi, Gordon K.   I. Title.

  D769.8.A6L96 2012
  940.53'73089956—dc22   2011015299

Printed in the United States of America

021012P

CONTENTS

၏ ၏ ၏

ACKNOWLEDGMENTS

I AM INDEBTED to those who have influenced this project, commented on previous drafts, and given advice and feedback on my research through formal and informal conversations. Frank Abe, Jo Arlow, Denise Bates, Jane Beckwith, Kathren Brown, Frank Chin, Frank Emi, Art Hansen, Lily Havey, William Hohri, Takashi Hoshizaki, Reeve Huston, Tiffany Jones, Tetsuden Kashima, Steve Koga, Dan Kubo, Katherine Morrissey, Eric Muller, Martha Nakagawa, Gary Okihiro, Greg Robinson, Laura Shelton, Kenji Taguma, David Wilson, and Meghan Winchell have all provided valuable feedback over the years. Yoriko Takasaku and Keiko Kakihara provided valuable assistance acquiring and translating (respectively) Japanese citizenship laws (the original Imperial Ordinance and subsequent Amendments). I owe special thanks to Karen Anderson, Elliot Barkan, Roger Daniels, Sarah Deutsch, Art Hansen, Joyce Hanson, Tiffany Jones, Ted Lyon, Jack Marietta, and Meghan Winchell for reading and commenting on drafts of the manuscript. Cheryl Lyon read and painstakingly edited an early draft of the entire manuscript, making the book more readable as a result.

Mary Farrell invited me to conduct oral histories with Gordon Hirabayashi and the Tucsonians when they first returned to Tucson in 1999. She has continued to champion this project as it has evolved over the years. Nicole Branton paired with me to conduct follow-up interviews and was a stellar project partner. Peggy Pascoe taught me how to become a historian, Matthew Dennis encouraged me to think more critically about historical memory, and Carlos Aguirre directed my attention to the history of crime and prisons. Jack Marietta gave generously of his time, edited several early drafts, and helped me become a better writer. Karen Anderson taught me to think more critically about race, gender, privilege, and propaganda and provided encouragement at some of the most crucial junctures of this project's development. Sarah Deutsch brought the topic to my attention, provided extraordinary support to finish the initial manuscript, and has continued to offer her expert advice and encouragement. I thank you all.

This project was funded through generous assistance from the following grants and institutions: the California Civil Liberties Public Education Program (CCLPEP), the P.E.O. Fellowship, the History Department and Graduate College at the University of Arizona, the Southwest Oral History Association, the Coronado National Forest, a Phi Alpha Theta Doctoral Scholarship, and the Charles Redd Center for Western Studies. The History Department at Utah Valley University provided me with an intellectual home through the final research phase of the project. California State University, San Bernardino (CSUSB), has been especially supportive, providing grants from the university, the College of Social and Behavioral Sciences, the Teaching Resource Center, and the History Department. My colleagues in the History Department and in the College of Social and Behavioral Sciences at CSUSB have provided a friendly and intellectually stimulating environment in which to teach, write, and work. Graduate research assistants Oceana Collins and Tom Hagen provided excellent support through the revision and editing process. My students at CSUSB have challenged me, engaged in discussions with me, and helped me think more deeply about citizenship and civil disobedience.

I would not have been able to write this book without the assistance of librarians and archivists across the country, including archivists at seven branches of the National Archives who guided me through the collections, even pointing out lesser-used record groups related to my research. Special Collections librarians and archivists made my research efforts more efficient and effective. Special thanks go to Jeff Burton, Mary Farrell, the Coronado National Forest, Martha Nakagawa, the National Archives, the White River Valley Museum, the Wing Luke Museum of the Asian Pacific American Experience, and Ken Yoshida for providing images for the manuscript.

This book would not have been possible without the individuals who shared their lives and their stories with me over the years, the individuals whose lives this book discusses. I thank Dan and Chris Kubo for opening up their home to me and my family, for granting me access to Yoshi Kubo's collection, and for answering endless questions about his life. Tucsonians Ken and Kay Yoshida, Susumu Yenokida, and Joe and Tee Norikane also opened up their homes to me, allowed me to interview them more than once, and made the research process a personally rewarding experience. Tucsonians Hideo Takeuchi, Noboru Taguma, and Harry Yoshikawa, as well as Frank Chin, Frank Emi, Gordon Hirabayashi, Takahashi Hoshizaki, Yosh Kuromiya, Martha Nakagawa, and Kenji Taguma, gave generously of their time in interviews and informal conversations.

I am grateful for the comments and suggestions provided by Scott Wong and the anonymous reader for Temple University Press. Their recommendations for revision made this a better book. I also thank the Temple University

Press board of directors and the *Asian American History and Culture* series edi-tors for publishing this book. Janet Francendese has been a model of patience, good humor, and professionalism in guiding the book through the publication process. Amanda Steele provided timely assistance in getting the images and permissions in order. I thank the editing and production staff—particularly Joan Vidal, David Wilson, Heather Wilcox, and Lynne Frost—for their pro-fessional expertise. I am especially grateful to Lynne Frost for her painstaking editorial assistance in the later stages of production. Any errors that remain, of course, are my own.

Finally, I thank my children, Forrest and Savannah, and my husband, Tom, for doing without me during the endless hours I have spent on this project. Their support made this work possible.

A NOTE ON TERMINOLOGY

cᴑᴐ ᴑᴐ

HE JAPANESE AMERICAN EXPERIENCE during World War II had a wide range of constitutional and legal repercussions, in part because the treatment of Japanese Americans was shrouded in euphemism. The words used to describe federal policies minimized the real impact these policies had on people and created lasting complications for those who tried to discuss the unconstitutionality of "evacuation" and "relocation." Scholars still grapple with the most appropriate terminology for these policies. For this study, therefore, I use a wide range of terminology, depending on the specific topic at hand, selecting those terms that best fit my interpretation of events. Because the terms used in this study are diverse, some of the choices I have made warrant specific explanation.

First are the commonly accepted terms used to describe generations of Japanese Americans and ways of identifying the entire group regardless of generation or citizenship. "Nisei" is a Japanese term that describes the second generation, or specifically the American-born children of Japanese immigrants. The first generation is called "Issei," the third generation "Sansei," and the fourth generation "Yonsei." "Nikkei" is a Japanese word for all Japanese Americans and does not differentiate between Japanese-born and U.S.-born persons of Japanese ancestry. "Kibei" refers to U.S.-born Japanese Americans whose parents sent them to Japan for their education. Finally, when referring to the entire group, I have left "Japanese American" unhyphenated to emphasize that ethnic Americans are not partial Americans. Scholars argue that hyphenating such terms as "Japanese-American" implies that the individual is half of each nationality and wholly nothing. Leaving out the hyphen promotes the idea that ethnic Americans choose for themselves elements of more than one culture to create their own unique identities.[1]

Even though popular usage continues to refer to the ten War Relocation Authority (WRA) centers as "internment camps" and the wartime treatment of

Japanese Americans as "internment," the term is appropriate for only a very specific legal category of confinement. When taking into custody enemy aliens or individuals suspected of specific and documented threats, the Department of Justice interned those individuals in federally regulated facilities. Some Japanese Americans, as well as German and Italian nationals, were legally interned in Department of Justice centers during the war. These individuals were interned because they were on a list of individuals identified as maintaining connections with enemy nations that would likely create a conflict of interest during wartime. The number of Japanese Americans "interned" was small compared with the total number of individuals forced into federal custody during the war.

The federal government never used the term "internment" to describe the confinement of the majority of Japanese Americans. A government propaganda newsreel that explained the "relocation" of Japanese Americans said, "They are not prisoners; they are not internees. They are merely dislocated people, the unwounded casualties of war."[2] The War Relocation Authority called its camps "relocation centers" to make it appear that the population had merely been moved from one place to another. This terminology is problematic because it is passive and extremely benign. It does not indicate the financial cost, the heart-wrenching personal losses, or the involuntary nature of the program. According to WRA terminology, individuals were evacuated from a military zone for their own safety and relocated to centers while they awaited a more permanent form of resettlement outside the temporary camps. This terminology denied all culpability and cloaked the involuntary nature of the program in euphemisms that did not accurately describe the legal condition of the "evacuees." Instead, scholars now prefer such terms as "forced removal," "exclusion," "confinement," "incarceration," and "detention" rather than "evacuation" and "relocation."[3]

Even during the war, people outside the WRA used alternative language to describe the treatment of Japanese Americans. President Franklin Roosevelt called the WRA centers "concentration camps." This term is not generally used today because of its close association with the death camps of Nazi Germany. "Internment" became the most popularly used term, but it is used in this study only when conveying the words of others and is enclosed in quotation marks to make it clear that this legal form of confinement should not be confused with the unconstitutional manner in which most Japanese Americans were held.

In recent years, scholars have experimented with words that emphasize the involuntary nature of Japanese American exclusion and confinement. These terms sometimes blur the lines between formal prisons and the civilian "relocation" centers. The terms "detained" and "detainee" are useful, because they make it clear that individuals were held against their will. Some argue that these words are too benign, pointing out that "detention" is a punishment for wayward schoolchildren. I disagree, as "detention center" is an accepted synonym for jail. "Detain," "detention," and even "detainment centers" were all used during the war by various government agencies, including the WRA, the solicitor general, the War Department, and the Office of Naval Intelligence. I prefer to use "detainees" when writing about Japanese Americans in the camps, because the word emphasizes the lack of freedom, the sense of limbo, and the lack of legal clarity that they experienced, not knowing how long they would be forced to live in the camps. "Incarceration" and "confinement" are also useful words that appear throughout the book. Incarceration is most often used in reference to jails and prisons, but the word is also used to refer to accused and convicted persons. Japanese Americans were accused of being a threat to national security and were "incarcerated" in camps that looked and acted like some strange hybrid of concentration camps and prisons, even though they lacked formal designation as prisons. "Confinement" avoids this direct reference to the prison system, but it is a fairly soft word, as sometimes the sick or infirm are confined. For the purposes of this study, I chose words that highlighted the similarities between the WRA camps and prisons for interpretive reasons. The areas in which the conditions and the administrative philosophies of prisons and the "relocation" centers overlapped provide analytic opportunities that help explain more clearly the administrative and ideological context for the wartime treatment of Japanese Americans.

Some argue that the formal names of the WRA camps should be used for historical accuracy; however, in deference to the historical memories of the Japanese Americans interviewed for this project, I chose to use the informal names they used to identify the three camps where they were detained. The Central Utah camp is commonly known as Topaz; the Granada camp (in southeastern Colorado) is commonly called Amache; and the Colorado River camp (in southwestern Arizona) is also known as Poston. Furthermore, there are two official names for the prison near Tucson, Arizona, where the Tucsonians and Gordon Hirabayashi served time. The Federal Bureau of Prisons called this facility the Tucson Federal Prison Camp, and the National Park Service now refers to the former prison as the Catalina Federal Honor Camp. In this volume I use the Bureau of Prisons name because it most closely aligns with the terminology used by the Tucsonians and Gordon Hirabayashi.

Prisons and Patriots

"A Footstep in the Sand of Time"

ᗑᕤᘒ

L ATE ONE EVENING, early in May 2002, I sat in a hotel room with a colleague, historical archaeologist Nicole Branton, after a very long day of traveling and conducting interviews. Together, we read from the wartime diary that Joe Norikane had so generously lent to us. Norikane stood defiantly against the government's attempts to force Nisei (Americans of Japanese ancestry) to accept partial, second-class citizenship during World War II when he resisted the draft, ultimately becoming part of a group of resisters who called themselves "the Tucsonians." We read the diary he kept from 1943 through 1944, believing that its pages would reveal the idealistic mindset of a young man preparing to take on his government in a courageous act of civil disobedience. What we found instead was a book chronicling Norikane's doubt and insecurity not about the war, the draft, or his civil rights, but about a girl. We read page after page about his social life, sports, and a whole lot of dancing.[1]

When we met with Norikane the next day to record an interview, he apologized for not having written about more important issues in his diary. We assured him that our impression was quite the opposite, because he wrote about the most important issue he was personally facing as a young man. He recorded the life of a young man coming of age, and he focused on what might be seen as the typical obsessions of a young man despite the fact that he was living behind barbed wire. What he wrote was far more important and eye opening than standard treatises on civil rights or the injustices of the draft ever could have been.[2]

Norikane, like the rest of the Nisei draft resisters of World War II, did not resist in a vacuum. His decision to challenge the government's restoration of his military obligations—after the assault on his citizenship rights that had come with the forced removal and incarceration of Japanese Americans—was shaped by the totality of his life experiences. His resistance represented a nuanced choice to defend a personal definition of his citizenship rights that stood in direct conflict with the state's understanding of his obligations. In the heat of the draft crisis of 1944, young Nisei men would either be called patriots for obeying the draft law despite their lack of citizenship rights or be accused of disloyalty, cowardice, and even sedition after being sent to prison for civil disobedience and noncompliance. Norikane chose prison, but he did so for complex reasons. He was devoted to the country of his birth, loyal to his family obligations, and insistent that the rights and the obligations of citizenship should remain in balance.

As Norikane sat down to be interviewed about his life and his resistance, he recalled that when he was in jail with some of the other resisters from the camp they all called "Amache"—one of ten government detention centers built to hold Japanese Americans after their forced removal from the West Coast and lower third of Arizona—none of them believed that they would get fair hearings or that their struggle for civil rights would be remembered. For decades they were forgotten, but Norikane always hoped that the stand he took in defense of his constitutional rights during the war might someday be recognized. If he left "a footstep in the sand of time," Norikane said, "somebody might look back on what was going on during the war and get curious."[3] He hoped historians and students might preserve the memory of his wartime stand for civil rights and, someday, finally understand why he went to prison during World War II for resisting the draft even though in his heart he remained a patriot and a loyal citizen. He stood against the draft not as a coward or a draft dodger but as a man who believed that the Constitution should be color-blind and should protect all Americans equally and without prejudice. Yet like others who resisted the draft, he had more reasons for his civil disobedience. As the eldest son in his family, he refused to risk death on the battlefield, which would mean leaving his aging parents without any means of support. He was disillusioned by his wartime treatment as an enemy alien when he had been taught his whole life that he was 100 percent American.

By the time Norikane died in the spring of 2003, he had left several footsteps in the sand of time. This book is an attempt to understand those footsteps and the context in which they were created, but not just in the simplistic terms of prisons and patriots that seemed to confine the government's definitions of his wartime choices. Between the extreme polarities of the prisons built to rehabilitate criminals and the battlefields on which patriots risked their lives to prove their loyalty lay a vast terrain in which real individuals negotiated their own definitions of citizenship. The gulf that divides prisons from patriots contains the history of Norikane, his friends the Tucsonians, and Gordon Hirabayashi, a man whom they admired very much.

HISTORIC CONTEXT

When the world went to war for the second time, many Americans fought their own wars at home. Americans, after all, were fighting around the globe in defense of democracy and freedom. But what did this mean when democracy and freedom were pushed to their limits within the United States? One group of Americans confronted this question in dramatic fashion. They called themselves the Tucsonians.

The Tucsonians' early lives epitomized the Nisei, or second-generation Japanese American, experience. They were born in America during the 1920s to parents who had immigrated to the United States from Japan. They were citizens of the United States by birth, born to parents forbidden from U.S. citizenship by racially restrictive laws. They attended public schools, studied American history, and sometimes enrolled in Japanese-language schools. They grew up in a world that combined elements of their parents' Japanese cultural traditions with American culture and history. They learned in American public schools that their citizenship guaranteed them equality and freedom as protected by the U.S. Constitution. But it was clear that race prejudice sometimes prevented them from enjoying full social equality.

This generation of Nisei found it hard to believe that political events beyond their control would jeopardize the one thing they believed was immutable: their citizenship. Before the war, many Nisei teens and young adults were, by their own admission, naively confident, even in the face of overwhelming race prejudice, that their citizenship alone had the power to make them 100 percent American. But in the context of war, their citizenship provided few protections. Wartime laws and government policies forced their removal from the West Coast and confined this dislocated population of Japanese Americans in War Relocation Authority (WRA) camps, places most regarded as a kind of prison, without due process of law. Other laws reclassified Nisei into ambiguous categories ranging from "non-aliens" to "enemy aliens" without any real change in their citizenship status. These wartime laws and policies forced all Japanese Americans to make painful decisions regarding how they would respond to the unprecedented suspension of their rights as a group and as individuals.

Although Japanese Americans had most of their rights taken away during World War II, they were not immune from state demands that they obey the law, peacefully cooperate with their own removal and incarceration, and two years into the war, accept the draft as a restoration of their "right" to serve in the military. In petitions, letters, and face-to-face negotiations with government representatives, Japanese Americans insisted that the rights and obligations of citizenship must remain in balance. The government could not restore military service obligations without first restoring rights to due process and to freedom of movement. Additionally, some believed they should be allowed to return to their farms and contribute to the war effort by producing food for the nation instead of being forced into military service as their only avenue of performing the duties of wartime citizenship. But the wartime state conflated rights with responsibilities and treated this racial minority group as an exception. Like a meat cleaver swiftly separating flesh from bone, the state divided Japanese American rights and obligations, promising that, as patriot soldiers,

Japanese Americans would be rewarded for military service with a restoration of their citizenship rights at some point in the future, yet threatening prison for anyone who refused to cooperate. Each individual had to face this challenge in his own way. And he did so under the watchful eyes of friends and family, neighbors and community leaders, many of whom believed that the way these young men responded to the draft would determine the postwar future of all Japanese Americans in the United States. It was a terrible burden for a young man to bear. No decision was easy.

This book focuses on the decisions made by one group—the group that began calling themselves the Tucsonians, because members had one thing in common: All ended up in the same federal prison near Tucson, Arizona, as punishment for their civil disobedience. Each decided to refuse the draft for his own reasons, and no two decisions were exactly the same. The friendships they developed in prison gave the group its name and sustained the men through repeated accusations during the war and for years afterward that they were disloyal cowards, not principled resisters. In their hearts, they knew differently. This stand was not a matter of simple loyalty or disloyalty. Fifty-five years after the war, the Japanese American Citizens League (JACL), the same organization that had ostracized them during the war and for decades that followed, recognized them as "resisters of conscience."

The Tucsonians shared much in common with a well-known resister, Gordon Hirabayashi. Based on his own understanding of citizenship rights and the Constitution, Hirabayashi refused to obey laws that he felt were unconstitutional and racially biased. His decision to resist was based on a complex personal concept of justice that also included his views on pacifism, Christianity (including his more recent identity as a Quaker), and the natural rights of man. But his resistance did not end there. In 1944, much like Norikane and the other Tucsonians, he refused to cooperate with the Selective Service and chose prison over compliance with a system that discriminated against him on the basis of race and violated his pacifist Quaker ideals.

Initially, Hirabayashi was, perhaps, more naive than the Tucsonians. In the early summer of 1942, the first year of the war, he knew the lower courts might not give him a fair hearing on his acts of resistance, but he had faith that the Supreme Court would rule that the racially based laws he had refused to obey were unconstitutional, and he believed that his test case would help clarify the status of all Nisei. But in the context of total war and racist assumptions about Japanese ancestry and national loyalty, the Supreme Court did not rule in his favor and instead unanimously upheld the military's right to restrict the rights of citizens along racial lines in an effort to prevent an unidentified, imagined disloyal few from committing future acts of sabotage. The courts upheld the War Department's decision to profile a group racially and to detain members before a single individual within the group had committed a crime. Japanese Americans were to be treated as if they were guilty until proven innocent. Using the war to justify extralegal measures to identify, to arrest, and to confine potential enemies, the War Department convinced Congress and President Roosevelt that its actions should not be tested according to normal civil law. Hirabayashi disagreed, and he felt that if he could not win a constitutional victory for all Japanese Americans, he would at least win a moral victory for himself through noncompliance.

The Tucsonians had the benefit of watching events unfold over the first two years of the war as they were forced to leave their homes and endure months in the filthy and overcrowded temporary detention centers the government euphemistically called "assembly centers," only to end up in concentration camps equally inappropriately designated "relocation centers" for what many assumed would be the duration of the war. By the time the Tucsonians stood before the judge for their resistance to the draft, most admitted they did not believe they would get fair hearings, and few were under any illusion that their cases would have any broad-based impact on Nisei rights. All they had on their side was their own commitment to their consciences and their insistence that a person's citizenship rights could not be divorced from his obligations at the whim of a wartime militarized state. Hirabayashi and the Tucsonians all fought what they believed were unjust laws in the same classic way. In resisting an unjust law, they had committed acts of civil disobedience and thus joined a long list of Americans who had faced the state as individuals and enjoyed the protections that the Constitution afforded them as dissenters. But alongside the relatively simple story of basic constitutional rights lay an even larger story of wartime citizenship—a story that involved a surprisingly complex web of reasons for wartime resistance, including obligations to family, religion, the natural rights of man, dual citizenship, and the belief that serving in the military was not the only way young men could perform their wartime duties as citizens. Some Tucsonians were willing to contribute to the war effort, but held out for the right to do so as independent citizen farmers rather than as soldiers in segregated units.

The Tucsonians and Hirabayashi were never incarcerated together, but they did serve time in the same federal prison camp in Tucson, and their periods of imprisonment there were separated by only a year. As the Tucsonians were being sent to Tucson for resisting the draft in 1944, Hirabayashi was sent to yet another federal penitentiary, McNeil Island in Washington State, for his own draft resistance. Their lives paralleled each others' during the remainder of the war and intersected once again fifty-five years later, when all of them were invited back to Tucson for a ceremony to rename the former site of the Tucson Federal Prison Camp as the Gordon Hirabayashi Recreation Site.

A CITIZEN'S DILEMMA

Visitors who stop at the Gordon Hirabayashi Recreation Site today can learn about the prison and about the prisoners who built the scenic highway that carries tourists from the saguaro desert valley floor up to the pine-covered and

Ribbon cutting, Gordon Hirabayashi Recreation Site naming ceremony, November 1999, Coronado National Forest, Tucson, Arizona. *Left to right:* Tucsonians Joe Norikane, Hideo Takeuchi, and Ken Yoshida; Coronado National Forest Supervisor John McGee; Gordon Hirabayashi; Congressman Jim Kolbe; Tucsonian Harry Yoshikawa; Heart Mountain resister Takashi Hoshizaki; Tucsonian Noboru Taguma; and Heart Mountain resister Yosh Kuromiya. *(Courtesy of Coronado National Forest.)*

sometimes snow-capped peak of Mt. Lemmon. This is a rugged and spectacular highway, yet few who drive on it stop to think about who built the road. But drivers who pull off the highway at Prison Camp Road learn that some of the prisoners sentenced to labor on the road faced what the interpretive kiosk calls "A Citizen's Dilemma." As they read the text on the kiosk, visitors are asked to consider the implications of this dilemma. "The resisters did not object to the draft," tourists learn, "but hoped that by defying the draft they would clarify their citizenship status." Some may ask, "If they were to share the rights and duties of citizens, why did the government forcibly incarcerate them and their families?" Good question. Others may think, "If their loyalty was in question, why were they being drafted?" Another good question. As visitors consider this dilemma and continue reading the kiosk, they learn about the context of Japanese American "relocation" during World War II and about some of the reasons why a prison without walls or fences was built on a mountain. They learn about Gordon Hirabayashi and the Tucsonians and about the other prisoners who helped build the highway. And they learn about the sacrifices that some Nisei made as members of segregated combat units in an effort to earn back their rights of citizenship.[4]

Few individuals ever face direct challenges to their citizenship in the way that Japanese Americans did during World War II. Most U.S.-born citizens

Gordon Hirabayashi Recreation Site Interpretive Kiosk, Coronado National Forest, Tucson, Arizona. In the background of the picture are the rock walls and stairs leading up to the site where the prison's administration building once stood. These are the most visible remains of the original prison. (*Courtesy of Coronado National Forest.*)

grow up with a vague understanding of their own citizenship, aware that being a citizen gives them certain rights and privileges and annoyed at times by the few obligations of citizenship, such as serving on juries, but usually content to think of citizenship as a static category that remains unchanged over time. Some people believe you simply either are or are not a citizen. But in reality, citizenship is not simple at all.

This book asks students and scholars of history to suspend what they think they know about citizenship. How do individuals learn about their own citizenship? How do these early lessons in citizenship shape their expectations as adults? If individuals can claim multiple citizenships, one by birth and another by ancestry, who gets to decide which citizenship they will claim, and which citizenship demands their loyalty? Which citizenship is the state obligated to recognize? Most important, when is a citizen obligated to obey the law, and when is a citizen obligated to disobey? And what role do the courts and prisons play in America's overall construction of the rights and obligations of citizenship? This case study—drawing on the deeply personal perspectives of a group of Japanese Americans at a time of extreme national tension—allows us to unravel the rights and obligations of citizenship to their core elements. In so doing, we can gain a better understanding of how citizenship is constructed, debated, and renegotiated.

PRISONS AND PATRIOTS: TELLING THE STORY

Joe Norikane's diary shaped this book's central argument that citizenship is a contested relationship between an individual and the state that evolves during the individual's life. Historians have long noted that individuals' interpretations of their own rights or demands for greater rights have sometimes led them into conflicts with state authority. At times, these conflicts have led to surprising triumphs of the least powerful groups over what appear to be overwhelming odds in favor of state authority.[5] In this way, the central thesis of this book is not new. Clearly, definitions of citizenship change over time, often in response to agitation from below. Historians of the role of women have also shown quite clearly and adeptly that citizenship rights and obligations vary greatly depending upon a person's status within a society, particularly the unequal statuses of gender, sexuality, and class.[6] Others have shown that racial barriers can hinder an individual's access to rights and protections of citizenship that more privileged members of society take for granted.[7] Linda Kerber articulated these arguments quite well in her 1997 presidential address to the Organization of American Historians in San Francisco. Citizenship is today a matter of great debate, and citizens' rights and responsibilities to the state are in "great flux" throughout the world, she told the audience. She continued, "The status of citizen, which in stable times we tend to assume is permanent and fixed, has become contested, variable, fluid." The concept of citizenship has been particularly fluid as the international climate has shifted from peace to war and back—again and again—and the concept is currently being further redefined as isolated economies give way to global markets.[8] The argument that citizenship is fluid and changes over time is certainly not new, and precisely because of this fluidity it is a matter that merits reexamination from time to time.

This book adds another element to the definition of citizenship. Citizenship is not simply a set of rights or obligations to be granted, won, or lost. Instead, citizenship is the *relationship* between citizens and the state, and is redefined over the life of the individual and in response to the state's changing political needs, a lesson still being learned in the context of America at war today. Additionally, citizenship, as a relationship between individuals and the state, changes from person to person. Depending on such categories as age, race, and gender, citizens experience the rights they can expect to enjoy and their obligations to the state quite differently. These negotiations become even more complex and personal when dual citizenship is a factor. The story told in this book helps us more clearly understand the fluidity of citizenship.

In addition to exploring the complexities and often misunderstood nature of citizenship and dual citizenship, the second major aim of this book is to use Japanese American history and the history of the resisters in particular to explore the politics and power of historical memory. The history of Japanese American draft resisters is one story that virtually disappeared, with a few notable exceptions, from the published historical record. It was only after 1988, when Japanese Americans achieved redress for their wartime treatment, that the story of their resistance returned to the mainstream. And not until the twenty-first century did the draft-resister story become a mandatory part of the Japanese American metanarrative.[9] The process by which the resisters made their decisions to refuse to obey the law and were then marginalized within their communities and within the historical record, followed by the transformation of their place in history to the role of "heroes" and "patriots" in the minds of a younger, post-Vietnam, post–cold war generation, is a major focus of this book.

Finally, as the title indicates, this book is a story of the duality and evolution of definitions of criminality (implied by imprisonment) and patriotism. The resisters were imprisoned for their civil disobedience during the war but were honored as patriots by some third- and fourth-generation Japanese Americans in 2002 for their courageous stand. Today, we still see these two terms—prisons and patriots—repeatedly manipulated according to the needs of the state and the claims of the people. Who is a patriot? What defines a prison? What rules define and confine the power of the state or the military to imprison people, and what rights to due process do these individuals have and under what laws? When is it patriotic to support the state with military service, and when is it patriotic to disobey the state in defense of the Constitution? By examining one case in which definitions of prisons and patriots changed radically over time, when the dual forces of prisons and patriotism were used quite effectively to quiet dissent in one historic context and then to elevate ordinary individuals to the status of heroes in another time and place, this book aims to refine our thinking about the power of terminology over the rights of individuals and over the legitimate wartime power of the state.

In researching the lives and wartime experiences of the Tucsonians, it became clear that the Nisei who resisted the draft were not alone in their protests. Hundreds of other Nisei and Issei (Japanese immigrants) also resisted the War Department's decision to restore Nisei obligations of military service as a test for future restoration of their full citizenship. In fact, the more I researched this curious episode in history, the more evidence I found that Nikkei—Japanese Americans as a whole, regardless of individual citizenship status—mounted a strong, diverse, and at times well-organized resistance first to voluntary military service in segregated combat units and later to the draft. It appears that the majority of Nikkei in at least two camps, Topaz and Amache, had at some point attempted to object to or had at least considered the possibility of refusing to cooperate with the War Department's recruitment of their young men into segregated combat teams without first demanding a full restoration of Nisei citizenship rights.

This book examines the resistance of Nisei in the narrow context of individuals refusing the draft and in the larger context of attempts to force the restoration of citizenship rights to all Nisei as a prerequisite to enforcement of the obligation of military service. The Nisei who resisted the government as individuals and refused the draft represent the most visible group because they ended up going to prison for their resistance. But there was a much broader effort that took the form of resistance against "loyalty" registration, as well as various approaches individuals and groups took to use the wartime obligation to serve in the military as a tool to renegotiate Nisei citizenship rights. The first book to comprehensively examine the Nisei draft resisters was Eric Muller's *Free to Die for Their Country: The Story of the Japanese American Draft Resisters in World War II*. Muller researched the resisters from the Heart Mountain, Minidoka, Tule Lake, and Poston relocation centers. He explains why federal judges ruled in radically different ways when hearing their cases: No two court rulings were exactly the same, even though all the defendants had committed the same crimes. Heart Mountain and Minidoka resisters received harsh sentences in maximum-security prisons, Poston resisters were fined a penny and sentenced to time served, and Tule Lake resisters had their charges dropped entirely, because Judge Louis Goodman said that being drafted from inside a concentration camp was "shocking to his conscience."[10] Muller's book made invaluable contributions to our understanding of the Nisei draft resisters, but *Prisons and Patriots* asks different questions and therefore tells a different part of the story. It examines groups of resisters not covered in Muller's book, as well as individuals who objected to the draft but who stopped short of committing acts of civil disobedience.

A complete history of Nisei resistance to the draft during World War II cannot be isolated to the story of overt acts of resistance but must also include the larger framework of others who attempted to resist without crossing over into acts of civil disobedience. It is important to address not only the question of why some resisted the draft but also the question of why more people did *not* resist the draft. And what were some of the other ways that Japanese Americans "resisted" the draft without committing criminalized acts of civil disobedience? Civil disobedience is not, after all, the only form of resistance.[11]

Through a combination of oral histories and archival research, this book's aim is to tell the story of a group of resisters who came to call themselves the Tucsonians, paralleled with the story of Gordon Hirabayashi, and through their combined life histories to unravel the unintended lessons of citizenship that led some to refuse to obey unjust laws. In so doing, the objective is to promote a better understanding of the important relationship between citizenship and civil disobedience and between the rights and the obligations of citizenship, particularly in times of war. The book also reveals the sometimes uncomfortably close relationship between the propaganda value of patriotism and coercive threats of criminal prosecution as dual mechanisms for squelching dissent.

UNCOVERING AND DOCUMENTING THE STORY

The research for this book began in 1999 as an oral history project. The purpose was to investigate the history of the prison where Gordon Hirabayashi and the Tucsonians were sentenced for their civil disobedience during World War II. The Coronado National Forest had decided to rename the prison site in honor of the prison's most famous inmate and to honor the other Japanese Americans who had also been sentenced to work in this road camp. Gordon Hirabayashi's Supreme Court test case was well known to historians at the time, but few historians had more than a general awareness of the Nisei draft resisters or had even heard of the Tucsonians.

After conducting several interviews, I turned to archival records for answers to specific questions. I wanted to know why Japanese Americans had been rejected from military service during the first year of the war, and then two years into the war were drafted from inside the camps. I wanted to know why the issue of dual citizenship was prominent in wartime documents but appeared infrequently and without satisfactory explanation in the secondary literature. And I wanted to understand what pressures kept some who seemed to support the idea of resisting the draft from following through with acts of civil disobedience. To answer these and other questions, I examined related documents of the Federal Bureau of Investigation (FBI), the Office of the Secretary of War, the Bureau of Prisons, the War Relocation Authority, the Office of the Provost Marshal General, and the Justice Department at the National Archives in College Park, Maryland. I also consulted District Court records in Denver, Colorado, and Seattle, Washington, as well as the papers of WRA lawyers housed in the library at the University of Arkansas in Fayetteville. The Bancroft Library (University of California, Berkeley) collection of the documents of the Japanese American Citizens League was also helpful. Some of my questions led me to individual personal collections housed in libraries and in the homes of resisters from Seattle, Washington, to Turlock and San Mateo, California. What I found in the archives answered many questions and raised new ones, inspiring me to keep interviewing and reinterviewing the resisters who had become central to the story.

Most traditional approaches to my core interest in the nature of wartime citizenship and civil disobedience would lead one to investigate the era's four main Supreme Court decisions that involved matters of citizenship and civil disobedience: the cases of Minoru Yasui, Gordon Hirabayashi, Fred Korematsu, and Mitsuye Endo. In fact, Peter Irons has already written that book, and it provides important insights into the ways in which these four individuals, backed by teams of lawyers and civil rights advocates, pushed the Supreme Court to rule, although imperfectly, on the fragile nature of wartime citizenship.[12]

Beginning with oral histories intended to interpret a historic site led me, and eventually this book, in a slightly different direction. I wanted to know what had inspired ordinary farm boys, sons of Japanese immigrants with only high school educations, to challenge the War Department's demands for their military service when these young men knew they stood little chance of winning in court. They not only lacked the backing of the American Civil Liberties

Union (ACLU) but also faced direct opposition from the JACL and their own communities. If these young men were brave enough to risk the stigma of felony convictions to defend their beliefs that a balance existed between the rights and the obligations of citizenship, surely others must have agreed. I wanted to know who had supported the idea of resistance and why more had not chosen prison over partial citizenship. I was also fascinated by the fact that some resisters had used wartime debates over dual citizenship in their own arguments against the draft and that some had even gone on to renounce their U.S. citizenship as a final act of defiance against the government's attempts to sever their citizenship obligations from their constitutional rights. I wanted to know why the men I met in 1999 called the federal prison I had just begun to research "summer camp," despite the fact that they had been sent to this prison to build a road through extremely rugged terrain through their own manual labor. Finally, I wanted to find out why debates over whether the JACL should apologize to the resisters had become so acrimonious and why some resisters had lived their entire lives holding secret their resistance against the draft.

A FRIEND ALWAYS TOLD ME, "Show; don't tell." In this book I have embraced that approach, unfolding the story of the Nisei draft resisters first and saving the theoretical analysis for last. Chapter 1, "Lessons in Citizenship," introduces pre-war debates over Nisei dual citizenship and legal battles over the rights of Nisei to own property. The chapter also describes the diverging histories of the first and second generations of Nisei, each of whom learned different pre-war lessons regarding the meaning of their American citizenship, framing vastly different responses to wartime challenges. Chapter 2, "Nisei Wartime Citizenship," explains the process by which Nisei gradually lost their rights of citizenship during the first year of America's involvement in World War II and highlights Gordon Hirabayashi's calculated attempt to challenge the constitutionality of the forced removal and incarceration of Japanese Americans without due process of law. It also explains why the War Department and Japanese Americans ended the first year of the war debating the efficacy and logistics of restoring Nisei "rights" to military service. Chapter 3, "Loyalty and Resistance," describes organized opposition to loyalty registration and War Department recruitment of volunteers for the newly created all-Nisei combat team. Chapter 4, "Gordon Hirabayashi in the Tucson Federal Prison," analyzes Hirabayashi's experiences in prison and the radicalizing effect that prison had on his resolve to refuse cooperation with racially based laws and the Selective Service process. Chapter 5, "The Obligations of Citizenship," explains how the crisis over the draft unfolded during the first few months of 1944, and reveals the intensely personal manner in which individuals explained their decisions to resist the draft, which led them into conflict with members of the Japanese American Citizens League and the courts, eventually leaving the resisters with felony convictions. Chapter 6, "Prison and Punishment," describes how draft resisters sentenced to the Tucson prison found that the conditions there were far better than during any other confinement they had experienced during the war, at least in part because the Tucson prison officials were more interested in rehabilitating their citizenship than punishing them for their crimes. In stark contrast, after leaving prison many resisters found that private individuals and communities were not ready to forgive them for their wartime crimes and instead punished them, sometimes subtly and sometimes more overtly. Chapter 7, "Reunions, Redress, and Reconciliation," looks at the lives the Tucsonians after President Harry Truman's pardon of all Nisei draft resisters. The chapter describes how the Tucsonians developed into a family of resisters through reunions that began almost immediately after their release, despite remaining victims of historical amnesia for decades after the war's end. The discussion reflects on the ways in which memories and official interpretive histories of Nisei citizenship and civil disobedience have changed over time, and it provides an analysis of the historiography of Japanese American resistance. The Conclusion unites the stories of Gordon Hirabayashi and the Tucsonians once again in a legal and theoretical analysis of the history of Nisei wartime citizenship, civil disobedience, and historical memory.

CHAPTER 1

Lessons in Citizenship

W HEN JOE NORIKANE was in third grade, his family moved from Yuba City to Walnut Grove, California. Before the move, Norikane had been one of only four Asian children in his school, but he never felt out of place and was never aware that his ancestry could differentiate him from the other kids. He participated in school plays, had Caucasian friends, and got along fine. When the family moved, his father took him to school in Walnut Grove for the first time. He said, "Joe, this is your school. It's the Oriental School." Norikane did not know what "Oriental" meant, but he quickly observed that every child had black hair and that no children had "white" hair at all. It took him a while to understand what segregation meant and to recognize this place as a segregated school.[1]

Norikane's introduction to race-based segregation typified the gradual process by which Nisei children came to understand the contradictions between the ideals and the limits of their American citizenship in a socially and racially segregated world, even though statistically it was unusual for Japanese American children to attend segregated schools. Japan and Japanese Americans, with the assistance of Theodore Roosevelt, fought successfully for the rights of Japanese American children to attend the mainstream public school system when the San Francisco School Board threatened segregation immediately following the historic San Francisco earthquake of 1906. The agreement held until 1921, when, in response to a growing population of children of Japanese immigrants in agricultural communities in Sacramento County, the state legislature approved an amendment to the California State Education Code that allowed school districts to create separate elementary schools for "Indians, Chinese, Japanese or Mongolian children," adding Japanese children to the list of children that could be segregated in elementary school. The only schools in California that took advantage of the amended education code were in Sacramento County. "Oriental" schools were located in Florin, Walnut Grove, Isleton, and

Courtland, where populations of Japanese families were heavily concentrated in agricultural communities.[2] Chinese, Japanese, and Filipino children attended "Oriental" schools in these communities until they graduated the primary grades and advanced to integrated high schools. Legal segregation for Nisei was sporadic and short lived, lasting only from 1921 until 1947, when *Westminster v. Mendez* ended race-based segregation in California schools.[3] The significance of Norikane's experience was not the literal circumstances under which he learned about race-based segregation. The significance is that as Nisei grew up in a variety of circumstances and came to an awareness of race at different times in their lives, each had to decide for him- or herself how to reconcile the realities of racism with the promises of equal American citizenship. No two Nisei learned the limitations of their citizenship in the same way growing up as children, so no two responses to their wartime loss of rights were exactly the same.

Norikane experienced the shock of being separated by race in grade school at a time when he did not know what racial difference meant and while he was learning about American history, the Constitution, and the ideals of American citizenship. This dichotomy makes his story a convenient and poignant analogy for many other Nisei, despite the fact that their individual experiences varied greatly. Some did not experience segregation on a massive scale until 1942, when they saw others who looked just like them locked up behind fences in places that looked remarkably like prisons. Then they soon found themselves in the same places, wondering what crimes they had committed by simply looking Japanese. When their shock, disbelief, and humiliation soon turned to guilt, anger, and, for some, resignation, all detained Nikkei, or Japanese Americans, had to reconcile for themselves the reasons that they were locked up without being given the rights of due process they knew were part of the American justice system.

The parallel story is the gradual process by which Nisei also learned what it meant to be citizens of the United States. Despite living in a world in which Nisei might not be able to swim in the community pool or sit anywhere they wished at a movie theater, or, in more rare circumstances, when they were sent to school with only "Oriental" children and no white children at all, Nisei learned in school that they were 100 percent Americans. They learned that Americans have rights under the Constitution that the government must respect, and they learned that America was created as a nation when proud men and women fought against the abuses of a government that failed to respect their rights. The personal ways in which Nisei understood the contradictions between racial inequalities and the promises of equal citizenship laid the foundation for the remarkably diverse ways in which Japanese Americans responded to their wartime treatment.

Citizenship is not static state policy or law. It is a dynamic, dialectical relationship between individuals and the state that changes over the life of a single individual. Citizenship adapts to the changing needs of the state. Citizenship is a process, a construction, and a complex relationship negotiated between individuals and the state. This chapter reveals the circumstances under which individual Nisei first learned the meaning of their citizenship and some of the unintended lessons the very young Nisei learned about their citizenship in the California public school system. As a whole, this book demonstrates the ways in which individual Nisei and the state negotiated their rights and responsibilities with each other, in peacetime and in war, resulting in a dynamic and contested relationship we call citizenship.[4]

NISEI BIRTH AND CITIZENSHIP

Many Nisei were born at a time when anti-immigration sentiments in the United States were beginning to reach a climax. As a direct result of the San Francisco school-segregation crisis, Japan and the United States had agreed to limit the flow of Japanese immigrant laborers with the Gentlemen's Agreement in 1907. Asian immigrants were barred from naturalizing to U.S. citizenship; only white persons and persons of African descent were allowed to naturalize. When members of Congress drew the boundaries between inclusion and exclusion along racial lines, they marginalized Asian immigrants and their children in lasting ways. Lawmakers wrote new laws targeting Chinese or Japanese immigrants but in language that limited the rights of "persons ineligible for citizenship," thus skirting the Fourteenth Amendment's requirement of equal protection under the law, regardless of race. Alien land laws, for example, prohibited "aliens ineligible for citizenship" from owning land and later from leasing or renting land for more than three years at a time. The Johnson-Reed Act, including the National Origins Act and the Asian Exclusion Act, severely limited immigration from southern and eastern Europe and prohibited the immigration of persons ineligible for citizenship entirely. It specifically prohibited the immigration of those coming from countries in the Asia-Pacific Triangle described in the 1917 Immigration Act, including Japan.[5]

At the same time that the legal, political, and social climate in the United States transformed Japanese immigrants into permanent aliens due to their inability to become naturalized citizens, lawmakers began scrutinizing the legal status of Nisei.[6] Until 1924, Japanese citizenship laws granted citizenship to all children of Japanese nationals, regardless of their place of birth. The legal term for this form of citizenship is *jus sanguinis,* or the right of blood. Germany and Italy are notable examples of other countries that followed this same model of citizenship. The United States, on the other hand, granted citizenship to all persons born in the United States, regardless of ancestry, beginning in 1868 with the Fourteenth Amendment to the Constitution: "All persons born or naturalized in the United States, and subject to the jurisdiction thereof, are citizens of the United States and of the state wherein they reside." The legal term for citizenship by birthplace is called *jus soli,* or the right of soil. Granting citizenship to all persons born within a country is typical of countries that received most of the world's immigrants, and at the turn of the twentieth century, the United States received more immigrants than any other single country. This rule had some notable exceptions, such as excluding Native Americans from automatic U.S. citizenship rights until 1924. In practice, U.S. citizenship could be granted on the basis of birth in country or inheritance by birth when U.S. citizens gave birth to children outside the United States. The extension of citizenship to children born abroad was neither automatic nor absolute, making it secondary to *jus soli* for the United States.

These sometimes contradictory methods of granting citizenship by birth and by blood theoretically gave Nisei children born to Japanese national parents on U.S. soil the right to claim dual citizenship in Japan and in the United States.[7] Lawmakers, many of whom assumed that Asian immigrants could not be assimilated into America racially, culturally, or socially, began questioning the legal status and loyalty of Nisei based on the presumption that all Nisei actually claimed dual citizenship. They found, however, that challenging Nisei rights in the United States based on the theoretical assumption that all Nisei were dual citizens was not effective. The U.S. government did not officially recognize Japanese citizenship law, just as it would not recognize the potential dual citizenship of any individual born in the United States, except for Native Americans.[8] Those who sought to limit Japanese Americans' rights within the United States tried repeatedly to strip Nisei of their U.S. citizenship rights based on the presumption that the bonds of race and ancestry as well as Japanese law made the children of Japanese immigrant parents subjects of the emperor of Japan.

In 1920, with hearings on the West Coast, members of Congress investigated problems related to immigration. In these hearings, congressional representatives considered what they believed to be the "problem" of Nisei dual citizens. Some political leaders argued with a fair amount of hysteria that Japan's policy of granting citizenship to the children of emigrants offered proof that it was planning a social—if not military—invasion of the United States as part of the country's attempts to expand its empire.[9]

When the House committee investigating immigration interviewed one future Nisei leader, James Sakamoto, about his dual citizenship, he described it as a mere legal technicality that did not interfere with his loyalty to the United States. When questioned before the House investigating committee in 1920, Sakamoto explained that he did not know if he was a dual citizen. Seattle was his home, and the United States his country. Sakamoto was a U.S. citizen and did not claim any other citizenship for himself. If ordered to serve in the Japanese emperor's military, Sakamoto replied glibly, he would "get out of it," but if called upon to serve the United States, he assured the committee that he would do so without hesitation.[10] Nisei dual citizenship was a matter of great concern to some lawmakers, particularly those who believed, due to their own racial biases, that Nisei were not capable of assimilating to American ways. Even Sakamoto's clear statement that he claimed only U.S. citizenship did not resolve some committee members' fears regarding a growing population of

U.S. citizens who could be claimed as citizens by Japan, even though the United States routinely ignored foreign claims on U.S. citizens.

In 1924, the same year Congress shut the door on legal immigration from Japan, the Japanese government revised its citizenship laws so Nisei born after this date would no longer be eligible for Japanese citizenship unless their parents registered children's births with a Japanese consulate within the first two week's of the children's lives. Furthermore, the new law allowed Nisei to renounce their Japanese citizenship more easily. Prior to this year, young men of military age (over seventeen) could not renounce their Japanese citizenship and, if they were residents of Japan, were obligated to serve in the military. After the law changed, they could renounce their Japanese citizenship and thus free themselves from any possible military obligation to Japan.[11]

In the wake of changes in Japanese citizenship law, the number of Nisei dual citizens in the United States declined steadily between 1924 and 1941. From 1924 to 1930, only one out of three children was registered with the Japanese consulate. During the same period, 40 percent of Nisei born before 1924 renounced their Japanese citizenship. In 1927, the consul general of Japan reported from San Francisco that more than fifty-one thousand of approximately sixty-three thousand Nisei, or slightly more than 80 percent, held dual citizenship.[12] Other reports using data from a census conducted under the auspices of the Japanese government indicated that by 1930, only 47 percent of Nisei in California held dual citizenship.[13] After 1930, fewer and fewer Japanese nationals declared Japanese citizenship for their children, and Nisei born before 1924 continued to renounce their Japanese citizenship. On the eve of World War II, as many as 70 percent of Nisei retained U.S. citizenship alone.[14] Although these statistics are only estimates that are subject to the biases of those keeping and reporting them, it is safe to assume that not all Nisei were dual citizens at the beginning of World War II, and the vast majority of those who might have been dual citizens in theory were completely unaware of their official dual status.

GENERATIONS OF NISEI

Children born in the United States to Japanese immigrants are identified by historians as Nisei, because they are literally second-generation Japanese Americans ("Nisei" in Japanese means "second") and because they shared many historical experiences as a generation. Japanese immigrants entered the United States inside a relatively small historical time period. The bulk of Japanese men immigrated to Hawaii and the United States between 1885 and 1907. The majority of pre–war bride Issei women entered Hawaii and the United States between 1900 and 1924.[15] The majority of Nisei were born between 1917 and 1925 (see Tables 1.1 and 1.2). Historians Yuji Ichioka, David K. Yoo, and Eileen Tamura are among those who demonstrate that Nisei shared experiences growing up in American schools, becoming the targets of assimilationists' efforts

TABLE 1.1 Nisei births in California from 1910 to 1930

1910 to 1920	Nisei births	1921 to 1930	Nisei births
1910	719	1921	5,275
1911	995	1922	5,066
1912	1,467	1923	5,010
1913	2,215	1924	4,481
1914	2,874	1925	4,408
1915	3,342	1926	3,597
1916	3,721	1927	3,241
1917	4,108	1928	2,833
1918	4,218	1929	2,355
1919	4,458	1930	2,220
1920	4,971		

Source: Statistical Reports of the Bureau of Vital Statistics, Department of Public Health, State of California, 1910–1930, as cited in Tsutomu Obana, "The Changing Japanese Situation in California," Pacific Affairs 5, no. 11 (November 1932): 959.

to foster rapid Americanization and serving as cultural and linguistic bridges of understanding between their parents and American society and between Americans and Japanese culture.[16] Nisei were pushed by assimilationists to reject their Japanese cultural heritage in favor of becoming fully assimilated Americans while growing up with parents who sent them to Japanese-language schools and taught them that certain Japanese values were superior to American ways. The tensions led many children of immigrants to seek a third path, a path Yuji Ichioka calls "dualism" and Vicki Ruiz calls "cultural coalescence."[17] Ordinary Nisei may not have used such terms as "dualism" or "cultural coalescence," but they knew they were navigating difficult terrain as they grew up as racial others in a racially ordered United States. Kazua Kawai wrote in 1926 that when he was "placed between the devil and the deep sea," he chose a third road. He refused quiet resignation to the power of race discrimination.[18] Children adapted the cultural teachings of their parents to their American-born lives in highly individualized ways, often finding a third road that suited them best.

Although it is true that all Nisei shared certain things in common, Nisei born before 1917 and after 1921 but before 1926 came of age and engaged in

TABLE 1.2 Issei and Nisei populations in California compared, 1910 to 1930

Population composition	1910		1919		1930	
	Number	%	Number	%	Number	%
Total Nikkei population	54,980	100	73,924	100	92,390	100
Issei	51,029	93	56,366	76	46,100	50
Nisei	3,951	7	17,558	24	46,290	50

Source: Statistical Reports of the Bureau of Vital Statistics, Department of Public Health, State of California, 1910–1930, as cited in Tsutomu Obana, "The Changing Japanese Situation in California," Pacific Affairs 5, no. 11 (November 1932): 960.

debates about their citizenship in very different historical contexts. They became distinct generations of Nisei. The first children born to Japanese immigrants in the United States came of age during and shortly after the first Great War. Approximately 19,441 Nisei were born between 1910 and 1917, all of whom became adults between 1918 and 1935 (see Table 1.1). This generation of Nisei grew up when they represented only 7 to 24 percent of the total Nikkei population (see Table 1.2). Public debates over immigration and restrictive legislation still focused primarily on their Issei parents.

By contrast, the majority of Nisei grew up during the Great Depression, when Nisei became the majority of the Nikkei population (see Tables 1.1 and 1.2). Approximately 27,837 Nisei were born between 1921 and 1926, and became adults between 1939 and 1944. This population of Nisei became the focus of attention during the registration and draft crises of 1943 and 1944 (discussed in later chapters). Each generation of Nisei came to understand the world, politics, their rights and duties as citizens, and the ideals of the Constitution and the politics of patriotism differently depending on when they were born and the historical contexts in which they came of age.[19]

The first generation of Nisei grew up and came of age in the post–World War I context of anti-immigration politics and the first Red Scare, which gave them specific experiences defending their citizenship and their loyalty in ways the younger generation of Nisei were not asked to do until World War II. This meant that for some Nisei, the ways in which government policies during World War II challenged their citizenship were familiar, and they were therefore likely to respond in ways that echoed conversations that had taken place before other Nisei were born. Sakamoto, for example, graduated from a high school in Seattle, Washington, just as World War I was ending, and by the time he was an adult, he had adopted an anti-Communist stance as one expression of his Americanism. In the 1930s, he editorialized in his newspaper, the *Japanese American Courier,* that members of the Communist Party should lose the privilege of voting in American elections. He believed that the Congress of Industrial Organizations (CIO) had become too militant in advocating the rights of labor and that the 1935 Wagner Act was too friendly to labor as well. Sakamoto became a major figure in Nikkei history when he organized an early version of what would later merge with Nisei organizations from California to form the Japanese American Citizens League (JACL). He hoped that his organization would help Nisei "blaze the trail into American life."[20] As the JACL matured into a national organization, it advocated Sakamoto's anti-labor, anti-Communist politics. In this drive against un-American activities, JACL members turned in names of suspected Issei Communists. And as the United States prepared for World War II, the JACL and its leadership collaborated with intelligence agencies to promote their own members' status as loyal citizens.

The younger generation of Nisei who were too young to remember the debates leading up to the landmark legal changes in 1924 (immigration restrictions for Japanese and major revisions to Japanese citizenship law) grew up at a time when debates over Nisei dual citizenship seemed to disappear. With the strongest legal barrier to Japanese immigration in place in 1924, Japanese citizenship laws revised, and the numbers of dual citizens declining every year, even lawmakers seemed satisfied that concerns regarding Nisei dual citizenship had been resolved, at least for a time.

PEACETIME DEBATES OVER
DUAL CITIZENSHIP AND LOYALTY

Between 1920 and 1940, the issue of dual citizenship was rarely discussed in Congress. Even though the United States had not yet formally entered the war, Congress passed the Selective Service Act of 1940 in anticipation of a need for more servicemen. This act provided the War Department with a legal mechanism by which it could compel adult males to serve in the military, but it also presented the War Department with a dilemma. The law included a provision that men would be drafted by lottery, drawing from populations throughout the country fairly and evenly, without prejudice. No one region or racial group would be overburdened by the draft, and the War Department was not allowed to exclude any racial group from service. Leaders within the War Department, however, and in the navy in particular, remained suspicious of Nisei loyalties, resulting in a resurrection of debates about Nisei dual citizenship.

The War Department sponsored legislation over the summer and into the fall of 1941 that would force Nisei to choose between their U.S. and Japanese citizenship. If this law passed, all persons with dual citizenship entering into military service or employed in government, not just Nisei, would have to take a formal oath of allegiance to the United States and denounce allegiance to all other foreign governments or give up their U.S. citizenship and be subject to deportation or, at the very least, confinement in a "concentration camp." This bill, presented under House Resolution (H.R.) numbers 5879 and 6109, received a great deal of support from legislators anxious to support the interests of the War Department, but it also became the subject of intense debate and scrutiny. The debate over the language, scope, and meaning of the bills reveals important information about how various agencies viewed Japanese Americans vis-à-vis their citizenship and loyalty, how far various politicians and government agents were willing to push the legal limits of the Constitution, and where the legitimate voices of dissent against the bill arose that eventually made it impossible for the bill to pass into law. Most important, these debates over H.R. 5879 and H.R. 6109 reveal that the issue of dual citizenship was at the forefront of discussions that led to the mass removal and incarceration of nearly one hundred twenty thousand Japanese Americans from the West Coast on the mere suspicion of disloyalty.

To clarify the dual citizenship status of certain persons in the country, the House of Representatives Committee on Immigration and Naturalization met on October 29, 1941, to debate War Department–sponsored bill H.R. 5879, "a bill to amend the Nationality Act of 1940 . . . for the clarification of the dual-citizenship status of certain persons, and for other purposes."[21] Japanese Americans were the primary targets of this bill. The War Department was concerned that a number of Japanese, Italian, and German Americans, all of whom might be claimed as citizens by enemy nations despite their U.S. citizenship, were being inducted into the military through Selective Service. Dual citizens, they argued, would be more likely to aid foreign agents in garnering sensitive military information than their counterparts who held only U.S. citizenship. Brig. Gen. Sherman Miles, acting assistant chief of staff, represented the War Department in these hearings. Miles claimed that many Americans worried that enemy nations might claim them as citizens and that they were anxious to have their citizenship clarified. Only those who wished to retain their dual citizenship, he argued, would oppose this bill.[22]

Representatives had many questions about the bill. If individuals refused to take an oath or to renounce their dual citizenship, would they lose their U.S. citizenship if they were born in the United States? Would this be allowable under the Fourteenth Amendment? Would U.S.-born citizens be subject to deportation or only incarceration for losing their citizenship? Was this law based on the idea that foreign governments might make claims on the obligations of their citizens who also happened to be U.S. citizens, or was it based on the likelihood that American citizens who chose to retain loyalty to a foreign nation might sabotage U.S. war efforts? In other words, whose agency did this proposed law represent—citizens' rights to choose their allegiance or the competing interests of foreign powers? Did the state already have powers at its disposal to handle this situation without passing a new law? For example, could the War Department just require an oath of allegiance and a renunciation of dual citizenship upon induction into the military? What purpose was this bill going to serve? Would a spy or someone intending to commit acts of sabotage not be the first person in line to make an oath of allegiance or to renounce his or her dual citizenship to avoid drawing any suspicion? Representative William T. Pheiffer (R-NY) said, "Is it not a case of burning down the barn to kill the rats?" Representative Robert L. Ramsey's (D-WV) comment hit a more serious nerve: "We have been talking a great deal about just how far we are going to permit a bureaucratic government to take charge of the whole country." If a decision regarding the loyalty and rights of citizens, deportations, and even confinement in "concentration camps" was to be made by one bureaucratic commissioner, Ramsey warned, then "it looks to me like it is rather dangerous."[23] The questions were endless, and each witness brought a different point of view to the debate, only adding to the list of questions but never fully resolving all committee members' concerns.

Not a single witness came out in direct opposition to the bill, not even JACL representative Togo Tanaka. Each witness explained that he or she supported the War Department's need to defend the country in a period of crisis, but each also brought up possible problems with a bill written so generally.

Tanaka accurately stated that most of the testimony he had heard portrayed Japanese Americans quite negatively and ignorantly. He explained that many who worried about "disloyal" Japanese Americans were stuck in the mindset of conditions that existed in the 1910s. Things had changed, Tanaka said. Nisei growing up in the 1930s, unlike Nisei born the decade before, were largely unaware of any technical relationship they may or may not have with Japan. The majority of Nisei knew of only their U.S. citizenship. Nisei were born in the United States and had been brought up attending American schools. Japanese Americans had achieved educational levels on par with other Americans and often above the average. Nisei leaders even cooperated with members of the Office of Naval Intelligence and the FBI, turning in names of Japanese individuals they felt had been involved with espionage. The vast majority of Nisei were quite anxious to prove they were loyal to the only country they knew.

Tanaka deftly handled questions that revealed the representatives knew little about Japanese Americans, as he tried to educate them in the most respectful yet convincing manner possible that Nisei coming into adulthood in 1941 were loyal to the United States. He ended by reading into the record the "Nisei Creed," written by JACL national secretary Mike Masaoka, explaining that Nisei wanted to be better Americans for a better America and that they were loyal and would not become bitter in the face of discrimination but would prove themselves worthy of equal treatment. After Tanaka finished reading the "Nisei Creed," the only question representatives had was how many Nisei held dual citizenship and would take Japan's side if war came tomorrow. Tanaka said he thought less than 10 percent would declare loyalty to Japan. The chairman of the committee, Representative Samuel Dickstein (D-NY), said even if that meant that one thousand of one hundred three thousand might declare loyalty to Japan, the number was too high. "Thank you, Mr. Tanaka," Dickstein said. "I think you have made a very nice statement."

It was clear from the tone of the rest of the hearing that Tanaka's testimony carried little weight with the committee. As had been the case with James Sakamoto's testimony before the House investigating committee in 1920, House representatives came to the hearings in 1941 with preconceived notions about race, nationality, and loyalty. Tanaka's testimony, like Sakamoto's testimony twenty-one years before, did little to assuage House committee members' fears that Japanese American dual citizenship, no matter how poorly understood or infrequently claimed, might become a wartime problem.[24]

Isidore Hershfield from the Hebrew Immigrant Aid Society represented those who believed the bills had been written so generally to avoid the appearance of discrimination against Japanese Americans that it would create even more problems than it sought to resolve, including witch hunts and neighbors spying on neighbors. Hershfield explained that according to the broad language of the bill, even he would be targeted by this bill: "I happen to be seventy years old, native-born of foreign parents," Hershfield said. "I am the typical case that many of you have been discussing." But Hershfield's parents had immigrated to the United States when they were just children, more than a hundred years before Hershfield gave his testimony, and from countries in Europe that no longer existed. Who would claim him as a citizen, he asked? Would it be Russia, who claimed Poland and Lithuania when his mother and father left these two countries? Or would he be considered a Polish dual citizen? Worse yet was the implicit accusation that because of his ancestral roots in these foreign countries, whose claim on him would be tenuous at best, he was not a good citizen. Did this mean that only Americans whose relatives came on the *Mayflower* were real, unquestionably loyal Americans? This bill, if passed into law, Hershfield suggested, would create a "boiling pot" of anger and suspicion, "and all of the witch hunting and babbling among neighbors and friends" would tear this country apart rather than give the country a greater sense of security, as the War Department desired. Until the suspect did something overt, Hershfield concluded, nothing could be done to him: "You cannot, as a practical matter, do anything to any man because he has this or that kind of belief or opinion, but the instant that he does an overt act, punish him, not by the possibility or threat of a man's deportation, but through the mechanics of the Department of Justice."[25] In other words, Hershfield urged the committee to rethink the bill and to refrain from assuming children of foreign-born parents were more prone to disloyalty than other Americans.

Commander Hartwell C. Davis, retired from the Naval Intelligence Office, argued that Hershfield had misunderstood the real point of the bill, and he called not for more restraint but for an even more aggressive approach to the War Department's concerns about disloyalty and dual citizenship. He suggested that the War Department just say, "This country is menaced by individuals who are engaged in subversive activities in this country, and then before they are able to commit any overt act for which they would undoubtedly be imprisoned and punished, to eliminate those suspects before they are able to do that and get from our country . . . put them in custodial detention so that they would not do any damage." He added that the government could not wait for proof beyond a reasonable doubt or hold off on investigating an individual until it was fully satisfied that he was a dangerous individual. "I think he should be incarcerated," Davis said. "That is what we aim to do in the Naval Establishment. . . . We aim to pick up these suspects."[26] In other words, these individuals should be picked up and incarcerated before they could do any harm. Davis's suggestion sounded outrageous in peacetime, but it became government policy just a few months later.

Several representatives questioned the constitutionality of Commander Davis's recommendation that the War Department place suspicious individuals in custodial detention first and investigate their loyalty second, but if war were declared, at least two representatives said they would agree with the commander's approach. Representative Noah M. Mason (R-IL) commented that he did not believe that the methods Davis recommended could be covered by civil law. They would have to come under martial law or be conducted under military control. Davis replied, "Of course, in time of war, or during the period of an emergency, it is very desirable to have some plan to put these suspects in custodial detention before they are able to do things during the war." Congressman Pheiffer replied, "Of course, Commander, what you are speaking of is an extra-legal process, which admittedly, would not stand the test in normal times, but our President saw fit to declare an unlimited national emergency. . . . [O]n a war basis there are a lot of things you are not going to test by legal precedents." The problem, Pheiffer said, was that the War Department was confronting a wartime issue while the country was "still in the twilight zone between war and peace." He asked, "How can we adopt such a direct method," when the country was not yet at war? "I am all for it," Pheiffer declared, and Mason echoed, "I am, too." "There is no use beating the devil around the bush at this time," Pheiffer concluded. "Let us cut out all of the red tape we can and not shoot at a target with a shotgun, and if we can evolve some such plan as you suggest, one that would fit into our peacetime legal structure, that is what we want to do, of course." "I have not a legal mind," Davis replied, "but I think there are enough brains in the War Department and the Navy Department in this country to work that out." "Of course, it is an anomalous situation," Pheiffer concurred. "We are dealing with war-time measures in peacetime." But the peace would not last. Japan bombed Pearl Harbor just one month after this hearing took place.[27]

Despite complaints that the language of the bill remained dangerously unclear, the subcommittee continued to revise the bill and pushed it through the House on December 15, 1941. By the time it reached the Senate, though, the peacetime constraints that prevented the War Department from taking a more direct approach to its problem were gone. The United States was at war. More than three thousand suspected disloyal individuals, predominantly Japanese, Italian, and German nationals, had already been identified by the Office of Naval Intelligence and the FBI and interned in Department of Justice camps. The bill died unceremoniously in the Senate.

The fact that H.R. 5879 died in a Senate committee mattered little, because the War Department found another way to achieve its goals through what became known as "loyalty registration" in 1943 (discussed in Chapter 3). The bill itself had garnered a fair amount of support, but it could not have passed into law as it was written. Japanese Americans were not the only citizens who retained citizenship in two nations. Germany and Italy, as well as Russia, Turkey, Switzerland, Greece, Bulgaria, Persia, and the Netherlands, granted citizenship to children born to nationals abroad. The political and economic power of these ethnic groups doomed any attempts to curtail the citizenship of Nisei with generalized legislation. And with the United States fully involved in the war, a more direct approach was possible under claims of military necessity.[28] Although early attempts to curtail the citizenship rights of Americans of

Japanese ancestry failed, the Japanese attack on Pearl Harbor became a catalyst for a series of policies and laws that severely limited the rights and freedoms of all Nikkei and eroded the very citizenship of Nisei.

NISEI CITIZENSHIP IN THE COURTS

Congress and the War Department may have concerned themselves with fears of Nisei loyalty to Japan in 1920 and again in 1941, but American courts were concerned first and foremost with the relationship of Nisei to U.S. laws and to the Constitution. The majority of Nisei, especially those born after 1917, were never called before Congress to testify about their loyalty or to resolve questions about dual citizenship, but they did grow up with a profound sense of the strength of their U.S. citizenship in the wake of legal battles over alien land laws. In the 1920s, courts at various levels played significant roles in clarifying Nisei citizenship in the United States. They ruled that Nisei were indeed citizens by virtue of the Fourteenth Amendment and by legal precedent and could not be singled out as having fewer rights just because they shared Japanese ancestry with their parents.[29]

THE HIRABAYASHI FAMILY

Gordon Kiyoshi Hirabayashi was born to Japanese immigrant parents on April 23, 1918, in Sandpoint, Washington. His civil disobedience during World War II would elevate him to a prominent place in American civil rights history and, like other Nisei who challenged their wartime loss of rights, Hirabayashi's resistance was rooted in lessons he had learned as a child. His family was unique in many ways, but in its struggle to establish itself in the United States through farming, it shared much in common with the majority of Japanese American families. The Hirabayashis' struggle against Washington state's alien land law illustrates the systematic erosion of Issei rights that took place in the United States from 1919 to 1923, as well as the limited strength of Nisei peacetime citizenship.

Gordon's parents, Shungo and Mitsu Hirabayashi, both came from a farming community in Nagano prefecture in Japan. Gordon's father, Shungo, immigrated to the United States in 1907 with seven classmates, some from his extended family. Seven years later, Shungo was paired with Mitsu in an arranged marriage. She joined him in the United States in 1914, and in 1915 they had their first son; Gordon was born three years later. When Gordon was two years old, the Hirabayashis' first son died, making Gordon the oldest child and conferring upon him heavy responsibilities later in life. The Hirabayashis also lost a child in infancy, but three additional sons and one daughter, along with Gordon, went on to long and successful lives.[30]

Both of Gordon's parents had studied at the Kensei Gijuku academy in Japan to learn English before coming to the United States, and it was there that both converted to Christianity. Rather than joining a denominational church, they became followers of Uchimura Kanzo, who founded the Mukyokai movement in Japan. Uchimura had studied theology at a Boston seminary, and he believed that Christianity would fit better into Japanese lives without the formal rituals practiced by Western churches. The Mukyokai movement that he inspired was dedicated to pacifism and a goal of "oneness" in belief and behavior. "They believed that religion should guide one's daily life," Gordon Hirabayashi said. "It should not be limited to Sunday service." As a child, Gordon felt that the religion of his parents was "too rigid and restrictive, but its emphasis on the oneness of belief and behavior left its impact."[31]

Gordon Hirabayashi credited his parents for laying the foundation for his own life guided by a marriage between principles and action. He described his mother as a remarkable woman—articulate and smart but able to sublimate her ambitions to fit in as an Issei wife. "A generation later," he surmised, "she would have become an editor, writer, or teacher." Instead, "as a Japanese woman in those years," she had to settle for encouraging her children to strive for more than she was able to achieve. "We were raised in a farming community, and there were many hardships as we grew up," Hirabayashi said, "but every one of us children went on to graduate from university and get advanced degrees." Gordon's father was known for his honesty and integrity, to the point, Hirabayashi said, that some called his father "stupidly honest" for refusing, for example, to place the best lettuce on top of the bin. All the lettuce should be the same, his father would say, and he would not deceive his customers in an effort to earn more money.[32]

When Gordon was just a year old, the family moved to a small farming community south of Seattle with three other Issei families (one of them headed by a cousin of Shungo's) who had also come from Nagano prefecture. In their new hometown of Thomas, Washington, the four families acquired a small farm, although they could not buy it outright. Washington had adopted an alien land law in 1889, forbidding the sale of land to aliens ineligible for citizenship. So the families purchased the land through a Caucasian intermediary named Alfred T. White and then created a corporation called White River Gardens, Inc., whereby the Issei farmers could own capital stock and control the farm without owning it directly or violating state law.[33] As they began to develop their forty acres, growing crops and raising their children in the Mukyokai Christian way, little did the families know that they would soon run afoul of increasingly restrictive alien land laws.[34]

ALIEN LAND LAWS IN CONTEXT

In the first few years after World War I, 1919–1923 particularly, state legislatures throughout the western United States bowed to renewed pressure from anti-Asian and anti-immigrant groups, labor unions, granges, and politicians to close loopholes in laws that excluded Japanese immigrants from the

White River Gardens families and a few friends in front of the Katsuno home, ca. 1921. *Back row (left to right):* Ishi Yokoyama, Teiko Kamikawa, unidentified man, Grandma Hirabayashi, Midori Hirabayashi. *On the steps:* Lillian Mizukami (girl), Roda Hirabayashi with Kujo Kamikawa (baby) on her back, Isami (Hirabayashi) Mizukami, and Mitsu Hirabayashi (both wearing hats). *Second row:* Unidentified man, Mr. Shirakata (carpenter who built the house), Toshiharu Hirabayashi, Nobuyuki Yokoyama, Tamiko Yokoyama (girl wearing bow), Wayo Katsuno, Yoshitake Hirabayashi, Gordon Hirabayashi (held by his father), Shungo Hirabayashi, Shoichiro Katsuno, and Itushi Kamikawa. *Children in front:* Martin and Grant Hirabayashi, Kazuko and Masako Yokoyama, Aiko and Peter Katsuno, Shuji Kimura, and Aiji Kamikawa. *(Courtesy of White River Valley Museum.)*

benefits of land ownership. Anti-Japanese groups made wild claims about the "threat" that Japanese represented in terms of economic competition and their allegedly excessive birth rate and leveled the general accusation that Asian immigrants were unassimilable; some even claimed that Japanese men posed a moral and sexual threat to white women.[35] Recent literature has shown that anti-Asian legislation came about not just because of pressure from those interested in eliminating what they perceived to be competition from immigrant groups but also due to top-down pressure from politicians who found that anti-immigrant, racist rhetoric was a powerful tool in exciting the voting population.[36] The laws were designed not just to make it difficult for Japanese immigrants to settle permanently but also to limit their role in agriculture to that of laborers, not farm owners. Those who chose to remain were put in the position of depending on Caucasians for employment.

The message these laws sent to Issei was clear: Japanese laborers were welcome, but Japanese farm owners were not. When historians examined the numbers, however, it became clear that Japanese owned only minuscule percentages of agricultural land. In 1913, when the California law was first enacted, the number of Japanese immigrants who owned land in the state, particularly agricultural land, was insignificant compared with the total acreage under cultivation. For example, in 1912, county assessors' reports indicate that Japanese farmers owned 12,726 acres of farmland. This represented only 0.001 percent of the total eleven million acres of improved farmland in the state. Japanese ownership increased from 1913 to 1920, likely because of the common practice whereby Issei purchased land in the names of their Nisei children or by forming corporations. Still, according to the California Board of Control records from 1920, as cited in Frank F. Chuman's *The Bamboo People,* Japanese farmers owned a mere 74,767 acres, an increase of only 62,041 acres in seven years, and leased another 383,287 acres, for a total of 458,054 acres farmed by Japanese Americans. The combined total represented 0.0164 percent of the total farm acreage (nearly twenty-eight million acres) reported in operation that year.[37] Despite the fact that competition for agricultural land was not as intense as it was perceived to be, stricter and stricter laws regarding land ownership did indeed succeed in reducing the acreage owned by Japanese immigrants and their families.

One aspect of the competition argument did have some basis in fact, however. Carey McWilliams points out in his historic book *Factories in the Field* that the remarkable productivity with which Japanese immigrants were able to farm a few acres and their introduction of truck farming and high-yield, high-end crops increased land values and put pressure on other farmers who were producing far less per acre. This argument not only speaks to the industriousness and education of Japanese farmers but also gives a more reasonable explanation for why so few immigrants farming so few acres could incur so much political wrath. McWilliams suggests that one of the political benefits of reducing an immigrant population to the position of farm laborers rather than farm owners is that when it becomes economically, socially, or politically desirable, it is far more expedient to dispossess a population of its position in society (sometimes by literally deporting people, or at least expelling them from their homes) if the population's attachment to the land and to the country is not permanent.[38] State laws could be written to prevent immigrants ineligible for citizenship from owning land, but states could not override the Fourteenth Amendment to the U.S. Constitution, which gave all children born in the United States the ultimate attachment to land and country: citizenship. This factor became pivotal, as rulings in a series of court cases that challenged the alien land laws between 1915 and 1925 hinged on citizenship rights conferred by the Fourteenth Amendment to U.S.-born Nisei, and the extent to which Issei would or would not be protected by the Fourteenth Amendment's equal protection clause.[39]

When California passed its first alien land law in 1913, individual families and entire communities devised ways of getting around the restrictions and challenged the law in court. The first test came from a case originating in Riverside, California. Neighbors complained that a Japanese family had purchased a house in the names of the family's citizen children, Mine Harada, Sumi Harada, and Yoshizo Harada. Jukichi Harada, the head of the family, was offended when neighbors tried to buy the house from him because they did not want a Japanese family in the neighborhood. When Jukichi Harada refused to sell, his neighbors complained that the Haradas were in violation of the alien land law. In response, on December 14, 1915, the Haradas' property escheated to the state (which occurs in cases where ownership of property is no deemed longer valid and the property reverts to the state), and the county of Riverside took the family to court. The resulting case, *The People of the State of California v. Jukichi Harada and Mine Harada, Sumi Harada and Yoshizo Harada,* was the first to address a list of questions related to the practical application and limits of alien land laws.[40]

The Harada case and others that followed it forced the state to deal with the dichotomy of racially restrictive laws that allowed only persons who were either white or of African descent to become naturalized citizens. California also had to contend with the Fourteenth Amendment to the U.S. Constitution, which protects the rights of all persons regardless of race or birthright citizenship. The Harada family was not the only family to purchase property in the names of their minor children, but it was the first to have this arrangement challenged in court. Judge Hugh H. Craig had to decide whether U.S.-born minors were able to own property, whether alien parents ineligible to own property could manage their children's estates as guardians, which application if any the equal protection clause of the Fourteenth Amendment had in this case, and whether property could automatically escheat to the state in cases of suspected alien land law violations without due process of law. Under typical application of property law, property would revert to the state—escheat—only when the owner had died without an heir and a hearing had been conducted to determine who, if anyone, remained eligible to inherit the property. In the context of the alien land law, property could escheat to the state if it was not rightfully owned by the alien. Nisei children, however, were not automatically considered eligible owners in place of their ineligible Issei parents. Litigants had to sue or appeal, arguing that the unusual nature of the escheat process constituted an unconstitutional taking.[41]

Judge Craig ruled that any citizen, no matter his or her age, had the right to acquire and to own real estate and that this right was protected by the Fourteenth Amendment. Therefore, the judge continued, Jukichi Harada, although ineligible for citizenship himself and barred from acquiring property in his own name, was not violating state law but instead was acting like any father might when he paid for, "improved, helped negotiate, [and] helped file legal papers" to provide his children with the gift of property.[42] Judge Craig concluded that because the children had a constitutionally protected right to their property, the state of California had no right to take it from them without due process. The property was returned to the Harada children, who retained ownership of the house until it was designated a National Historic Landmark in 2001 and given to the city of Riverside in August 2004 to be cared for by the Riverside Metropolitan Museum.[43]

Ironically, California Attorney General Ulysses S. Webb agreed with Judge Craig's ruling. Webb supported the California alien land law and believed that it was a necessary deterrent to continued Japanese immigration. He was known for his vigorous prosecutions of cases that involved transfers of ownership from Issei to non-Issei so Japanese immigrants could avoid losing their land in the wake of the new law. But in this case, he recognized the right of all citizens, including minors, to the full protection of the U.S. Constitution. Webb wrote a letter in response to an inquiry he received regarding the Harada case: "Can a Jap boy or girl born in Calif. Acquire & hold Real Estate?" His response: "In reply, section 1 of the Fourteenth Amendment of the Federal Constitution provides: 'All persons born or naturalized in the United States and subject to the jurisdiction thereof are citizens of the United States and of the state wherein they reside,' and any citizen of the United States and of this state may acquire and hold real estate in California."[44] The matter, according to Attorney General Webb, was quite simple: Alien Japanese could not own land, but their citizen children could.

In response to the legal loopholes exposed by this first legal challenge to California's alien land law, James D. Phelan, noted anti-Japanese crusader and Democratic candidate for the U.S. Senate who ran under the slogan "Keep California White," joined forces with the Sons and Daughters of the Golden West, the American Legion, the California State Federation of Labor, and the California State Grange to place an initiative on the 1920 ballot that would replace the 1913 law. Leading up to the election, voters were barraged by anti-Japanese propaganda supporting the initiative in newspapers, magazines, and movies. On November 2, 1920, voters approved the new law by a three-to-one margin. The law became effective on December 9, 1920, putting into place a number of added measures: Aliens ineligible for citizenship would no longer be allowed to lease land. Criminal penalties were established for anyone who failed to account for lands held on behalf of ineligible aliens or minor children. Most importantly, the new law made it clear that it was illegal for an ineligible alien to provide funds to purchase land in the name of another person. Purchasing lands through a citizen intermediary would be interpreted as an attempt to evade the alien land law, in which case the property would automatically escheat to the state.[45] The coalition that had been created to lobby for a more restrictive alien land law, the California Oriental Exclusion League, proposed a five-point program that extended beyond the question of alien land-holding and beyond the power of the state. They argued for complete cancellation of the 1907 Gentlemen's Agreement and absolute exclusion of

Japanese immigrants, including a ban on the immigration of picture brides. They also lobbied for a permanent ban on Asian-immigrant naturalization to U.S. citizenship and a corresponding amendment to the U.S. Constitution that would deny birthright citizenship for children of aliens ineligible for citizenship. Even though the California Oriental Exclusion League was successful in achieving stronger barriers to alien land ownership, they would not in peacetime—nor during World War II—succeed in dismantling the Fourteenth Amendment's guarantee of citizenship to Nisei.

California's new alien land law was tested almost immediately and, as in the Harada case, the dispute involved the issue of Nisei citizenship and Nisei rights to own property. In 1922, the California State Supreme Court handed down a landmark decision regarding the right of a two-year-old Nisei child, Tetsubumi Yano, to hold property in the state of California despite laws forbidding her parents from doing the same. The California State Supreme Court affirmed that the children of Japanese immigrants were citizens by birth and that their parents had equal rights to guardianship over their children despite the fact that they were aliens. The case emerged when Hayao Yano received a notice from the Superior Court of Sutter County, California, denying him the rights of guardianship over the estate of his two-year-old daughter. His daughter was the owner of fourteen acres of land, and Hayao Yano and his wife cared for the property on her behalf. Prosecutors claimed that the only reason Tetsubumi owned the land was because her father and mother were aliens, ineligible for citizenship, and thus prohibited by California state law from owning land themselves. The prosecution argued they had purchased the land in their daughter's name in a deliberate attempt to circumvent the law.[46]

In deciding the case, the court ruled that because Tetsubumi Yano was a citizen, despite her youth and the motivations of her parents she was privy to all the rights of property assured to other citizens of the United States. It also ruled that being an alien did not mean that Hayao Yano had forfeited his guardianship rights as a parent. The court cited the equal protection clause of the Fourteenth Amendment to the U.S. Constitution and the legal precedent set in the 1886 case of *Yick Wo v. Hopkins,* wherein the court had ruled that even though immigrants from China were ineligible for U.S. citizenship, they were regarded as persons and were thus protected by the Fourteenth Amendment. The court concluded, therefore, that Tetsubumi Yano's parents could not be denied guardianship over her estate.[47] This case provided a powerful legal precedent regarding Nisei rights to property and their birthright citizenship despite the permanent alien status of their parents. The *Yano* decision was followed by similar cases wherein the courts upheld the rights of minor children to own property.

In 1921, shortly after California's enactment of its more restrictive alien land law, the state of Washington strengthened its own law, adding measures very similar to those enacted in California. It would no longer be legal for aliens ineligible for citizenship to hold major shares in a corporation holding property or for aliens to hold any major interest in agricultural lands. Washington's revised law touched off a new set of complications for the farming effort of Gordon Hirabayashi's family and the other Issei families participating in the White River Gardens stock company.

To comply with the new law, Shoichiro Katsuno, the primary stockholder in White River Gardens, transferred his 1,997 shares of stock (the vast majority of the shares for the company) to his Nisei daughter, Yoshiko Katsuno. In 1922, Malcolm Douglas, the prosecuting attorney for King County, Washington, charged Taka[48] Hirabayashi, White River Gardens, Inc., and various other individuals with violating the alien land law, and the farm escheated to the state. Douglas claimed that even though the majority of the stock shares were in the name of a citizen, this citizen was the minor child of an alien ineligible for citizenship. Since Shoichiro Katsuno, the father of Yoshiko Katsuno, was the president of White River Gardens as well as the manager of the farm, the court denied that his child held majority interest in the farm, ruling instead that individuals named in the case had committed subterfuge in their attempts to hide the fact that aliens controlled the agricultural lands in question even though a citizen was the majority shareholder of record. The Katsunos and Hirabayashis appealed, arguing among other things that a citizen's right to own land is protected by the Fourteenth Amendment to the U.S. Constitution regardless of the age of the citizen or the legal status of a minor's parents. Debates that arose from this case not only challenged Issei efforts to farm their own land in spite of state legislative attempts to bring an end to any form of Japanese immigrant control over agricultural lands but also raised questions about the legal rights of minor citizens and the limits of Issei rights to guardianship over their children's estates.[49]

Politicians and anti-Japanese organizations that had supported revisions to California's and Washington's alien land laws became aware that further amendments were needed to counteract the effects of the *Yano* decision. By 1923, both states had refined their laws to prohibit Issei guardianship over Nisei property. In 1925, the Washington State Supreme Court ruled on two appeals that addressed whether or not laws that prohibited Issei guardianship over Nisei landholdings were a violation of the Fourteenth Amendment's equal protection clause, as the California State Supreme Court had ruled in the *Yano* case, or whether the revised laws had been written in a way that could withstand this constitutional test.

In the case of *Washington v. Kosai*, the Washington State Supreme Court ruled that the Issei parents held no real interest in a dairy farm purchased in the name of their Nisei minor son. The Kosai parents were paid a very small sum, only $100 a month, for managing the dairy and milking the cows. The profits generated by the farm were also small. According to the evidence presented, "the gross income from the land from the date it was taken over by the trustees, June 7, 1921, to September 12, 1923, was $16,558.79, and that the expense of operation was $15,797.87, leaving a net balance of $706.92." The court concluded that even though there were aspects of the case that were "suspicious," they were only "suspicious." There was no just cause to take property away from a U.S.-born citizen, regardless of his age.[50]

In its ruling on *Washington v. Hirabayashi* (the White River Gardens appeal), the Washington State Supreme Court held that the Issei parties to the case had clearly intended to defy the law: Issei were directly engaged in running the farm; producing and selling the harvests; taking in profits; and improving the land with houses, outbuildings, farm equipment, and livestock. Only after enactment of Washington's stricter laws did Shoichiro Katsuno transfer his stock shares to his minor child. Despite this transfer, Issei control and interest in the farm remained unchanged. The court's ruling against the families reaffirmed state control of the farm, which earlier had escheated to the state. The families were allowed to continue to occupy and farm the land but were forced to rent it from the state of Washington. Notwithstanding the fact that these families had lost ownership of their farm and faced the inevitable hardships that accompanied farm life, they continued to work together to create a Mukyokai Christian community in which to raise their children and to weather the changes that were to come.[51]

Despite many setbacks, the importance of the citizenship rights of the Japanese was not totally ignored by the courts. For example, Washington State Supreme Court Justice Oscar R. Holcomb, who wrote the majority decision in *Washington v. Kosai,* went further than the facts of the case to comment on the important relationship between honoring citizens' rights to property and loyalty: "In any event, the state, although mighty, cannot insist upon the allegiance of all its citizens unless it deals justly with all its citizens, and it cannot deal justly if it confiscates the property of its own citizens without just reason."[52] Court decisions such as those in the Yano and Kosai cases gave Nisei a powerful role in Japanese families, even if that role was contested and in some cases insufficient to protect families from losing their land. Nisei children could offer their parents some degree of legal security in a nation in which the parents could not become citizens. This was a powerful lesson in the strength of Nisei citizenship.

YOSHI KUBO AND THE CORTEZ COLONY

Most Nisei who owned property for the family, especially those who lived in predominantly Japanese American communities in California, did not have to fight the courts to retain their property rights. Nisei property ownership and corporation-owned property were strategies that helped families establish a sense of permanence and stability despite the alien land laws. Some Nisei, such as Yoshi Kubo, grew up understanding that the strength of their U.S. birthright citizenship gave them not only the right to own land but also the strongest claim to Americanism. This understanding of citizenship and his status as a farm owner laid the most important foundation for Kubo's decision to the resist the draft during the war.

Kubo became a property owner when he graduated from high school, but his family had farmed its own land from the time it moved to Cortez using the same method the Hirabayashi family had used in Washington. When the Kubo family moved from Sebastopol to Cortez, California, it began farming a ranch called "Sunny Acres." This land was owned by the KK Company, which had acquired it in 1920. When Kubo graduated from high school in 1933, he purchased his own farm on Pepper Street. This farm was not adjacent to the Kubo "home place," but it was still in the town of Cortez. Two years later, in 1935, the KK Company deeded Sunny Acres to Yoshi Kubo, giving him ownership over both farms.[53]

Cortez was the third of three colonies started by Abiko Kyutaro. Abiko was one of the most influential men in Japanese America, having started the *Nichibei Shimbun* (*Japanese American News*) and organizing three Japanese American farming colonies in Livingston, Cressey, and Cortez. Abiko was confident that anti-Japanese hostilities could be combated through education and by encouraging Japanese immigrants to settle permanently in the United States, proving to Americans that they were committed to education, industriousness, and community.[54] The farming communities that Abiko inspired stand out in Japanese American history because of their owners' success in gaining ownership over their lands and their unique success in retaining ownership and resettling on their farms after their exclusion during World War II.[55]

The Cortez colony was first founded in 1919 on the eve of alien land law reforms and a renewed wave of anti-Japanese hostilities and rhetoric.[56] Having learned from other successful cases of Nisei land ownership, Abiko established this colony, where families like the Kubos were able to purchase farms under the protection of a corporation, or in the names of Nisei who were of age.[57] The community organized further to protect members' interests, creating the Cortez Growers' Association, which allowed Japanese Americans to compete more effectively in the California agricultural market.[58]

Kubo and other future Tucsonians, including Susumu Yenokida, grew up in Cortez in a vibrant and growing Japanese American farming community, a community that despite its flaws was tightly knit and provided young Nisei a sense of security and pride. Kubo attended Ballico Grammar School and graduated from Livingston High School in 1933. After graduating from high school, he started farming his own land. This had been his father's occupation, and he was proud to continue farming in the same community in which he had grown up. He spent the next eight years making improvements to the farm and became a member of the Cortez Grower's Association in 1941.

Wartime exclusion laws forced Kubo to hand over his farm to a less-qualified caretaker while he was sent to languish in frustration in some sort of prison camp in the desolate southeast corner of Colorado. For Kubo, the war undermined his citizenship rights in shocking and profound ways. He believed that, as a farm owner and a citizen, he should have been allowed to stay on his own land and to contribute directly to the war effort as a farmer.

LESSONS IN CITIZENSHIP AND ASSIMILATION

Nikkei made strategic choices to assimilate to American ways based on a foundation of core Japanese cultural values and their own identities as American citizens. Along with instilling a strong sense of pride in being Japanese, Issei parents passed on to their children values that had an enduring impact on the way Nisei children interpreted their own experiences growing up. They taught their children to value education and to obey authority. Children also learned that duty and loyalty should start at home and radiate outward and that they must perform their duties of loyalty and service to family first, *ken* (community) second, and nation third. Seen in this light, the selective assimilation chosen by some Nikkei represents a different way of thinking about assimilation that emphasizes the agency and power of those who chose assimilation on their own terms, not on their acceptance of dominant scripts that told them they must assimilate because of their racial inferiority.[59]

Children applied the lessons that they learned about obedience, education, and good behavior in public school. Yenokida remembered that his parents' first expectation for him was to behave or, in other words, not to be a "troublemaker at school." Second, he was to listen to his teachers and do what they asked. Finally, he was supposed to learn whatever lessons his teachers expected him to learn. For Yenokida, this meant learning English, which was very difficult for him as a child. With the generous assistance of his teacher and the support of his parents, Yenokida stayed after school every day for several years to practice his English rather than going home to help on the family farm. If learning English was what Yenokida needed to do to get ahead, or at least to keep up in school, his parents believed that focus was more important than performing chores at home.[60]

With all the support his parents lent to his early education, Yenokida remembered that before the war he expected to go on to college after graduating from high school. Yenokida was not alone. Contemporary studies of Nisei in the 1920s and 1930s note their success in school and tendency to stay in school. Some Nisei remembered that higher education was a value and an expectation that they and their parents shared. This was but one expectation that shifted dramatically after the United States entered World War II.[61]

Some parents, educators, and Nikkei leaders urged Nisei to surpass their white counterparts in school and at work. In 1930, this belief was published as an editorial in the *Nikkei Shimin*. The author writes, "in technical or commercial vocations, we cannot afford to work with talents *inferior* to Americans. . . . It is not enough to be their equals. . . . [W]e must *surpass* them—by developing our powers to the point of genius if necessary" [emphasis original]. The author opines that those who complained about racial discrimination and prejudice were misguided and that their complaints merely revealed their own lack of initiative and inferior talents. Nikkei authors published their support of an early version of the "model minority" ideal or myth—that the way to beat discrimination was to surpass whites—in journalistic and academic writings. It was up to Nisei, they argued, to make sure that America would accept them based on their superior talents and skills. Some scholars added that Nisei efforts to assimilate could go only so far and that at some point America would have to accept Nisei efforts for full assimilation to take place. Yet the idea that it was up to Nisei to initiate the process of assimilation and acceptance into American society remained strong in Nikkei-authored literature from before the 1920s through the early 1930s.[62]

Nisei were not the only ones who learned in school and from family that selective assimilation and excelling beyond the achievement standard of their white counterparts could help them succeed later in life. Chinese Americans also learned this early version of the model minority myth or ideal. Norikane attended Japanese school for an hour or more each day after grammar school. Whenever a test was coming up at the Japanese school, children would use their big American geography textbooks to hide their Japanese books while they studied for their exams. Norikane remembered with some amusement that the teacher thought they were studying geography, until one day when she discovered they were actually studying Japanese. Norikane recalled the scene many years later:

> I think it was in 7th or 8th grade, the teacher caught us and said, "You people don't need another language. All you need to learn is English." And this Chinese boy, Richard Chang, I remember him, he stood up and said, "I think you're wrong, teacher. If I've got the same ability as the white person, and I go out and fight for a job, you think the white person is going to give a job to a Chinaman? To Chinese or to the white person? White person's gonna get it, you know. If I want a job, I have to be better than the white person to get a job. That's how it is. By learning another language, I'm ahead, so I could get a job. So, if they're going to communicate with Chinese people I'll be able to get a job after that." The teacher never did say anything after that.[63]

When Norikane went home and told his mother about the incident, she replied, "Gee, the Chinese people teach that, too?" Norikane was familiar with this lesson. He learned it in Japanese-language school, where his teachers told him, "There is always discrimination, so you'd better prepare for it."[64] They would have to become more qualified, or, as the editorial in the *Nikkei Shimin* said, Nisei would have to "surpass" whites. It would not be enough to become their equals.

Japanese and Chinese immigrant communities struggled with questions of how they could most effectively prepare their children for a world in which racial segregation and exclusion dominated the Asian American experience but in which international trade and understanding was still critical, more so than ever. Chinese communities throughout the United States, but especially in California, started looking to Chinese-language schools as not only a way to combat *de facto* segregation but also a way to prepare children to be able to work in China, to trade with China, or at a minimum to communicate effectively within Chinese American communities as adults. As time passed, Chinese American children's fluency in English quickly surpassed their basic familiarity with Chinese. Chinese-language schools became more focused on language as a result, but the schools also sought to provide children with some ties to a Chinese education. Chinese-language schools were designed to teach children language skills as well as lessons in Chinese geography, history, civics, and "moral character." No central authority regulated Chinese-language schools in the United States, so significant differences existed between one school and the next and one region and the next.[65] But the central goals of each reinforced the idea that Richard Chang had expressed in Norikane's class: Chinese American children would get ahead in life most effectively if they had more than just an American education.

Japanese-language schools had also been designed to provide Nisei with options to work in or to trade with Japan as adults, to communicate effectively within Japanese American communities, and to maintain a sense of their cultural heritage and language roots. But some Japanese Americans argued that the schools should be abolished to encourage Japanese Americans to become 100 percent American. Seattle Japanese Consul Ohashi Chuichi wrote an essay arguing this point in 1925: "It will be necessary to educate Nisei children as complete American citizens. . . . Half-baked Americans are neither American nor Japanese." He believed Japanese-language schools would fuel future anti-Japanese agitation and pointed out that Nisei citizenship was not absolute. Proposals had been made in the past to rewrite the Fourteenth Amendment in an effort to deny citizenship to children born to "aliens ineligible to citizenship." According to Ohashi, this was reason enough to reform Japanese-language schools in an effort to encourage Nisei to become 100 percent Americans. If Japanese was to be taught to Nisei children, it should be offered in the public schools where Japanese children could learn Japanese side by side with Anglo American children. Nisei could not become effective cultural bridges between Japan and the United States, he argued, unless they were fully accepted by mainstream white Americans. Although Ohashi had support among some Issei, others argued that the effect of Americanization on Nisei threatened their sense of moral integrity to a dangerous degree. Japanese-language schools could teach children the importance of Japanese morals and the practical necessity for being 100 percent American at the same time.[66]

AMERICANIZATION AND CITIZENSHIP
IN PUBLIC SCHOOL

While Issei parents and Japanese-language schoolteachers taught the younger generation of Nisei that they would always experience discrimination in their lives, Nisei also learned in public schools that the United States stood for principles of democracy and equal citizenship. California embraced progressive educational reforms in response to the state's diverse population. Since the end of World War I, California had experienced constant influxes of new immigrants and rapid urban growth. In step with, and at times ahead of, reform movements throughout the country, California schools attacked problems associated with growth and immigration by intensifying their Americanization programs.[67]

In 1929, California initiated its own study of the problems of public school education in the state and outlined recommendations for reform. The study concluded that citizenship education was of paramount importance to any reforms. In a survey of state laws throughout the nation, California was already one of fifteen states that required training in patriotism, citizenship, American ideals, and the Constitution in its public schools. Oregon, Washington, and California were included in the list of states that required citizenship training by law. In 1929, as a result of this study, California revised its own statute. The new statute declared it was the duty of all teachers to educate students in the principles of morality, justice, and patriotism. This new emphasis on a moral basis to education included basic lessons in honesty and work. The new law declared that teachers could inculcate in students a sense of patriotism if they helped students truly comprehend the "rights, duties, and dignity of American citizenship."[68]

Far from embracing white supremacy, racial inferiority, or American values to the exclusion of all else, the final recommendations of the state's report encouraged educators to teach international understanding and sympathy. California had experienced firsthand the increasing interdependence of nations. Because of the growing national diversity in its schools, the commission strongly suggested that schools make a commitment to help their students comprehend the nature of this diversity and to develop a sympathetic understanding of the living and working conditions of people from around the world.[69]

Educators in California facilitated a "trickle down" of modern racial ideologies through these reforms.[70] Such universities as Stanford and Berkeley supported research to reform California public school education. The University of Chicago trained or worked closely with the faculty and students in universities throughout California and the West. Robert Park was prominent among sociologists of the Chicago School. He proposed that culture was not determined by race.[71] If educated properly, children could become, in the words of one elementary school principal, 100 percent Americans regardless of race or ancestry.[72] Although it took longer for this new and seemingly egalitarian vision of race, culture, and assimilation to reach the public at large, educational reforms brought these ideas quite quickly to young children attending California public schools in the 1930s.

For Nisei enrolled in the public schools, the lessons that came out of California education reforms taught them that despite social discrimination, as citizens they retained an inalienable claim to all the "rights, duties, and dignity of American citizenship," regardless of their ancestry or race.[73] They were American citizens. As minors, they were too young to shoulder the responsibilities of citizenship, but they could enjoy some of the rights of citizenship and begin untangling for themselves the contradictions between the equality of citizenship and the social inequality of race.

Learning about the rights of citizenship and the dignity of being Americans by birth made a deep impression on young Nisei. The effect of citizenship training in the schools was especially strong on those Nisei who entered school after these reforms were in place. Nisei children born after or near 1924 not only missed early national debates over Japanese American dual citizenship and loyalty but also entered public schools during the years of the Depression and New Deal politics, after liberal educational reforms in California were in place, and at a time when the older generation of Nisei were organizing politically.

UNINTENDED LESSONS IN CITIZENSHIP

Educators were well intentioned in their efforts to accelerate the pace of Nisei assimilation through citizenship training, but they could not resolve the conflicts between equal citizenship and social discrimination that children faced every day. By teaching children patriotism or love of country through the lens of equal citizenship and what they called 100 percent Americanism, teachers invited criticism from students and inadvertently taught young children to discern for themselves the difference between the ideals of their citizenship and the reality of a racially ordered society. This launched a set of unintended lessons in citizenship.

Nisei children passed along to their friends some of the most powerful yet unintended lessons of citizenship. Norikane witnessed one of these lessons when his friend, Charles Shishida, dared to confront his principal about the incongruity of teaching 100 percent Americanism in a segregated school. After a fight broke out between Chinese and Japanese students at the Walnut Grove Oriental School, where a Japanese student had called a Chinese student a "Chink," the school principal tried to instruct the students in equality and racial understanding as she broke up the fight. The principal said, "You're no Chink and you're no Jap! You're 100 percent American, so I don't want you to ever call names, you understand that?!" Remembering the scene, Norikane said Shishida stood next to him, and when he began to speak, the principal inquired, "Yes, what do you want?!" Shishida stated what was obvious to the rest of his classmates: "If we're 100 percent American, why aren't we in the other school up there?" referring to the all-white school only a half mile away. Norikane said the principal was stunned by the question and hardly knew how to respond—"None of your business! Give that boy an 'F' in deportment! That's just how it is, and it's going to stay that way!"—and then she walked out of the gym, leaving the children behind with many unanswered questions. Norikane said that even at the end of his life, he still could not figure out why

Thomas School third and fourth grade, posed in front of the school, ca. 1926. *Front row:* Dorothy Putnam, Shigeyoshi Iseri, Henry Miyoshi, Kiyoji Horiuchi, Frank Arima, Gordon Hirabayashi, Shooko Teraoka, Tetsuo Kamo. *Middle row:* Catherine Eastman, Rose Yamada, Mae Iseri Yamada, unknown girl, Tsuruye Inouye, Itsuko Tsujikawa, Matsue Nomura, Mary Tsukamaki, Mieki Teraoka, Kenko Natori, Lillian Yamada, Helen Casebeer, Evelyn Eastman. *Back row:* J. Arthur Stewart; Harry Carr, Jr.; Robert Olson; Edward Moore; Bennie Portman; Frank Kosai; Mineo Kamo; Maxwell Ortwein; Shigeharu Horiuchi. *(Photographer unknown. Courtesy of the White River Valley Museum.)*

Shishida got an "F" in deportment, a general category determined by a student's demeanor, attendance, and overall "citizenship" in school.[74] By assigning Shishida a failing grade in deportment, this principal passed on a very powerful message to all students who witnessed the scene: It was not good manners to point out the obvious contradictions between the lessons in 100 percent Americanism students learned in school and the obvious forms of race distinction that existed all around them.

The contradictions between lessons in citizenship as taught in the schools and at home did not end when segregation ended. Schools in Walnut Grove were segregated only up to high school, and then students attended integrated schools. This, according to Norikane, set up Asian American students for even more problems. One day the gym coach asked Norikane and his friends, "What's the matter with you Orientals? You're cliquish. . . . You never mix." Norikane remembered none of them had the nerve to stand up to him, but if they had, they would have asked him what he expected. Norikane recalled:

They put you in a segregated school from the beginning, and they show you that's where you belong. You don't belong with the whites. And then all of a sudden you go to high school and they expect you to mingle with them? So we just always stayed together. When we graduated from grammar school we [were] always together.[75]

There seemed to be no end to the contradictory lessons learned by Nisei. Stay separate, but then integrate. You are all equal, but not equal enough to attend the same school or to get the same jobs.

Although Shishida received an "F" in deportment for speaking up against segregation in school and Norikane showed respect by holding his tongue, teachers regularly encouraged their Nisei students to "speak up" and to become more American in their classroom behavior. Hirabayashi mentioned that, for him, growing up in a Japanese home became a real problem when he went to school. His teacher would encourage him by saying, "Speak up, Gordon! What do you think about that? Let's hear your view." But, as Hirabayashi recalled, "The Japanese value system told me not to blurt out anything that was only half-baked, bringing shame to me and my family, and I frequently sat like a sphinx in school."[76] Even though it took some time for Hirabayashi to tell authority figures what was on his mind, he seemed to retain his commitment not to blurt out anything that was half-baked. By the time he did speak up, he had given his ideas and values plenty of time to mature and to crystallize, so he spoke with conviction and strength.

Norikane continued to have direct confrontations with segregation and discrimination, but for some young Nisei, experiences of interracial cooperation dominated daily life. Ken Yoshida remembered cooperation more than conflict. When Yoshida was about eight years old, his family moved to the Santa Maria valley in Southern California. In the first town he lived in, Guadalupe, about 90 percent of the population were Japanese. But Guadalupe did not have its own school, so Yoshida and the other children were bused to the nearby town of Santa Maria. By the time Yoshida was in high school, he estimated that the school was made up of at least 40 percent Japanese students. "We got along alright," because, as Yoshida said, they were all farmers. They all had a common basis for understanding one another. Cooperation and friendship characterized race relations in Yoshida's school experience. "In fact," he said, "in the town of Guadalupe they had so many Japanese, they used to bring rice balls to school . . . and their Caucasian fellows would bring their sandwiches, and when they'd eat together, they'd trade off."[77] He went about his business, until World War II changed it all. It was not until his family was forced to move to the Tanforan Assembly Center in 1942 that Yoshida faced overt race discrimination for the first time.

It may be hard to believe that Nisei who grew up in the 1930s in California could say that World War II was the first time they were personally confronted with outright race discrimination, but stories like this are repeated quite frequently in oral histories. The most commonly segregated public spaces were pools, movie theaters, and golf courses. During the Depression, when most

Nisei were growing up, these were luxuries that they could ill afford. Neighborhoods might be informally segregated or might be segregated through housing covenants, but for young people growing up, this was not yet a major issue. In fact, in many of the neighborhoods where Nisei grew up, particularly in the urban areas of Los Angeles, Japanese American children were exposed to a remarkable diversity of ethnicities and races, laying the groundwork for postwar inter-ethno-racial cooperation instead of reinforcing their own marginality.[78] Nisei might have had to adjust career goals based on fields of study and professional occupations that were closed to them, but, again, young people adjusted and made the most of being young. When I compared notes with oral historian Richard Potashin, he agreed that it was quite common for Nisei to report that they did not experience race discrimination when they were growing up. It was only after being asked pointed questions about segregated housing, theaters, and limited careers that individuals agreed that some forms of race discrimination may have surrounded them, but they were not always willing to say that they had been personally affected on a day-to-day basis.[79]

Hirabayashi explained this seeming lack of race discrimination in his own way. It was not that he and others did not encounter problems—they did. As he put it, "I grew up in the midst of discrimination and injustice, violations of what I believed to have been the Bill of Rights." When asked how he could possibly have had such strong principles about the Constitution and fair play his whole life, living in a world dominated by race-based discrimination yet not having a major problem before World War II, he said that he did not know how to overcome what he saw. He did see people all around him, Japanese and Chinese workers in particular, who lacked the power to end the various forms of discrimination that seemed out of step with the Constitution. So, the only thing Hirabayashi felt he could do personally was to resolve to be a strong advocate of constitutional principles and to vow to live those principles. It was not until discriminatory laws were written that applied only to persons of Japanese ancestry during the war—laws that, as Hirabayashi said, required nothing of him except that he be of a particular ancestry—that he was forced to make a move. That personal intrusion of an unjust law created the conflict. To go on living life without altering one's behavior became a criminal act, but only if you were of Japanese ancestry. The personal intrusion into daily life changed the nature of race-based discrimination. It was impossible to ignore.[80]

Growing up in the midst of a world ordered by racial hierarchies, children grew up having ordered their own lives in ways that minimized invasive confrontations with race discrimination and segregation on a day-to-day basis. This meant that Nisei experienced significant levels of shock and trauma when they were forced to leave their homes and to move into camps where they were surrounded by all Japanese faces during World War II. Yoshida's shock when the government began treating him like an "enemy alien" during the war, after getting along fairly well while growing up, was a common reaction among Nisei. Many Nisei grew up for some time without realizing that their ancestry could limit their citizenship rights. They had become accustomed to some forms of social inequality but still believed in the fundamental constitutional guarantees of their birthright citizenship.[81]

No matter how diverse life was for Nisei children growing up, regardless of whether they experienced racial discrimination firsthand, World War II changed everything, and not a single Nisei escaped the effects of the wartime forced removal and confinement of Japanese Americans. They responded to these wartime changes in ways that revealed their own unique takes on their formal and informal lessons in citizenship. Public school education, whether in segregated or integrated settings, had a profound influence on how children learned their places in the nation. Educators intentionally shaped their lessons around changing ideas about race and citizenship. Their lessons gave children a sense of equality and their rights as citizens, laying the foundation for wartime civil disobedience.

Growing up in peacetime, Nisei became acquainted with a rights-based introduction to citizenship. As children, they exercised their rights to public school educations but lacked the political right to vote and the obligations of service to the state. The courts upheld their rights to ownership of property and to equality before the law, and as children they passed on some limited legal rights to their parents through guardianship over them and their estates. They were taught in school, as mandated by state law, of the power and sanctity of their citizenship and about the important role that resistance to colonial rule had played in creating an American democracy of which they were a part. So, due to age and to the absence of war, Nisei were not expected to fulfill obligations related to their citizenship other than the more ideological obligations of good behavior in school, obedience to the law, and loyalty to the country. The strong foundation in rights-based citizenship certainly played a significant role in determining Nisei reactions to their wartime experiences just a few years later.

For Norikane, his childhood lessons in the complicated nature of his own citizenship became all the more ironic when his family was placed in a racetrack better suited for holding animals than humans. As he stood in the assembly center, Norikane remembered the incident in the gymnasium of the Oriental School when his friend challenged the principal about the real definition of 100 percent Americans. Her words rang loudly in his ears as he tried yet again to reconcile for himself what it meant to be 100 percent American at a time when citizenship offered no protection against incarceration for wearing the face of the enemy. He said, "So this is what it means to be 100 percent American? That's a bunch of bull," and he started down his own path of personal resistance, demanding that his birthright citizenship be considered good enough, even in times of war.[82]

CHAPTER 2

Nisei Wartime Citizenship

O N A SATURDAY MORNING in California only a few months after Japan had bombed Pearl Harbor, a young Nisei boy heard a knock at his door. When he opened the door, he found a police officer standing on the porch. The officer could sense the boy's fear and began joking around to put him at ease. The child's father joined them. They were both relieved that the policeman had not come to take the father away. The FBI had taken many other fathers from their homes in the hours and days following Japan's attack on Pearl Harbor. This policeman explained that he was inspecting the homes of Japanese families to search for firearms that he needed to confiscate. The man had one gun that had been given to him as a gift, but which he had never fired. The policeman told him that if he had a son that was of age, the father could turn the firearm over to this son, but because the man did not, the policeman had to take it.[1]

It is ironic that the policeman would have been satisfied leaving a gun in the home of an Issei, an enemy alien, if he could have turned the gun over to his citizen son. Most historians interpret such stories as the beginning of a transfer of power from Issei to Nisei.[2] Often overlooked is the confidence many Americans had in the power of citizenship at the beginning of the war. Historian Alice Yang Murray emphasizes this early confidence in the protections of Nisei citizenship, even pointing out statements made by Gen. John L. DeWitt very early in 1942 that indicated that he believed Nisei had certain rights that could not be violated.[3] From a Nisei perspective, it was not a foregone conclusion that they would end the year locked up in camps under government control. Even as rumors spread of an evacuation of Japanese Americans from the West Coast, government officials, Japanese American Citizens League (JACL) leaders, and private individuals debated the extent to which Nisei rights should or could be proscribed based on exaggerated and often misleading notions of military necessity.

When World War II began, Nisei had little reason to renegotiate their relationship with the state as citizens. Then the state changed the rules of citizenship, recasting Nisei as nonaliens or as enemy aliens. This chapter explains the crisis regarding Nisei citizenship as it evolved early in the war. When conflicts arise, where is citizenship decided? The courts do not have sole claim to the question, even though we continue to rely on the courts for definitive answers. Do the individuals themselves choose their citizenship through declarations of loyalty and patriotism? Is citizenship then a matter of the heart and mind? Does the federal government decide, or do the states? During the first year of the war, Nisei lost many of their most basic rights of citizenship. This chapter also discusses various responses to these attacks on Nisei citizenship by the courts; by the federal, state, and local governments; by private race-baiting organizations; and by Japanese Americans themselves. The outcome of these debates redefined Nisei citizenship in the context of war.

Japanese Americans clearly did not remain silent as their citizenship came under attack. Leaders of the JACL, proclaiming themselves spokesmen for all Japanese American citizens, reenacted conversations about loyalty and Americanism that they had with congressional investigation committees in 1920, when the country was faced with the immediate post–World War I crisis over immigration. The younger generation of Nisei just coming of age during World War II were left frustrated by debates over loyalty, patriotism, and 100 percent American citizenship. JACL accommodation was not a popular choice with the majority of Japanese Americans. The bulk of Nisei, born between the early 1920s and early 1930s, had learned in school that their birth in the United States gave them 100 percent American citizenship. When faced with an erosion of that citizenship, though, few dared to resist immediately. The few who did resist, most notably Minoru Yasui and Gordon Hirabayashi, initiated test cases that would demonstrate how far the courts would bow to military authority and wartime hysteria to justify restricted citizenship for suspect dual nationals. Most Nisei waited and watched as events beyond their control eroded their standing in the nation and recast them as suspect citizens at best and enemy aliens in the extreme.

This chapter explains Hirabayashi's civil disobedience in this context of a crisis over Nisei citizenship. The chapter also shows how Nisei became divided over the meaning of their changing status in a country at war with the nation of their ancestry and the official language of euphemism that cloaked it. Hirabayashi responded to the violation of his own rights with civil disobedience, but most Japanese Americans were less sure of how they should respond. Government officials from the FBI, the Office of War Information, and the War Department became concerned about what they perceived to be the growing problem of male juvenile delinquency among the incarcerated Nisei population. They began discussing ways in which these young men might be given the chance to serve in the military as a cure to growing discontent and a turn toward what looked like disloyalty in the camps. Violence erupted as Japanese

Americans struggled to find appropriate and effective responses to the gradual erosion of Nisei citizenship and the wholesale violation of Nikkei civil rights.

PEARL HARBOR

When Japan bombed Pearl Harbor, most people living on the U.S. mainland could not locate Pearl Harbor on a map, and fewer still understood the implications of this attack. Nisei youth were no different. An attack by Japan against a remote naval base in the Pacific seemed of little relevance to their lives. Joe Norikane was playing basketball near his home in California when he heard the news. At first, he did not even believe what he had heard. When a member of the opposing team repeated the story, he realized that it was true. But a game was on, and even his friends said, "Hey, we can't be talking about that . . . let's play basketball!" The news may have seemed irrelevant then, but, Norikane recalled years later, that night it became a nightmare.[4]

The nightmare began when the FBI put into motion a plan to arrest a prepared list of Japanese Americans whom intelligence agencies believed might pose a threat to national security. Many families responded to these arrests with fear and trepidation. Some tried to anticipate the arrests by removing cause for suspicion. Families buried or burned anything that demonstrated their ties with Japan. Tee Norikane remembered the day her family decided to burn anything Japanese, such as books, dolls, and kimonos. Tee Norikane lamented the loss of her dolls the most. However, she could get rid of a doll, but she could not change her face or the fact that she was Japanese, too. Fear of arrest and fear of drawing accusations of Japanese loyalty led some young people to stop speaking Japanese even at home, frustrating their parents, some of whom could speak little English. Some families even stopped eating rice and instead ate hamburgers and stews in an effort to appear more American.[5]

As Nikkei families defended themselves against accusations of disloyalty, they also became aware of a growing crisis of suspicion within their own communities. Rumors grew that Japanese Americans were turning in names of other Japanese Americans they suspected of Japanese sympathy. Susumu Yenokida grew up in a JACL-dominated town. In Turlock, California, some men stood out as community leaders and fit the profile of those the FBI had been arresting all over California, but they were never taken into custody. Yenokida remembered that these men who had not been arrested had sons who were prominent JACL leaders. The families of those who lost their fathers and husbands became suspicious; to many Nikkei, the correlation between those who were not arrested and JACL membership became startlingly clear. As a result, some Issei men actually found relief in being arrested by the FBI. At least they would not be suspected of spying or of being a government stooge or *inu,* a derogatory term meaning "dog" or "traitor."[6] Yosh Kuromiya's family made a joke of the situation, even packing a bag for his father and keeping it near the front door in case he, too, was arrested. Family members told him, "Well, this is your care package when they come after you." The Kuromiya family did not expect the father to be arrested, though, because he was not a prominent man within the community. As Kuromiya put it, his father was always too busy trying to make a living. Preparing for the unknown, though, gave the family at least a small sense of control over an unpredictable situation.[7]

Informants deflected criticism that they were betraying their own people with arguments that they were merely acting out of patriotic duty and in the interest of national defense. This rationalization did not change what looked like betrayal to many Nikkei. By turning over Issei names to U.S. intelligence agencies, JACL leaders fostered bitter resentment between Japanese Americans at large and JACL members. Few understood the implications of this early cooperation between the JACL and the government, and even fewer could foresee the full-scale evacuation of Japanese Americans from the West Coast that loomed large on the horizon.[8]

LOYALTY VERSUS CITIZENSHIP

The War Department justified evacuating all Japanese Americans from the West Coast based on the claims that it was impossible to determine which Japanese Americans were loyal to the United States and which were not. It became clear early in the war that these same leaders believed citizenship provided little proof of loyalty. As early as January 4, 1942, Gen. DeWitt declared that he most suspected the citizen Nisei of disloyalty. He looked to his legal assistant, Col. Karl Bendetsen, for assistance in creating a legal means to exclude all persons of Japanese ancestry from the West Coast. Bendetsen, a military lawyer, had been assigned to help DeWitt manage his role as commander over the Western Defense Command. In Bendetsen's legal opinion, certain areas of the country could be off limits to anyone, "whether they are citizens, white or Jap or black or brown." Individuals without permits to enter the area could be prohibited. Thus, California politicians and unsubstantiated popular hysteria supported the exclusion of all Japanese from the West Coast, but the movement would be presented to the public and the courts as a military decision, based on the assumption that all persons of Japanese ancestry were suspects and potential saboteurs.[9]

In the face of government claims that loyal persons of Japanese ancestry could not be differentiated from disloyal persons, the JACL went to great lengths to prove its organization staunchly loyal to the United States. Some observers even charged that JACL members became overzealous, even belligerent, in their attempts to prove their loyalty.[10] At the first wartime convention of the JACL held on January 11, 1942, delegates voted to require that all members sign a loyalty oath:

> I, _____, do solemnly swear that I will support and defend the Constitution of the United States against all enemies, foreign and domes-

tic; that I will bear true faith and allegiance to the same; that I hereby renounce any other allegiances which I may have knowingly or unknowingly held in the past; and that I take this obligation freely without any reservation or evasion. So help me God.[11]

This oath provided a means for Nisei to declare their allegiance to the United States and to forswear allegiance they may or may not have held to the emperor of Japan by way of dual citizenship. The JACL leadership remained keenly aware of the fears that pervaded congressional debates in the 1920s over Nisei dual citizenship and the War Department's failed attempts to sponsor legislation that would have required such an oath of dual citizens in 1941. With no such law in place, the JACL tried to resolve the issue by creating its own oath of allegiance that included a renunciation of any foreign allegiances.

Despite JACL attempts to prove Nisei loyalty, Japan's attack on Pearl Harbor became a catalyst for a series of policies and laws that severely eroded the strength of Nisei citizenship. The attack also functioned as a catalyst to bring to the surface questions about Nisei citizenship from a variety of sources, not all of which were legal. The Selective Service on the federal level, the civil service on the state level, and petitions supporting mass removal on the local level all attacked Nisei constitutional and civil rights.

LAWS ERODE NISEI RIGHTS

On February 4, 1942, the military established a curfew for enemy aliens. This restricted the freedom of movement of Issei, but not of Nisei. Enemy aliens would have to remain in their homes from 8:00 P.M. until 6:00 A.M. and remain within five miles of their homes. At the same time, the military encouraged all who were able to move voluntarily from the West Coast and to resettle farther east. A few chose to resettle voluntarily, but not many. Most preferred to stay in their homes as long as possible and to abide by the curfew law.[12]

On February 19, President Franklin Roosevelt signed Executive Order 9066, which allowed military commanders to designate military zones from which "any or all persons may be excluded." In practice, this meant all persons of Japanese ancestry. On February 26, the evacuation began, but only in specific areas, such as Terminal Island off the coast of California near Los Angeles. On March 2, Gen. DeWitt created military zones along the West Coast and declared that all German and Italian aliens and Japanese aliens and nonaliens could be forced to evacuate these zones if necessary.

In an attempt to stall or even to prevent a mass evacuation of all Japanese Americans from the West Coast, Carey McWilliams (a well-known journalist, author, lawyer, and civil rights advocate for migrant workers' rights in the 1930s and advocate for Japanese Americans' rights during World War II) urged a congressional investigation into the situation. The Tolan Committee hearings were the result of well-meaning individuals' efforts to prevent civil rights abuses, but they began after President Roosevelt had already signed Executive Order 9066. To make matters worse, the Tolan Committee was largely composed of congressional representatives who believed falsely, based on sparse, inaccurate, and fabricated evidence, that Japanese in Hawaii had contributed to the successful attack on Pearl Harbor. The Tolan Committee would not achieve what McWilliams sought: a reversal of what promised to become a massive attack on the civil rights of an entire ethnic population without due process of law.[13]

Leading officers of the JACL testified before the Tolan Committee early in March. Instead of resolving concerns about loyalty and sabotage, their testimony actually reinforced critics' fears that it was impossible to tell who among Japanese Americans was loyal and who was disloyal. On March 7, 1942, Tokie Slocum, Togo Tanaka, Sam Minami, Fred Tayama, and Joseph Ninoda all appeared before the Tolan Committee as members of the United Citizens Federation and as prominent members of the JACL. Slocum explained that as a veteran of World War I, he realized that no price was too high for victory in the war. If evacuation became necessary for Japanese to prove their loyalty, Slocum declared, "I'll lead them." He continued, "No one appreciates the spiritual value of citizenship more than I do." In response to Slocum's enthusiasm, investigators asked whether he was overplaying his hand. One investigator warned, "Beware of Greeks bearing gifts." Gushing declarations of loyalty might be used to hide the intentions of those who plotted against the United States.[14] Nisei had no credibility once they had become racialized suspect citizens in the eyes of the Tolan Committee.

James Sakamoto, former president of the JACL, agreed with Slocum that, if necessary, he would support limited freedoms for Japanese Americans to curb growing fears of Japanese sabotage. He testified before Congress that it might help the U.S. government and Japanese Americans to cooperate against growing racial hysteria if Japanese Americans voluntarily placed themselves under protective custody:

> Let me say, incidentally, that this public hysteria, if we do not watch out, is going to cause disunity, and that is what Hitler is looking for, and I believe that is what Japan is looking for, too. Now if it is going to help to curb public hysteria, and if it will help the end of national unity, why not put all of us under protective custody? Or, better still, if you care to, why not place the alien Japanese parents of ours under our custody? For instance, I can give you one concrete plan. We can have a registration system where every alien must report, let us say, twice a week, to our Japanese-American Citizens League headquarters, and if they do not come in to register twice a week, we will report those persons to the Federal Bureau of Investigation, and a check-up will be made.[15]

One investigator asked Slocum how the government could rely on the JACL to police the Japanese alien population. It was not just aliens, after all, whom congressional investigators suspected of disloyalty. He asked, "Do you have any members—I am speaking of your national organization—do you have any members who have what is called 'dual citizenship'?" Sakamoto replied, "Yes, I believe we have some who are still called dual citizens, although I will have to say this much for them," and he repeated what he had told the committee two decades earlier: Most Nisei knew little about their citizenship with Japan and held allegiance only to the land of their birth, the United States. Some JACL members were dual citizens of Japan and the United States by law, but by feeling and patriotism, they were only Americans.[16]

Academics, church leaders, labor leaders, and lawyers spoke against the evacuations and were bolder in their criticism of the pending constitutional abuses than were the representatives of the JACL. Notable among those who testified in defense of Japanese Americans' rights to due process was A. L. (Abraham Lincoln) Wirin, counsel for the Southern California branch of the ACLU. He said, "There must be a point beyond which there may be no abridgement of civil liberties . . . whether we are at war or peace."[17] James Omura, a noted writer, newspaperman, and critic of JACL collaboration with the government, was more blunt in his criticism of the planned evacuations, asking whether the Gestapo had come to America. In a statement submitted to the Tolan Committee, Omura writes, "Is citizenship such a light and transient thing that that which is our inalienable right in normal times can be torn from us in times of war?"[18] Despite some testimony urging congressional leaders to prevent a massive assault on Japanese Americans' civil and humanitarian rights, many more who testified seemed to assume that the mass evacuation had already become inevitable.

Toward the end of March, despite the best attempts of civil rights advocates and JACL testimony proclaiming extraordinary loyalty to the United States and suggesting that members control surveillance over their alien parents, government policies closed the door even tighter on Nikkei rights and freedom, initiating the most drastic transformation of Nisei wartime citizenship. On March 18, Roosevelt created the War Relocation Authority (WRA). On March 21, Congress imposed penalties for any who refused orders to evacuate the military zones. On March 23, DeWitt issued his first Civilian Exclusion Order, giving "aliens and non-aliens" of Japanese ancestry one week to evacuate Bainbridge Island in the Puget Sound of Seattle, Washington. On March 24, Public Proclamation 3 included Nisei in curfew restrictions. Once Nisei became "non-aliens" and subject to the same exclusion and curfew orders as enemy aliens, they became in a very practical sense marginalized as they had never been marginalized before.[19] By the end of March, it became clear that Nisei were gradually losing the protections of the Constitution.

In what appears to have been a final effort to prevent the involuntary incarceration of all persons of Japanese descent, Sakamoto promised continued support and loyalty "under all but impossible conditions." His proposal was telling and stood in sharp contrast to the offers that fellow JACL leader Mike Masaoka made in private. Sakamoto made this proposal to Roosevelt:

> Mr. President, we have protested our loyalty in the past. We have not been believed. We are willing to assume the burden of continuing to demonstrate it under all but impossible conditions. . . . Give us some refuge in the heart of the country far removed from even the suspicion or possibility to do harm. We have helped to feed the nation in the past. Let us continue to do so now that it is needed [even] more. Only let us do so freely and not under that compulsion made notorious in an enemy country. We do not have to be driven to work for a country in which we believe for ideals more precious than our life-blood.[20]

Sakamoto's petition for continued voluntary relocation is important. Forced removal could only reinforce the implicit guilt of all those affected. Through voluntary compliance, Nikkei could demonstrate loyalty and patriotism. This emphasis on loyalty through voluntary sacrifice was important then and remained an important tool in the JACL attempt to rehabilitate the Japanese American reputation and image during and after the war. A sacrifice made under threat of criminal prosecution would not translate into evidence of loyalty and patriotism the same way voluntary sacrifice would, and Sakamoto knew this as he pleaded with the president to put off mandatory evacuations of the West Coast and to consider the alternatives, no matter how drastic the alternatives might be.[21]

While Sakamoto requested a voluntary resettlement program, Masaoka proposed the formation of an all-Nisei suicide battalion. He believed that Japanese Americans could "illustrate the extremes to which they were willing to go" to safeguard their homes and could demonstrate their loyalty in two ways. A "suicide battalion," Masaoka suggested, "would go anywhere to spearhead the most dangerous missions. . . . To assure the skeptics that the members of the 'suicide battalion' would remain loyal, the families and friends of the volunteers would place themselves in the hands of the government as 'hostages.'" The War Department rejected Masaoka's plan, saying it was "not the practice of the government to require 'hostages' or to sponsor such 'suicide battalions.'"[22]

The policy changes that most directly redefined the state's relationship with Japanese Americans removed Nisei obligations to serve in the military. The War Department not only rejected Masaoka's proposal for an all Nisei "suicide battalion" but also tried to halt Nisei inductions into the military almost entirely. The War Department had failed in its attempt to push H.R. 5879 through Congress, which would have made it impossible for Nisei to enter the military without first renouncing any loyalty to Japan and reaffirming their loyalty to the United States (discussed in Chapter 1). Declaration of war motivated the War Department to end Nisei inductions without congressional approval. This process was uneven at first. Some Japanese Americans already drafted under the 1940 Selective Service Act were discharged, while others were relegated to menial, noncombat duties. After Japan attacked Pearl Harbor, the War Department worked directly with the Selective Service to stop drafting Japanese Americans. The Selective Service requested that draft boards reclassify some Nisei from Category 1-A (citizens available for service) to IV-C (aliens not acceptable for service). The use of IV-C for Nisei is extremely significant, as the categorization was one concrete way in which Nisei literally lost their citizenship statuses and were reclassified as enemy aliens despite their rights to citizenship under the Fourteenth Amendment. It was also illegal, as Roger Daniels points out, because the Selective Service Act of 1940 clearly prohibited this kind of race-based discrimination.[23] But normal civil law did not apply to many wartime policies restricting the rights of Japanese Americans, and a precedent for refusing the service of Japanese in the navy already existed. The navy had stopped accepting Japanese into service in 1907 because of questions it had about loyalty and citizenship. The War Department followed the navy's lead when it stopped accepting Japanese Americans into the military until a system could be worked out to assess their loyalty and to resolve questions about Nisei dual citizenship.[24]

It took months for the Selective Service and the War Department to formalize their plan to stop inducting Japanese Americans, and in the meantime, the Selective Service started worrying about the legality of its actions. In June 1942, the Selective Service requested information from the War Department that might help speed up the process of converting all Nisei over to IV-C status. It urgently needed to finish the reclassification of Nisei to IV-C if the War Department and navy remained unwilling to accept Nisei inductees so they would not be counted in the population of draft-eligible citizens.[25] The War Department finally agreed. It distrusted Japanese Americans' loyalty, but it desperately needed some people with Japanese-language skills for translation and familiarity with Japan's geography for map making. In a letter dated June 17, 1942, Secretary of War Henry Stimson gave Gen. Lewis Hershey, director of the Selective Service, the official signal to stop inducting Japanese Americans.[26] In this case, the War Department's decision not to accept Japanese American inductees necessitated a corresponding decision on the part of another federal entity: the Selective Service. The gradual erosion of Nisei citizenship came about one decision at a time and one agency at a time, the combined effect of which led to a devastating list of unintended consequences.

As a result of this delayed and drawn-out process of transferring individual Nisei over to IV-C status, combined with the fact that citizens could appeal to their draft boards for reclassification, some Nisei ended up with several different Selective Service statuses during the war, and it took years for some Nisei to receive notices that their classification had been changed to IV-C. Future resister Yoshi Kubo did not receive notification of his IV-C status until March 1943, even though the reclassification process began more than a year earlier and even though as a farm owner he had rightly appealed for an agricultural deferment. His Selective Service status changed so frequently, it led to a feeling of complete distrust and anger for the Selective Service system by the time he was returned to I-A status and received his draft notice in 1944.[27] Hirabayashi had more changes in his classification than most. According to an FBI report, he was reclassified seven times in two years.[28] Despite the lag time involved in notifying individual Nisei about their new Selective Service statuses and the confusion that multiple changes in status caused, the shift to IV-C was eventually applied to all Nisei, recasting them as enemy aliens despite no official change in their statuses as U.S.-born citizens.[29]

The State of California implemented its own interpretation of Nisei dual citizenship when it summarily fired all Nisei from civil service positions. The state made the assumption that under Japan's citizenship laws, all Nisei were dual citizens; in the context of war, they were then by extension enemy aliens. The state fired all employees on the basis that they had withheld information about their employment, misrepresented their citizenship, and were thus ineligible for one of the most important perks of citizenship, civil service employment.[30] This process began with questionnaires asking for details regarding how closely Nisei maintained cultural ties to Japan. They were asked about past visits to Japan, about their Japanese-language skills, and whether individuals maintained membership in organizations with ties to Japan. The California Senate called for the termination of all Nisei employment despite Attorney General Earl Warren's warnings that firing individuals on the basis of race would be unconstitutional.[31]

On April 2, 1942, the California state personnel board began the process of terminating Nisei employees. Those who had been told to "stay home" after President Roosevelt signed Executive Order 9066, without being formally terminated, were definitively fired. On April 13, letters were sent to the remaining Nisei employees, explaining that they were being terminated on the basis of "fraud in securing employment," among other charges. The documents sent to Nisei civil service employees claimed universally and without individual evidence that all Nisei were citizens of Japan, that they were all "able to read and write Japanese," that they had attended Japanese schools where they were educated by "officials of the Buddhist Church," and that they were members of "Japanese organizations" that were "violently opposed" to America's democratic form of government. The JACL planned to fight these blanket charges in court, but the actions of the Western Defense Command were moving along so rapidly toward the mass exclusion of Japanese Americans that more pressing crises soon overwhelmed concerns of wrongful termination.[32] The State of California determined that in the case of Nisei, it would ignore the Fourteenth Amendment guarantee of citizenship by birth and instead recognize only the possibility that Nisei were eligible for foreign citizenship.

Nongovernmental groups began calling for the mass removal of Japanese Americans from the West Coast, especially from California, and complained that one of the problems facing the country stemmed from Nisei dual citizenship. The Joint Immigration Committee, a reorganized anti-immigrant group that in part included the old Asiatic Exclusion League and was supported by small business owners who opposed Japanese immigration, began organizing around a new exclusion goal. On January 2, 1942, it issued a manifesto that was reprinted in newspapers throughout California, arguing that Japanese Americans were "totally unassimilable" and could not be trusted in a time of war. The manifesto proclaimed, "those born in this country are American citizens by right of birth, but they are also Japanese citizens, liable . . . to be called to bear arms for their Emperor, either in front of, or behind, enemy lines." The manifesto argued that "Japanese language schools" served as "a blind to cover instruction similar to that received by a young student in Japan—that his is a superior race, the divinity of the Japanese Emperor, the loyalty that every Japanese, wherever born, or residing, owes his Emperor and Japan." The Native Sons of the Golden West and the California American Legion supported this manifesto. They argued that "all Japanese who are known to hold dual citizenship . . . be placed in concentration camps." Shortly after the Joint Immigration Committee published its manifesto, Warren and Ulysses S. Webb, the present and former attorneys general, respectively, began advising the committee about how it might effectively persuade the federal government to remove all Japanese Americans from California and the West Coast. The Native Sons argued further that it was precisely because of efforts to exclude Japanese from immigrating and owning land and failed attempts to deny "citizenship to offspring of all aliens ineligible to citizenship" that the Japanese had attacked Pearl Harbor in the first place. Local chapters of the Native Sons responded by passing resolutions of their own, which demanded that the federal government remove all Japanese Americans from the West Coast.[33]

The gradual erosion of Nisei citizenship rights seemed complete when the Western Defense Command and Fourth Army Wartime Civil Control Administration began posting notices up and down the West Coast ordering all persons of Japanese ancestry, aliens and "non-aliens," to prepare for mandatory evacuation. Heads of Nikkei family units were ordered to report for further instructions at civil control stations, where each family would be assigned an identification number in preparation for the mass-evacuation orders. Then families packed all that they could carry, sold what they could not for pennies on the dollar, and made final arrangements to store what was left. The first stop for most evacuated families was a temporary holding facility euphemistically called an "assembly center," where detainees waited for the more permanent camps to be built. In all, approximately one hundred twenty thousand individuals were forced into government custody at great personal cost for what many believed would be the duration of the war.

GORDON HIRABAYASHI

Hirabayashi was supposed to register for "evacuation" like all other Japanese Americans from the Seattle area for what would become the largest forced removal and incarceration of one ethnic group without the benefit of due process in U.S. history. But Hirabayashi refused. He had no other choice. Like others who had committed acts of civil disobedience before him, he felt that

Gordon Hirabayashi as a
student at the University of
Washington in the 1940s.
*(Photo by Sharon Maeda.
Courtesy of the Wing Luke
Museum.)*

he could not cooperate with a law that so clearly violated his understanding of the Constitution.[34] He had studied the actions of World War I resisters, had read the political writings of Jawaharlal Nehru about passive resistance and the independence movement of India, and had become a conscientious objector (CO), a Quaker, and a member of the Fellowship of Reconciliation. As Hirabayashi embarked on his journey through the courts and on to prison, he was self-consciously aware of how his actions fit into a long history of passive resistance and civil disobedience.

Despite the punctuating effect of Japan's attack on Pearl Harbor and the racial hysteria and wartime fears that this attack provoked, Hirabayashi had no reason to believe that his rights would be curtailed on the basis of race. But when laws began to erode Nisei citizenship rights gradually over the first few months of the war, doing nothing was not a choice Hirabayashi could make. He either had to comply with the law and turn himself over to the government for processing and forced relocation into a detention facility, or he could refuse to obey the law and go to jail. He chose the path of resistance.

Hirabayashi's civil disobedience was based in part on his educational and personal experiences leading up to the war. Hirabayashi enrolled at the University of Washington in the fall of 1937. He spent his first two years of university life working hard to pay his way. He worked as a "school boy" in the home of a doctor, where he earned room, board, and $5 in pocket money each month. In 1939, the Sociology Department hired him as a statistician under the National Youth Authority program that paid students $15 a month to work two hours a day, five days a week on campuses across the country. This program, Hirabayashi remembered, allowed some young people to attend school during the Depression who might not otherwise have been able to enroll in the university. In Hirabayashi's case, the job allowed him to focus his energies a little closer to campus.[35]

Besides working hard to earn a meager living and going to school, Hirabayashi became involved in extracurricular activities at the university. He had been a member of the "HI-Y," a branch of the Young Men's Christian Association (YMCA) for high school students, while he attended Auburn High School. He continued his "Y" membership at the University of Washington. The university "Y" was located in Eagleson Hall, home of many student clubs, where liberal thinkers and guest lecturers led students in thoughtful discussions about the world, politics, and the student Christian movement. The intellectual environment of Eagleson Hall attracted Hirabayashi, inspired him to attend school year-round, and eventually became his home when an opportunity opened up for him to take a room in the basement of the building in exchange for maintaining the furnace.[36]

The YMCA was a part of the international Christian student movement, with roots in the nineteenth century.[37] As the YMCA evolved as an organization into the twentieth century, it became more closely aligned with the international student movement and the antiwar movement, especially on U.S. campuses. YMCA leaders became vocal participants in campaigns against militarism on campuses and elsewhere. By the 1930s, other organizations, such as the Fellowship of Reconciliation (FOR), joined the YMCA in drawing students into politics to support antifascism and pacifism. By 1940, FOR looked to the YMCA and its female counterpart, the Young Women's Christian Association (YWCA), as an important partner coalition that could provide leadership for students and potentially attract new recruits for the antiwar movement. FOR's student membership continued to increase through 1941, but after the United States entered the war at the end of 1941, support on campuses waned. FOR continued to support an anticonscription campaign throughout the war years under the leadership of A. J. Muste. Nonviolent civil disobedience became a popular topic of conversation among campus groups that gathered to discuss pacifism.[38]

During the summer of 1940, Hirabayashi was given a scholarship to attend a YMCA student leadership seminar at Columbia University. This leadership seminar was called the President's School, and it brought together students from universities across the country. Hirabayashi enrolled in a course on Christianity and one on leadership. He was exposed to political debates raging at the time and met Norman Thomas, a well-known socialist and pacifist, previous candidate for mayor of New York, and candidate for president of the

United States. Thomas impressed him with his oratory skills when Hirabayashi heard him argue for and against the lend-lease bill, a bill that if approved promised to move the United States another step closer to direct involvement in World War II. The environment in which Hirabayashi studied over the summer inspired a rapid maturation of his religious and political ideas. He later compared the experience to a graduate-level educational experience and said it was fundamentally important to the later decisions he would make during the war.[39]

Hirabayashi recalled that students tried to make the most of their free time while they were in New York, and they created a committee to decide what they would do during each free period. They took advantage of the inexpensive public transportation and sometimes even free admission to museums, lectures, and concerts. More important, Hirabayashi became acquainted with leaders in the peace movement by attending lectures organized by FOR and the War Resisters League. He met such influential figures as Frank Olmstead, executive secretary of the War Resisters League, and Muste, executive secretary of FOR, whose arguments against war shaped Hirabayashi's own stance on the subject.[40]

Hirabayashi returned to Seattle a devoted pacifist. He and his companions who had spent the summer in New York at the YMCA President's School registered as COs after the Selective Service Act of 1940 went into effect. They met on campus as a group and became very close friends. Among this group was Howard Scott, a young "idealist," as Hirabayashi called him. He was from Marysville, Washington, and came from a family that was not well to do and shared much in common with Hirabayashi. They became life-long friends, sharing leadership positions at the university YMCA; Scott served as president and Hirabayashi served as vice president. They also shared a commitment to pacifism and helped organize a small group of like-minded university students, just as FOR had encouraged them to do.

Hirabayashi became the head of this small group of COs, and it was in this capacity that he had his first opportunity to confront authority as a pacifist. Col. Edward Kimmel, Hirabayashi recalled, was in charge of the campus ROTC and also served on the university's YMCA board. He was concerned that the small group of COs was using Eagleson Hall as a meeting place, so he interviewed Hirabayashi about the group's intentions. "Why do you people have to meet?" he asked. "We meet for the same reasons any other student group with special interests meets," Hirabayashi replied. "We believe that students who share our feelings about serving in the military should know there are other individuals with similar views." Hirabayashi recalled that this was his first experience confronting an authority figure over an issue he felt went against his conscience. He explained in an oral-history interview:

Having been raised in a Japanese community, where conformity is a basic virtue, I was going against the tide. My position on most orders was to comply. I have since wondered if, had I been living at the Japanese American Students Club with 150 others, I would have responded as I did. When the chips were down and Japanese Americans were evacuated from the West Coast and interned, very few of them took a stand, even though they bitched about the treatment.[41]

Hirabayashi made a direct connection in his mind between his training in New York, his decision to become a CO, his involvement with the interracial YMCA, his early experiences confronting authority over his right to meet with other COs, and his later decision to refuse the government's exclusion order.

Hirabayashi and Scott took their commitment to pacifism a step further when they decided that it was time to stop meeting with the Quakers casually, a group that had welcomed them in fellowship since their return from New York, and to take on the responsibility of membership. Hirabayashi recalled that his family's commitment to the Mukyokai Christian movement had unconsciously guided his decision to become a Quaker.[42] He became a Quaker as an adult, but this religious conversion represented a continuity of belief that began early in his childhood.

On the morning of December 7, 1941, Hirabayashi went with Scott to the Friends meeting to enjoy a Sunday morning Quaker service. When they came out, Hirabayashi heard someone say, "I heard on the radio that Japan has bombed Pearl Harbor. We are at war!" Like every other American, Hirabayashi was stunned to hear the news. It did not seem real, but it did not take long for the reality to set in. The next day, Hirabayashi went to class, and even though he did not feel any negative reaction personally, he started hearing rumors that a few Japanese Americans had been picked up and detained. A relative owned a grocery store in the city and was a leader in the community. When he was picked up and his son saw his dad behind bars, the son broke down.

Trauma mixed with resignation dominated the feelings of most Nisei students whom Hirabayashi knew at the University of Washington. He recalled later that students were resigned to the fact that their parents would probably experience difficulties, but, as Hirabayashi said, "it never occurred to us that we who were born in the U.S. would be restricted." When Hirabayashi assured his father that he would take care of things if his parents were interned as "enemy aliens," Hirabayashi's father replied, "Hey, if we can be interned, it could happen to you, too." But Hirabayashi and his friends were certain they were safe. "You don't understand," he told his father. "We are citizens! They won't do that to U.S. citizens." Hirabayashi and his friends believed this so strongly that even as they were being picked up and forced to leave their homes, "even as it was happening," he said, "we could not really believe it was happening to us!"[43]

Charitable organizations tried to lessen the humanitarian crisis from which Japanese Americans suffered as a result of the early stages of mass removal and registration for detention. The Council of Churches formed a Japanese American Emergency Committee. Arthur G. Barnett, Hirabayashi's future attorney, remembered, "There was panic in the air." Japanese American families did not have enough money to live on. Some families were without their main sources of support when the FBI arrested community leaders, especially Issei men, in the early weeks of the war. Japanese families also lost access to their bank accounts when the accounts of "enemy aliens" were frozen. Families were afraid of what might happen to them and were in desperate need of assistance. The Council of Churches tried to help. Barnett said, "We were constantly making overtures to the political authorities and the army to be less strict and to set up ways and means where the Japanese could even get groceries and food to eat, and to do something about coming out to calm the panic in the air." But, he explained, "We did not get very far."

Barnett and Hirabayashi crossed paths during the early months of the war. Among the few places the Council of Churches Japanese American Emergency Committee could find to meet were the very places that Hirabayashi called home: the University Friends Meeting and Eagleson Hall. In addition to dealing with the need for basic access to food and living expenses, once orders started coming down for Japanese Americans to register for removal from their homes and temporary detention at the Puyallup Fair Grounds, various organizations, including the Quakers and the Council of Churches, stepped in to help those who were suffering. Barnett recalled:

> Some of the Japanese who were removed to Puyallup included the very young and the very old and people would get sick. And so the Quakers very frequently asked to co-operate to the extent of transporting these people to doctors and hospitals out of Puyallup into Seattle and other places. I went down and visited that camp several times, and talked to people there which included a couple of lawyers, including ex-reserve corps officers. . . . It was really quite a traumatic experience for everybody. Everything had been done so fast that there were no fit human habitations. The barracks were divided off between families with just blankets hanging between them. It was a sad, sad looking thing. I can't remember seeing any mattresses; all I saw were bags which were filled with straw.[44]

Hirabayashi was one of the Quakers who helped families make the trip to Puyallup. He saw the desperation of families trying to store their belongings, settle their affairs, and pack what they could carry only to face the trauma and humiliation of confinement in a makeshift camp barely fit to house humans. This experience made a strong impression on Hirabayashi.

When it was clear that Japanese Americans were facing a crisis, Hirabayashi decided that he would have to drop out of school. He did not enroll in courses for the spring term and instead volunteered his time with the American Friends Service Committee (AFSC). The AFSC was created in 1917 in an effort to provide pacifists a way to serve the country during World War I without engaging directly in military service. Instead, members drove ambulances, provided medical services for the troops, and worked hard to help rebuild communities after the end of the war. The organization became well known throughout World War II for its efforts to ease the strain that government policies had brought to Japanese American families. Hirabayashi had expected that he would work for the AFSC until he was sent to a CO camp due to his IV-E Selective Service status as a CO. The Civilian Public Service (CPS) camps were designed to provide COs a way to be "drafted" to perform work of national importance instead of bearing arms in active military combat. The creation of the CPS demonstrated an important step forward in the way the country handled individuals who refused to bear arms for religious or intellectual reasons. Hirabayashi's CO status meant that if drafted, he would go to a CPS camp. He did not realize at the time that normal processing of Nisei through the Selective Service had already come to a halt.[45]

Hirabayashi volunteered for the Friends Service Committee, helping families prepare to leave their homes and driving them to Puyallup, the Western Washington Fair Grounds. Hirabayashi watched in disbelief as Japanese Americans suffered, lending a hand when and where he could. He recalled the situation years later: "The situation was intense and there were all kinds of rumors. . . . It was a period of disbelief."[46]

Despite Hirabayashi's confidence that his citizenship would protect him, he began discussing the harsh reality all Japanese Americans were facing with his friend, Bill Makino. Makino had a very difficult time commuting to campus once the war began, so Hirabayashi offered him a top bunk in the furnace room of Eagleson Hall where he resided. They began discussing their diminishing rights. Both agreed that they could not accept being treated like enemy aliens, because they were good American citizens. They agreed to stand together, because, as Hirabayashi said, "sometimes it can be lonely . . . taking a tough stand alone."[47] But Makino was the oldest and only son of aging parents, who begged him not to resist. Hirabayashi understood that Makino's first responsibility was to his family. When Hirabayashi explained his feelings to his parents, who themselves were unsure when they would be ordered to leave their home and were even less sure where they would be sent, they begged him to rethink his decision. With the future so uncertain, it was important to keep the family together. Even though his parents were younger and could rely on the support of Hirabayashi's younger brothers, his mother in particular warned her son that they may never see each other again. She urged him to stay with the family. Hirabayashi was torn, emotionally. His mother explained that discrimination always existed. "They don't hire Japanese as engineers," she said, and "they won't hire teachers." With all the injustices, she told her son, they could change some things, but they could not change them all: "Right now, let's not get separated." She cried and warned Hirabayashi that there was no telling what might happen to him. He might get sent away for good, or he might even face a firing squad. Still, Hirabayashi could not reconcile cooperating with an unjust government order. He apologized to his parents, but he could not accompany them. He would have to resist.[48]

In the process of deciding to resist the Exclusion Order, Hirabayashi started taking smaller steps to resist, and he started documenting his experience in a diary. As he recalled many times throughout his life, he had been accustomed to obeying the law, and at first, even when curfew was extended to Nisei on the basis of race, he obeyed. He said that his university friends were always very helpful in reminding him of curfew, warning him when it was nearly time for him to head home. One night, Hirabayashi recalled, he was rushing home from the library to be in his dormitory before the beginning of curfew, and it occurred to him that he was going out of his way to obey a law that was profoundly unjust. All his friends were allowed to remain in the library, studying for class, yet because of his ancestry, he was forced to change his habits, to leave the library, and to remain in his dormitory not because of anything he did or might do but because he was Japanese. He said that he took the first step toward resistance at that moment. He returned to the library and refused from then on to alter his behavior to accommodate an unjust law. On the night that he first broke curfew, May 4, he also started keeping his diary, in which he documented other times when he deliberately disobeyed this law. These decisions would have a profound impact on the outcome of his court case.[49]

On May 16, 1942, Hirabayashi went to the law office of his friend, Barnett, to turn himself over to the FBI rather than registering for detention at Puyallup. When the two arrived at the FBI offices, they were expected. Barnett had called officials to announce their intention to present the FBI with a statement explaining why Hirabayashi could not comply with the law. Barnett and Hirabayashi did not realize that the FBI already had a copy of his statement. Only days earlier, Hirabayashi had inadvertently dropped a copy on the sidewalk. A woman, concerned about its contents, called the FBI and asked officials to come pick it up. Agents accepted the statement anyway and read it over.[50]

Hirabayashi titled his written statement, "Why I Refused to Register for Evacuation." Hirabayashi explained:

> This order for the mass evacuation of all persons of Japanese descent denies them the right to live. It forces thousands of energetic, law-abiding individuals to exist in a miserable psychological and a horrible physical atmosphere. This order limits to almost full extent the creative expressions of those subjected. It kills the desire for a higher life. Hope for the future is exterminated. Human personalities are poisoned. The very qualities which are essential to a peaceful, creative community are being thrown out and abused. Over sixty per cent are American citizens; yet they are denied on a wholesale scale without due process of law the civil liberties which are theirs.[51]

Under these circumstances, Hirabayashi declared that cooperating would mean granting his own consent "to the denial of practically all of the things which give me incentive to live."[52] He refused so he could maintain his Christian principles, and he said it was his duty to defend the very principles for which the nation lived.

Special Agent Frank Manion finished reading Hirabayashi's statement and then, under advice from Assistant U.S. Attorney Gerald Shucklin, drove Hirabayashi to the Maryknoll Mission House, where the army was processing Japanese Americans for transfer to Puyallup. When Hirabayashi was handed forms to register for removal, he refused. Manion explained that Puyallup was the only place they could send him. In a letter to his friend Eleanor Ring, Hirabayashi explained that he simply had to refuse again. "Since registration seems to be a necessary preliminary for evacuation," he wrote, "I suppose I'll be going elsewhere." But where that would be was unclear. While government agencies debated what they should do with Hirabayashi, he was temporarily detained in a schoolroom under the guard of two privates. He wrote in a letter to Ring:

> Since 12:15 [P.M.], I've been in this erstwhile schoolroom with two splendid privates Earl Holly of Tennessee and Joseph Jones of Alabama. Boy! Have they got the accent! After three hours of all kinds of interesting conversation, I thought I'd write a bit. Earl and Joe are now looking boringly out of the window; Earl looks about ready for a snooze. Things are so quiet here on Jefferson Street, the sun out, and the air lazy—it is very difficult to think or realize that all that has happened in the last three weeks have happened.[53]

Despite the uncertainty of Hirabayashi's future, he found comfort in the support of his friends, especially Ring. More clearly than anywhere else, one can see Hirabayashi's identity as a resister forming in his letters to her. Hirabayashi had been in love with her and said that if the war had not separated them, they likely would have married. Separated by war, though, what was to remain of their friendship played out in letters.

Unable to sway Hirabayashi in his decision to resist participating in any part of the relocation process, Special Agent Manion "interviewed" Hirabayashi at length. What was motivating this young man? Why was he taking such a risk? Hirabayashi recalled his explanation in an interview years later: "I knew something of court cases as a student. I had read of World War I and the constitutional cases," cases that involved the war resisters, "but it wasn't a high priority in forming my decision." His main priority was rooted in his religious principles. As Manion explained in a report he wrote to FBI headquarters on this case, Hirabayashi refused based on "the principle of the Society of Friends [Quakers] that each person should follow the will of God according to his own convictions and that he could not reconcile the will of God, a part of which was expressed in the Bill of Rights and the United States Constitution, with the order discriminating against Japanese aliens and American citizens of Japanese ancestry." "These forceful words," legal historian Peter Irons notes, "bear remarkable similarity to the letter composed two decades later by Martin Luther King in the Birmingham City Jail. . . . Religious conviction and constitutional concerns are separately powerful. Joined in struggles against discrimination, they lead to acts of legal significance." In comparing the actions of the few who challenged these wartime policies to the highest court in the nation (Minoru Yasui, Fred Korematsu, and Mitsuye Endo), Irons calls Hirabayashi "the moralist."[54]

After hours spent waiting in limbo and a two-hour "conversation" with Special Agent Manion, Hirabayashi was finally sent to King County Jail, where he began a journey that resembled that of other historic figures, such as Henry David Thoreau and Martin Luther King. It was first in jail and later in prison that Hirabayashi developed his strongest, firmest understanding of the moral and ethical principles by which he would gauge his future acts of resistance. He learned from fellow inmates, as he approached them in deliberate acts of fellowship, and he developed an active theory of citizenship through his continued acts of purposeful passive resistance. In a letter to Ring, Hirabayashi said:

> Here I am at the County Building. . . . My apartment is called "The Federal Tank" by the residents. I am the 22nd person to be admitted to this exclusive fellowship. Just the other day, Thomas Masuda had lost his membership. . . . There is an interesting group of fellows here, very international in appearances: a couple of Negroes, swell fellas; 3 other Japanese (2 Nisei, and one alien for alien registration shortcomings); an Italian; and others. . . . I am looking forward to becoming better friends with these fellows. If I ever get ambitious enough, I ought to write a personality sketch of each housemate. My roomie is a fellow by the name of Adams, who's here because of Selective Service shortcomings; failure to take a physical—negligence, I think. There's another fellow—a Jehovah's Witness, whom I'd like to know better, but on whom I've used the wrong approach so far. On my two approaches so far, I've received two sermons on how to be an effective witness![55]

Hirabayashi learned quickly that prisons and jails are not at all what he thought they would be, and he had a lot to learn from his fellow inmates. Prison was not a place filled with "dangerous," "awful people" as some people assumed, especially during wartime. Instead his first fellow inmates seemed to look after Hirabayashi and viewed him as some sort of "innocent babe" in need of protection. One fellow gave him an extra blanket, claiming that he did not need it. Hirabayashi wrote Ring that his offer "made me very humble—and sad, reminded me of my Mother."[56]

After Hirabayashi spent the weekend in jail, Captain Michael Rivisto tried one last time to get him to register voluntarily for entry into an assembly center. Rivisto was stationed at the Western Defense Command Headquarters for "Japanese Exclusion Area A" in Seattle, Washington, and was in charge of the transportation of individual Japanese Americans to the "Puyallup Assembly Center."[57] He was under pressure to make sure that the northwest sector of the

Western Defense Command carried out the removal and exclusion orders with 100 percent compliance. The Presidio in California had already declared that its sector had been cleared of Japanese Americans with 100 percent success, so now it was up to Rivisto to persuade Hirabayashi to register, because, according to Rivisto, Hirabayashi was the last holdout in Seattle. This conversation was deeply disheartening to Hirabayashi. He had thought that after the dust settled, there were probably be "fifty to a hundred guys like me with whom maybe we can get a mass case going." Instead, Rivisto told him that he was the only holdout.[58] Of course, this was not exactly true: Others had disobeyed curfew and exclusion rules, but the important thing was that no mass movement was forming as Hirabayashi thought it might.

Hirabayashi's primary concern, then, was that he could not voluntarily agree to his own removal. He suggested, in the spirit of cooperation, that if Rivisto were to have some men come and pick him up, carry him to a car, drive him to a center, and drop him off behind the fence, Rivisto would be able to report that his sector had finished the removal process and Hirabayashi would still be able to hold to his principles that he could not voluntarily submit to removal. Hirabayashi recalled, "It seemed like for a split second or so he's thinking about it." But, laughing, he remembered that Rivisto said, "We can't do that. That would be breaking the law."[59] Hirabayashi was amused that the government could justify forcing one hundred twenty thousand people to leave their homes involuntarily, but it would consider forcing him into one of the camps involuntarily to be illegal. The conversation also left him with the impression that he was truly alone in his resistance. He did not know that Yasui had already started his legal challenge against curfew, nor did he know that Fred Korematsu had refused to relocate from the San Francisco area, not from an idealistic standpoint but because he was in love with a girl. Rivisto was disappointed that he would not be able to declare his sector to be in 100 percent compliance with the exclusion order, but because Hirabayashi remained firm that he would not voluntarily register, Rivisto had no choice but to take him back to King County Jail.[60]

In jail, Hirabayashi had a lot of time to think, to read, and to sleep. He told Ring that he not only was catching up on his sleep but also had read much of Catherine of Siena's *Dialogue,* which presented the spiritual life of man as explored through a series of dialogues between the Eternal Father and a human soul. Hirabayashi wrote to Ring, "Sometimes I think it's about my specific problem." Throughout his correspondence with Ring as he moved from jail, to prison, to freedom, and then back to prison, he inserted quotes from and references to the intellectual material he was reading about spirituality and Quaker mysticism, democratic theory, and civil disobedience. Hirabayashi was self-consciously aware that he had indeed become part of an exclusive fellowship of resisters and intellectuals.

Hirabayashi received support from dear friends, the Quakers, FOR, and even, after time, his parents. His mother had cried as she tried to convince her son not to take this stance against the government, and Hirabayashi carried a terrible burden of guilt for refusing his mother when she begged him to keep the family together. After she had been sent to Tule Lake, one of the ten permanent WRA sites of confinement, she realized that some Japanese Americans looked up to Hirabayashi for his courage. Hirabayashi wrote to Ring that his mother even seemed a little proud of him. Shortly after arriving at Tule Lake, two women came to visit. These women were from Terminal Island, the first place where Japanese Americans were forced to leave their homes even before the program for mass removal had been fully developed. They told Hirabayashi's mother, "We heard that the parents of the guy who is fighting in Seattle jail [arrived] today, so we came out to say welcome, and to say thank you for your son." His mother was lifted by this visit, and her letter telling him of the experience removed the terrible burden of guilt that Hirabayashi had been carrying.[61] This recognition from other Issei women of her son's sacrifice was extremely meaningful and would be sharply contrasted with the scorn that the mothers of draft resisters would suffer as people told them not to be too proud, because their sons were in prison.[62]

As Hirabayashi prepared for his trial, he worried about the effect this would have on his loved ones, but he relished the support that started pouring in from the outside world. He received approximately three letters a day, and sometimes more. He met with his lawyers to plan their approach, because this was not just a personal case of resistance, despite Hirabayashi's strong convictions that shaped the case.

Some lawyers and politicians in the Seattle area were deeply disturbed by the mounting civil rights violations being carried out in the name of national security, and Hirabayashi presented them with an outstanding opportunity to test the constitutionality of these wartime policies. Even before Hirabayashi's arrest, rumors started to spread that a principled young man was preparing to resist the exclusion order. Mary Farquharson was a lawyer and a politician. She represented the University District and was a member of the ACLU. She paid a visit to Hirabayashi to see whether he intended to carry through his plan to resist and to ask whether he intended to turn his resistance into a test case for the entire program of Japanese American mass removal, exclusion, and detention. He said he had no specific plans beyond his own personal position on the issue. Farquharson explained that a group in Seattle was upset about the way Japanese Americans were being treated, believing that this policy was a serious test of everyone's civil liberties and citizenship.[63]

Farquharson asked whether Hirabayashi would mind receiving this group's support to turn his resistance into a test case, and he agreed, happy to have the support. Farquharson began organizing a legal defense fund for Hirabayashi, and although Barnett offered his legal services at first, Barnett found other lawyers to assist him in carrying the case forward. Barnett brought his law partner, John Geisness, on board, and later both lawyers transferred representation to Frank L. Walters. Walters was not particularly experienced in constitutional test cases, but he was an experienced lawyer and a member of the American Legion. Barnett hoped that his strong record of Americanism and patriotism might dissuade the judge from dismissing this trial as a leftist attempt to undermine America's war effort.[64]

While Hirabayashi awaited his trial, he met with his defense team and other supporters. Floyd Schmoe visited Hirabayashi frequently while he was in jail. He was a close personal friend and adviser. Schmoe was a lifelong Quaker and had been a pacifist in World War I, volunteering for the AFSC in lieu of combat service. When the United States joined World War II, he headed up the regional office of the AFSC and eventually left his position teaching forestry at the University of Washington to assist Japanese Americans through the relocation process. His relationship with Hirabayashi was deep, and he supported him in many ways in and out of jail. His friendship and advice sustained Hirabayashi. Farquharson also made frequent visits, sometimes bringing along guests. One time she brought Thomas to meet with Hirabayashi. While he was a student in New York in 1940, Hirabayashi had heard Thomas debate such issues as the lend-lease bill. He had also voted for Thomas when he ran for president of the United States on the socialist ticket. Thomas met with Hirabayashi to lend him his personal support, clearly sharing Hirabayashi's philosophy. Thomas had been the secretary of FOR, helped found the ACLU, and was a devoted pacifist. But the personal encouragement he gave Hirabayashi was the most meaningful.[65]

Hirabayashi was indicted on May 28, 1942, for violating Public Law No. 505, which made violating Civilian Exclusion Order No. 57 and curfew a federal crime. When he had turned himself into the FBI, he carried with him a briefcase that contained his diary documenting every time he had disobeyed curfew. Even though Hirabayashi's intent was only to challenge the Civilian Exclusion Order, the FBI discovered that he had also violated curfew, and so he was indicted accordingly.

Hirabayashi was arraigned on June 1, 1942, at which time he entered a plea of "not guilty." Walters replaced Geisness as lead attorney on June 11, 1942, and began fighting this case on procedural grounds in an attempt to get the case dismissed before trial. He first filed a demurrer, a legal document in which the defendant argues that the facts in the case may be correct (Hirabayashi did not contest that he violated curfew or exclusion orders) but contends that there is no legal basis for the charges against the defendant. In this case, Hirabayashi's lawyers argued that due to the fact that both laws were racially prejudiced, the court had no constitutional basis for charging Hirabayashi for violating the laws. Curfew and exclusion orders violated the due process clause of the Fifth Amendment to the Constitution. Walters also noted that Public Law No. 503 was "too indefinite and too uncertain to be valid criminal statute" and that it was unconstitutional, because it "fails to define any crime or course of conduct the violation of which will constitute a crime.'" Civilian Exclusion Order No. 57 was equally unconstitutional, because it denied Hirabayashi due process, it allowed unconstitutional forms of search and seizure of property, and it delegated to military commanders powers that are "arbitrary and capricious and fail to show or set up any sufficient or reasonable basis for the classification of persons subject thereto." Walters cited a long list of cases to support his argument and submitted these to Judge Lloyd D. Black for his ruling.[66]

Walters followed up on his demurrer with a plea in abatement on June 29, 1942, in which he argued the case on the basis of Hirabayashi's citizenship. He wrote that Hirabayashi had been born on April 23, 1918, in King County, in the state of Washington. He was a citizen of the United States by birth and "has always borne and does now bear, true, full and complete faith and allegiance to the United States of America and the government thereof." Hirabayashi had never been and was not then a "native, citizen, or denizen or subject of the Empire of Japan"; furthermore, Walters explained, Hirabayashi "has never borne and does not bear any faith or allegiance to the said Empire of Japan, or to the Emperor or the government thereof." The indictment, Walters argued, did not address the citizenship status of the defendant, which was another reason the defense argued that the indictment was "unlawful or void."[67]

Judge Black was not amused, nor was he persuaded by Walter's approach. His response revealed his personal attitude about civil liberties in wartime. Judge Black rebutted Hirabayashi's first line of defense not with a careful legal analysis of the Constitution but with a diatribe on the wartime conditions under which this case was brought to court. After rebuking Hirabayashi's attorneys for not following proper procedure, for not asking for permission to file a plea in abatement, and for other procedural errors, he went on to rule on the defense's motions.

Since Japan's attack on Pearl Harbor, Judge Black noted, the country had been engaged in a total war against "unbelievably treacherous and wholly ruthless" enemies "who intend to totally destroy this nation, its Constitution, our way of life, and trample all liberty and freedom everywhere from this earth." "It must be realized," Judge Black wrote, "that civilization itself is at stake in this global conflict." Black concluded that "the decision of this case must be in the light of unprecedented world conflict which so suddenly engulfed this nation, in the light of this being a declared Military Area, in the light of the dangers that would confront us if defendant should prevail, in the light of the advantage to this nation and actually to those of Japanese ancestry from the orders and proclamations which defendant attacks."[68] Clearly, the judge was not on Hirabayashi's side.

As Hirabayashi and his attorneys prepared for trial, the prosecution planned its approach as well. Two of its key witnesses would be Hirabayashi's parents. The prosecution would have no problem demonstrating that Hirabayashi had, indeed, broken the law. That was not a matter that was in contention. But it was also interested in proving that Hirabayashi was without a doubt "Japanese" and that as a Japanese American Hirabayashi was subject to wartime laws that restricted his movement and eventually ordered his removal from the West Coast.[69]

Hirabayashi's parents were subpoenaed to appear in court and were transported from Tule Lake, the WRA camp located near the northern border of California, to King County Jail, where they would remain throughout the trial. Hirabayashi recalled that one night the guard brought a new inmate into the "tank." Hirabayashi had been elected "mayor" by the other inmates, so he was in charge of placing the new inmate in a bunk. Hirabayashi complained jokingly that the guard should wait for a more humane time of day to bring in new inmates, not realizing that the man he had taken into custody was Hirabayashi's own father. Hirabayashi's realization was bittersweet. He was glad to see his father and happy that he would be able to see his trial, but he was upset that the prosecution treated its own witnesses like criminals. Hirabayashi noted in a letter to Ring that despite the humiliation of being held in the jail, his parents were spared the shock of incarceration, because they were transferred not from freedom but from another kind of prison:

> One thing helped. Coming from a concentration camp to here is not nearly as bad as coming here from a home. So the restrictions, custody, food, sleeping quarters, etc, did not undergo quite the change were it from another circumstance. And yet, it is bad. Were it not for me, they would not now be here.[70]

Hirabayashi's parents had been placed in the jail because the government could not keep them anywhere else under the exclusion orders. They were not allowed to return to Seattle, even under court orders, under conditions of freedom. Their only option was to be placed in jail.[71]

Hirabayashi's parents were brought to court to testify that he was Japanese and to demonstrate that Hirabayashi was raised in a "Japanese" home. Because his parents could not speak English well enough to testify without translation, Hirabayashi served the court as translator, which inadvertently reinforced for the court that he had some ties to Japan, even if they were based solely on family and language.

Despite his lawyers' emphasis on his rights as a U.S. citizen, even the court chose to emphasize his ties to Japan. The same tactic was used in Yasui's case. Yasui was a young lawyer living in Portland, Oregon, when the war started. He was deeply troubled by the earliest signs that Nisei were going to lose their constitutional rights. When the curfew was extended to citizen Nisei, he decided he would initiate a test case, confident that this was a law that could not stand up in court. But his case became complicated when the prosecution argued not only that the law should apply to him because he was "Japanese" but that, because he was eligible for Japanese citizenship, he had actually given up his U.S. citizenship when he worked for the Japanese consul in Chicago. Even though the Supreme Court overturned this specific ruling—a person could not lose his or her U.S. citizenship just by working for a foreign consul—

it did show that the courts were ready to use the concept of dual citizenship to justify restrictions against Nisei.

The prosecution encouraged this relationship between assumptions of Nisei disloyalty and an assumption that all Nisei were dual citizens and therefore were suspected of disloyalty. In its memorandum to the court, the prosecution team wrote about Yasui's case for the District Court of Oregon: "Citizenship, conferred by birth, may bare little relationship to the status of an individual as a loyal member of our body politic."[72] When District Judge Black gave his opinion on Hirabayashi's case, he made less direct connections to dual citizenship but implied that because of racial ties, it would be impossible to distinguish a Nisei from a Japanese soldier in the event of an invasion. He wrote, "Of vital importance in considering [whether curfew and exclusion orders violated Hirabayashi's rights] is the fact that the parachutists and saboteurs, as well as the soldiers, of Japan make diabolically cleaver use of infiltration tactics. . . . They are shrewd masters of tricky concealment among any who resemble them . . . with the aid of any artifice or treachery they seek such human camouflage and with uncanny skill discover and take advantage of any disloyalty among their kind." Quoting next from the Constitution's preamble declaring the right to "provide for the common defense" of the nation, Judge Black moved easily between his own assumptions of race-based loyalty, the "tricky" Japanese, and his analysis of the Constitution.

Hirabayashi realized quickly that he would not win his case at the district court level, especially when he heard the judge instruct jurors to consider only the facts of the case. Did Hirabayashi fail to obey curfew? Did he fail to register under the exclusion orders? If so, the jury could return only one verdict. In light of these instructions, it took the jury only a few minutes to deliberate and to return a guilty verdict.

Hirabayashi had predicted a guilty verdict just days before his trial. In a letter to FOR, he said that he would soon be going to court. "My long awaited trial will be held," but he predicted that following the trial, "I shall win an extension on my room and board scholarship here." But this was "not a feeling of desperation," he explained, "only a realization of the climate of the day":

> I do not blame the court for that which I expect. The court seeks to perform its patriotic duty. Realism points to two important elements—race prejudice and war hysteria. Yet my idealism does not permit me to surrender. I am somewhat aware of what was and is; I have a glimpse of what ought to be. I seek to live as though the ought to be is.[73]

Of course, living life as if what "ought to be" was reality would bring risks, such as the risk of imprisonment. This consequence was clear, but Hirabayashi did not fear the risks. There are always "risks in such an endeavor," he wrote, "but as Nehru says: 'Danger seems terrible from a distance; it is not so bad if you have a close look at it. And often it is a pleasant companion, adding to the zest and delight of life.'" Hirabayashi concluded the letter, "May we continue to grow in the simple truths of life. In deeper fellowship, Gordon Hiraba-yashi."[74] Hirabayashi had clearly found a deeper sense of his own values and commitment to fighting for justice in jail. This experience would spur him on to resist again when faced with an impossible choice between obeying the law and upholding his sense of moral and constitutional rights. Until then, he held out hope for his appeal, believing that once the Supreme Court heard his case, he would be vindicated.

From the time Hirabayashi first refused to register for removal to the time of his conviction and appeal, he remained in county jail. By the end of January 1943, he was still in the county jail. He had been held there for more than eight months, and his incarceration seemed to have no end in sight. Jail was meant to be a temporary holding cell, not a place for long-term confinement. Under normal circumstances, someone like Hirabayashi would have been released on bail. He had a defense fund and many supporters, so money was not the issue. When a judge asked him why he remained in jail, even while he was waiting out the appeals process, he replied that it was because he was in the exclusion zone. If he could not be freed to the streets of Seattle and upon release would be transferred directly to the custody of the WRA, he said he could not leave the county jail. Hirabayashi's lawyers started working on an alternative solution: Perhaps he could move directly from jail to freedom out-side the exclusion zone. Walters began corresponding with the WRA to gain a special exception for his client. But the WRA insisted that if Hirabayashi were released from jail, he would have to be transferred directly to a WRA camp. So his lawyers helped him apply for permanent leave from the camps to work for the AFSC in Spokane. This was an odd request, as he was never admitted into any of the camps, and the WRA refused on those grounds. Finally, in February 1942, thanks to Schmoe's additional assistance, Hirabayashi was given per-mission to be released from jail to work with the AFSC in Spokane. There he worked with people in Minidoka, Idaho, and Heart Mountain, Wyoming, who were seeking opportunities to get out of the camps and to relocate to a town outside the exclusion zone that was a little closer to home than the big cities of Chicago or Cincinnati.[75]

LIFE IN CAMP

Life in America's concentration camps was not easy for anybody. For young people just coming of age or those who had just entered their adult years, incarceration seemed especially difficult. For most Nisei, their forced evacua-tion from the West Coast and imprisonment as "enemy aliens" stood in sharp contrast to their prewar associations with Americans of all backgrounds and races. Being isolated and confined just when they expected their lives might take off in exciting directions was more than many could bear.

The lack of legal classification left those confined to the camps, politicians, and historians to this day without words to define the containment areas. President Roosevelt called them "concentration camps," as did many Japanese Americans confined by their barbed wire fences. Some called them prisons. An old sign left behind after the end of the war remains in the Topaz Museum, identifying the WRA camp in the deserts of central Utah as a "prison camp." Those WRA officials hired to run the facilities and dedicated to their own principles of justice and fair play continued to call them "temporary relocation centers" in an attempt to deny the implications of this mass violation of civil rights. The lack of appropriate terminology for the prisons that Japanese found themselves in indicated that the words that people chose to use in the absence of adequate official terminology played a role in supporting the propagandist view that this was an unfortunate wartime necessity being carried out by a paternalistic but fair state or in laying the foundation for creative forms of resistance.[76]

The guilt associated with incarceration transformed Nisei from citizens to enemy aliens in a profoundly personal way. For Kay Yoshida, it was not until her family entered the Tanforan Assembly Center that she internalized a sense of shame for being Japanese. She recalled wondering why the government had forced Japanese into racetracks and fairgrounds hastily converted into holding facilities. "Who's out there that's going hurt us?" she thought. Kay laughed when she remembered thinking that, because she soon realized it was she the government deemed dangerous. When "you see a nervous young man," Kay recalled, "a soldier having his gun pointing at you, you begin to realize. . . . You're in some kind of prison." Her next thought was quite natural: She wondered what terrible thing she had done to deserve being there. The transformation of the Nisei generation from citizens to detainees in government camps created deep-seated guilt that many carried with them for the rest of their lives.[77]

Paul Kusuda summarized the feelings of many Nisei and their dwindling faith in the power of their American citizenship and the U.S. Constitution. In a letter to his former teacher, he wrote, "Time and time again, I have argued that America is not a democracy for white people only. . . . Was I wrong? . . . God help us all if I am or was because what a future is in store for everyone in a false democracy!" Blind faith in the promise of American democracy and citizenship did not last long in camp.[78]

NISEI CITIZENSHIP UNDER ATTACK

Nisei like Paul Kusuda had good reason to wonder whether American democracy really was only for white people as Nisei continued to come under attack even after they were confined in the camps. During the summer of 1942, the Native Sons of the Golden West and the American Legion filed lawsuits designed to deny not just Japanese Americans but the U.S.-born children of all persons ineligible for citizenship the right to vote. On July 2, 1942, John T. Regan, grand secretary of the Native Sons of the Golden West, filed suit against Cameron King, registrar of voters in San Francisco, aiming to force him to eliminate all Japanese names from the voting rolls. James Fisk, of the Alameda County American Legion, filed a similar suit demanding that all Japanese Americans be dropped from voting rolls. Former California Attorney General Webb represented Regan and Fisk. He argued that the government never intended to grant citizenship to children of Asian immigrants. Congress passed the Fourteenth Amendment as reparations for slavery, he argued, not to provide excluded classes, meaning Asian immigrants' American-born children, with the rights of citizenship. He criticized the Supreme Court decision that expanded interpretations of the Fourteenth Amendment to guarantee equal citizenship to children of Chinese immigrants born in the United States, calling *U.S. v. Wong Kim Ark* "one of the most injurious and unfortunate decisions" ever handed down by the Court. He fought to win a dramatic reinterpretation of one of the most important constitutional amendments that had been ratified to defend individuals against race-based discrimination. This attack on Nisei citizenship attracted the attention of Japanese Americans and anyone else who valued the protections of the Fourteenth Amendment.[79]

Critics attacked Webb, Regan, and Fisk for targeting Japanese Americans' citizenship rights on racial grounds, particularly during a war against fascist states where such overt discrimination might actually be sanctioned. After all, Germany had passed a series of Nuremberg Laws, gradually stripping Jews of all rights and segregating them to confined camps. To those who were paying attention, the growing attacks on the civil rights of all Japanese Americans and the citizen Nisei in particular appeared dangerously similar to German attacks on the rights of Jews. Charles R. Garry spoke out against Webb on behalf of the National Lawyers' Guild, saying that he hoped the judges would remember that when the nation was at war, international opinion must be kept in mind. He said, "What would our Allies think if we came out today and said, 'only those are Americans who are whites'?" The *Pacific Citizen,* the newspaper of the JACL, denounced the lawsuits, calling them "a bitter Hitlerite attack against the right of Asiatics to hold American citizenship." The lower court and the federal court of appeals denied the suits as unconstitutional, citing the very case that Webb declared deplorable, *Wong Kim Ark.* The lawsuits may not have succeeded in ending Nisei suffrage, but word spread quickly among Japanese Americans that such groups as the Native Sons were in the process of attacking their citizenship directly. Those seeking to take away Nisei suffrage kept the lawsuits alive until the Supreme Court finally upheld the lower court's ruling on May 17, 1943.[80]

Rufus C. Holman, a Republican senator from Oregon, introduced a constitutional amendment that was perhaps even more threatening than the lawsuit brought forth by the Native Sons. If ratified, the amendment Holman introduced would have ended dual citizenship entirely by prohibiting children of immigrants from automatic citizenship by way of the Fourteenth Amendment. As with the case of the 1941 War Department–sponsored bill, the Holman bill threatened the citizenship of a much larger and more powerful voting block of Americans: German and Italian Americans, among others. Yet the bill's mere presence in Congress, combined with the lawsuits designed to disenfranchise Nisei, posed a serious threat to their security in the nation and reminded all Nikkei that even though their situation was already quite precarious, things could get much worse. Their citizenship rights had been ignored, and now some members of Congress sought to strip them of their citizenship entirely. Examples of other proposed actions against Japanese Americans included a proposal to place all persons of Japanese ancestry living anywhere in the United States into the camps, regardless of geographic location, and a call to deport all persons of Japanese ancestry, regardless of loyalty or citizenship to Japan. Even though none of these rather extreme proposals came to fruition, they represented threats to security that Nisei faced in the United States. It would be up to Nisei to try to prove that they really were 100 percent American to win the acceptance of the American people, even if the U.S. government remained skeptical.[81]

Dual citizenship remained a crucial and yet poorly understood issue throughout the war and became one of the focal points of debates over whether Nisei in particular deserved any protections of due process in this time of hysteria and wartime crisis. In fact, each attempt to remove additional rights from Japanese Americans brought the issue of dual citizenship to the forefront, from the *Regan v. King* case to proposals before Congress to incarcerate all persons of Japanese ancestry living in the United States. Dual citizenship seemed to provide racially motivated demagogues with some justifications for ignoring the Constitution or attempts to revise the Fourteenth Amendment to strip certain groups of their U.S.-born citizenship.

In an attempt to weed out fact from hysteria, WRA attorneys wrote several summaries of the citizenship status of Nisei to clarify questions that administrators and local project attorneys had about these growing threats against Japanese Americans' rights. Much of this literature focused on what dual citizenship was, how many Nisei retained dual citizenship, and how they could renounce their Japanese citizenship if they so desired. These reports debunked myths that all Nisei were dual citizens, but they were not widely circulated and did nothing to protect Nisei from ongoing attacks on their citizenship. And even though most Nisei remained quite unconcerned or even unaware of their own dual citizenship status, evidence abounds that some U.S. government leaders and racially motivated groups, such as the Native Sons of the Golden West, were not only ill-informed about Nisei dual citizenship but also determined to keep it at the center of any debate regarding how much further the government could strip Nisei of their rights, using convoluted and weak legal arguments to do so.[82]

MILITARY SERVICE AND NISEI

Not long after Japan attacked Pearl Harbor, military leaders realized that they would need to recruit Japanese-language specialists to fight the war in the Pacific. Recruiting Japanese Americans for military service on a limited basis, particularly those with basic skills in Japanese, became essential despite the inherent contradictions when these recruits came from the WRA camps. On July 17, 1942, Lt. Col. Kai E. Rasmussen began his tour of WRA facilities to recruit candidates for the Military Intelligence Service (MIS) Language School in Savage, Minnesota. A far more guarded, secretive recruitment of Japanese Americans had already succeeded in expanding the language program originally located at the Presidio in San Francisco, so the military knew that it must expand this program and its recruitment efforts in the most logical place: the WRA camps. Along with increasing recruitment, the location of the program had to change, because the MIS could not train Japanese Americans for highly sensitive military work in the very region deemed too sensitive to allow any persons of Japanese ancestry to remain—namely, the coastal port area of San Francisco.

Even at the earliest point, the military was forced to adjust to the contradictions of its own policies and its own need to win the war as it struggled to justify its race-based exclusion of Nikkei from the West Coast without due process. Lt. Rasmussen was interested first and foremost in candidates fluent in Japanese with at least an elementary knowledge of written Japanese. Rasmussen was looking for U.S.-born Japanese schooled in Japan, who were able to read Japanese newspapers but had solid academic backgrounds in English. Ironically, this profile fit the most suspect population in the camps: Kibei. By the end of 1942, the MIS had recruited 179 candidates for its language program.[83]

Between June and July, individuals within the War Department debated the possibility of recruiting Nisei on a massive scale. Some suggested that offering young people a way out of camp (and into the military) might diminish the alienation and disillusionment many Nisei were suffering as a result of their confinement. Juvenile delinquency had become a major concern for WRA administrators and the FBI within the first few months of the camps' existence, and both agencies wrote that the confinement of young men had become particularly worrisome. Scott Rowley, project attorney for the WRA at Poston, Arizona, suggested that the conditions in camp were to blame for the problem: Young people did not have enough meaningful work or activities with which to fill their time. He charged the WRA with failing in its "obligation to boys" in particular. Most Nisei young men would arrive at manhood while in the camps and would not be able to learn about manhood from "practical experience." J. Edgar Hoover lamented the fact that the vast majority of detainees were between the ages of ten and twenty-five. He wrote, "Some of them are now embittered because they are United States citizens and are being handled as they are." The growing problem in the camp, Hoover concluded, was not disloyalty but a rise in what he called criminal behavior and delinquency.[84]

Critics within the military argued that prohibiting Nisei from military service for the duration of the war might permanently alienate a population that in all likelihood remained loyal to the United States even after its forced evacuation from the West Coast. On July 22, 1942, members of the Western Defense Command staff wrote a memorandum on the problems that would arise from disallowing Nisei into the military, calling the present policy "indefensible." They addressed their concerns to Chief of Staff Gen. Joseph T. McNarney:

> The present treatment of persons of Japanese ancestry born in the United States is to preclude almost every possibility of future serviceable citizenship. Some intelligent action looking to a chance must be made to provide an opportunity for these persons to demonstrate their loyalty and their right to live as free people in this country after the war. This must be done or they must all be returned to Japan after the war. If this is done then as many as are sent become added to our enemies abroad.[85]

Pushing the ultimatum further, the report stated that if Nisei in the camps were declared permanently ineligible for service, those already in the military would have to be discharged, reassigned to the reserve corps, and placed in the WRA camps for the duration of the war.[86]

The problem remained that there was no way, according to some, to test Nisei loyalty.[87] Lt. Col. William A. Boekel, assistant to Col. Bendetsen, suggested a program of segregating "presumptively loyal Nisei" from potentially disloyal Kibei and Issei. Nisei should then be afforded "all the rights of citizenship as quickly as possible," Boekel continued, "inclusive of the rights, as well as the corresponding obligation to serve in the armed forces." Gen. DeWitt's staff agreed with Moffitt's emphasis on segregation. They added that Nisei could prove themselves loyal through military service while Kibei would remain in custody until they proved that they were not disloyal—a task that would be nearly impossible from behind barbed wire.[88]

In these discussions, it is important to note that the issue of loyalty or disloyalty among Nisei women never came up. Only the matter of manhood and the disillusionment of young men drove these discussions. Debates about loyalty, citizenship, and military service in relation to Nisei during World War II turned on concepts that, during war, men were considered either citizens or potential saboteurs. Women were never discussed directly in those terms, but they would find a way to enter the debate as mothers of potential soldiers and much later as volunteers for the Women's Auxiliary Army Corps.[89]

The international propaganda value of readmitting Nisei to military service prevailed as the most popular justification. The Japanese government had already used the segregation of Japanese Americans into WRA camps as evidence that racial lines were clearly drawn in the United States, much as they were being drawn in Germany. When the United States "does not recognize [Nisei] as being good enough to fight alongside Caucasian troops," the government only reinforced Japanese propaganda.[90]

Elmer Davis, director of the Office of War Information, agreed that allowing Nisei to volunteer for service would disprove Japanese propaganda circulating in the Philippines and in Burma suggesting that the United States was fighting a race war. After passing individualized tests of loyalty, Davis suggested, Nisei should be allowed to enlist in the army and the navy. It must be a matter of choice, he emphasized, not a matter of conscription. "It would hardly be fair to evacuate people and then impose normal draft procedures," Davis wrote, but "the voluntary enlistment would help a lot."[91]

President Roosevelt was swayed by the propaganda value of allowing Japanese Americans to volunteer for the military but remained deeply skeptical of their loyalty. He suggested that a compromise solution might be to keep them stateside. Secretary of War Stimson responded quickly: "The effect on India and elsewhere of the yellow man voluntarily fighting for the white would be substantial." But keeping Nisei stateside, he wrote, would be a "faint-hearted compromise." Any propaganda value the military hoped to gain by accepting volunteers would be lost if they were not used in full combat.[92]

When Roosevelt asked Secretary of the Navy Frank Knox for his reaction to the proposed induction of Japanese Americans, he stated clearly and emphatically that he would not accept Nisei under any circumstances. His decision remained policy throughout the war and became a major point of contention among Nisei. If they were loyal enough to serve in combat for the army, they asked, why could they not serve in all branches of the military? The limited basis on which Nisei were eventually admitted back into military service became the principle basis of future resistance to the draft.[93]

JAPANESE AMERICAN CITIZENS LEAGUE COLLABORATION

At the end of November 1942, the JACL held an all-camps summit in Salt Lake City, Utah, to discuss the organization's future and the problems that were arising in the camps. In this meeting, representatives suggested that the government should restore normal Selective Service procedures for citizens of Japanese ancestry, even those in the camps. The idea, simply put, was to allow Nisei to serve their country on the same basis as other Americans and thus prove their loyalty in combat. More importantly, JACL delegates hoped to prove extraordinary loyalty among Nisei, who would be willing to accept their most basic obligation of citizenship even after their rights had been suspended. This position was not popular among the general population of Nikkei in the camps and only reinforced the strong reputation the JACL had acquired for cooperating with the government instead of defending the civil rights of Japanese

Americans. The Selective Service had already reduced Nisei to the category of enemy aliens, yet JACL leaders insisted that military service remained the best way Nisei could demonstrate loyalty and earn their citizenship rights.

Delegates representing the JACL from all ten WRA camps voted unanimously in favor of requesting that the Selective Service apply to Japanese Americans on the same basis as other citizens and forwarded this resolution in a telegram to President Roosevelt.[94] What they did not know was that the War Department had already decided to readmit Nisei for service. Now it was just a matter of determining the best way to recruit soldiers. During a phone conversation on November 6, 1942, Col. Karl L. Bendetsen and Col. M. W. Pettigrew agreed that organizing a military unit of Japanese Americans would be an excellent idea. They knew that Assistant Secretary of War Gen. John McCloy was personally interested in the idea and was making plans to implement the program. Pettigrew mentioned that initially only single men, and predominantly eighteen- to nineteen-year-olds, would be drafted. To clarify, Bendetsen said, "You are viewing it not only from the standpoint of conscription but also from a voluntary basis, both ways." "Oh yes," Pettigrew replied. Conscription would be put back for a while. "I think a damn good recruiting campaign will get a lot of them to volunteer," Pettigrew said, but the draft would come eventually. He continued, "As a matter of fact, the way conscription is going to work before long any single man is going to be a prime suspect anyhow. . . . However from a morale standpoint the more people we can get to enlist [voluntarily] the better." Pettigrew asked Bendetsen for his help in gathering the final data so the plan could be put into operation. Bendetsen agreed and assured Pettigrew he would put men on the project immediately, and he did.[95] The following morning, Pettigrew sent a memo to McCloy that provided a progress report on his efforts to gather statistics on the number of Nisei men available for service. The idea of an all-Nisei combat team was taking hold, and Pettigrew had the numbers to support it. He continued writing McCloy through November and December, reiterating that available statistics supported the formation of a Nisei unit.[96] But a unit of Nisei could not be created overnight, especially after so much damage had been done to Nisei morale and citizenship rights.

For the time being, the War Department had decided to readmit Nisei for military service, but the methods of doing so would evolve gradually over the next two years. News of the JACL's petition requesting such a change sparked outright violence among detainees when the delegates returned from the summit meeting. Masked assailants attacked Tayama, a prominent JACL leader, when he returned to Manzanar. In Poston, Saburo Kido, the national JACL president, was beaten nearly to death. Both camps were rocked by protests and violence. The first was the Poston Strike in November over living and working conditions, ending with peaceful negotiations but with administrators clearly alarmed at the breakdown in relations between the administration and Japanese Americans and among Japanese Americans over such issues as the JACL's collaboration with the government and its request that the War Department reinstate the draft for Nisei. The Manzanar Riot, on the other hand, ended with two dead and prompted an early form of isolation for what the administration considered to be "troublemakers" in camp. Conditions in the camps were deteriorating rapidly.[97]

The Manzanar incident was publicized widely in newspapers, particularly in the Hearst papers. Nativist groups, such as the Native Sons of the Golden West, along with congressional leaders and the FBI questioned how the WRA had allowed things to get so out of hand. Kentucky Senator Albert B. Chandler led an investigation into the administration of the camps and accused Dillon Myer, director of the WRA, of coddling inmates. Assistant Secretary of War McCloy testified before Chandler's investigative committee that the WRA needed to implement the segregation of agitators from the general population of loyal inmates throughout the camps. Senator Mon Wallgreen of Washington argued instead that administration of the camps should be handed over to the War Department and introduced a bill that would abolish the WRA completely. Everyone agreed that the camps were becoming a liability and a public embarrassment, but no one could agree how to solve the crisis.[98]

As the first full year of war drew to a close and the new year began, Nisei looked back on the events of 1942 and pondered their future. Hirabayashi was eventually released from jail to help Japanese Americans relocate to Spokane. His work for the AFSC involved educating businesses and citizens of Spokane about the skills and labor that Japanese Americans could bring to the town and how they were hard-working, friendly Americans. Through his work, he also traveled to WRA camps, specifically Minidoka and Heart Mountain, and spoke on occasion with young people about his court case and the principles that drove him to resist unjust laws. And he continued to write to friends, supporters, and Ring about the need to keep up the fight. Writing to Ring's parents, who had been mentors and supporters of Hirabayashi throughout his ordeal, Hirabayashi said:

> Many things have happened to me since my incarceration here. I have appreciated very deeply all of the acts of kindness and concern on your part. But the thing which gives me greatest joy in is the feeling of one-ness I get out of a realization that we are both pledged to a common cause—the cause of human decency. Through your example I have learned how to act toward a person who is down whether he is out or not. . . . We are traveling on a long and rough trail; I feel, however, that we are on the right path. May we never deviate, and may we always remember the source of all our incentives and inspirations.[99]

Most Nisei had not yet come to terms with their battles and were only beginning to realize the extent to which the government had betrayed their trust. They could not know that the War Department was working on a plan to draft them into the military. For many Nisei, military service was the last thing on their minds after losing so much. Many Nisei had begun the year with confidence that their citizenship would protect them during the war, but over the course of one year, they had become "non-aliens" and in some instances had even been classified as "enemy aliens," despite their birth in the United States and the guarantees of citizenship promised by the Fourteenth Amendment. And they did not yet know the outcome of congressional bills and court cases that threatened to strip them entirely of their U.S. citizenship.

By the end of 1942, the JACL drew sharp criticism for its petition to restore the draft for incarcerated citizens, its collaboration with intelligence agencies, and, in the end, its decision to promote cooperation with exclusion as one way that Japanese Americans could contribute to the war effort. A growing number of detainees accused the JACL of "selling the Japanese community down the river."[100] Regardless of whether the JACL was responsible for "selling" Japanese Americans down the river for their collaboration and, according to some critics, overly zealous cooperation with government policies restricting Nisei rights sparked a debate that would span more than sixty years and persist into the twenty-first century. Japanese Americans asked whose fault the evacuation was. Could the JACL have done anything more to stop it, or was collaboration the only way to prevent even worse abuses of Nikkei rights? What prevented more from resisting as Hirabayashi did? These were questions no one could answer with any certainty, but they created major rifts within families and communities that would take more than a lifetime to heal.

CHAPTER 3

Loyalty and Resistance

❦

Life was going its calm and orderly, if somewhat unnatural, way in Topaz, Utah, on the afternoon of January 28, 1943. . . . The teletype stuffed away in a corner of the telephone exchange room in administration building "A" began to clatter out a message. A few moments later, the operator laid a message before Mr. Hughes, who studied its wording carefully. Then suddenly he began to act. Telephone bells jangled in the offices of the division chiefs. It was as though an electric current on the loose was flashing through Topaz.

—Russell A. Bankson, WRA community analyst at Topaz

THE TELETYPE MESSAGE that set off a flurry of activity in Topaz on January 28, 1943, came from Secretary of War Henry Stimson, who announced that the War Department had created a combat unit exclusively for the Nisei. Nisei volunteers could enlist for military service during a loyalty registration program. War Department representatives would come to Topaz in two weeks to begin the process. Shortly after Stimson's announcement, the War Relocation Authority (WRA) announced that it would conduct its own loyalty registration program for all Nikkei ages seventeen and older. The War Department and the WRA hoped their registration programs would work in tandem to accelerate efforts to clear detainees for relocation and to hasten the eventual closure of the camps.

The Nikkei detained at Topaz organized resistance to those aspects of registration that most threatened their citizenship rights. Issei leaders successfully persuaded the War Department to revise the loyalty registration questionnaire in a way that would not force them to choose between loyalty to the United States and their Japanese citizenship. The Nisei were less successful. At the heart of Nisei resistance to registration was resistance to the War Department's efforts to recruit Nisei men into a segregated combat team before their citizenship rights had first been restored. Issei demands could be met by revising the registration form itself. Nisei were asking for changes that were far more substantive. Debate over Nisei registration at Topaz marked the beginning of broad-based resistance against what would become a full restoration of Selective Service for Nisei without a full restoration of their citizenship rights. The registration process itself represented a continuation of War Department efforts to force Nisei to resolve questions about their dual citizenship and to profess undivided loyalty to the United States before making them eligible for military service.

This chapter focuses on Topaz for two reasons. First, resistance against registration took place in all the camps, but to different degrees. The most studied examples are Manzanar and Tule Lake; few if any historical studies even mention resistance at Topaz. Yet during registration, some observers believed that resistance at Topaz was the most serious of all the camps. This might indicate that efforts to suppress dissent at Topaz ended up being more successful in the long run than the resistance itself. The fact that resistance to registration at Topaz has all but faded from historical memory makes the analysis of the event in this chapter important on its own terms. The second reason Topaz is important to this particular narrative is because only seven men resisted the draft from this camp (and only four of the seven served prison sentences for their resistance). In a camp that exhibited such spirited resistance against a segregated military just one year before, this small number of draft resisters serves as one example of how successful the government and private individuals were in suppressing dissent in this case. By contrast, even though residents of Amache questioned registration and voiced their concerns, they did not organize any broad-based resistance efforts until the draft was reinstated the following year. Amache is the principle topic of Chapter 5, "The Obligations of Citizenship." Together, Topaz and Amache serve as striking examples of the variety of forces that government and civilians used to quiet dissent and to encourage overt patriotism in the face of civil rights abuses and a diminishing civil society.[1]

THE BROADER CONTEXT OF WARTIME CITIZENSHIP

During World War I and World War II, the government filed complaints against individuals who had obtained citizenship through fraudulent means and stripped them of their citizenship. The Supreme Court upheld this practice as constitutional, as those who held reservations in their hearts at the time they naturalized as U.S. citizens had obtained their citizenship through what it called "fraud" and "deceit." The numbers of those who lost their citizenship through this same process during World War II increased, particularly those who challenged the loss of their citizenship in the courts, but these cases involved the outright loss of citizenship that individuals had at one point gained through the naturalization process.[2] In additional cases, the majority opinions in federal appeals court cases stated that the strength of allegiance and loyalty should increase over time, becoming stronger the longer an individual resided in the United States. Subsequent acts of disloyalty, then, indicated that the original oath was invalid, because "the seeds of such feeling were fertile within him at the time of his naturalization, and the burden shifts to the defendant" to prove that his oath of allegiance was sincere at the time and his or her feelings of disloyalty materialized after naturalization.[3]

What about the citizenship of those born in the United States yet whom the government suspected harbored loyalty to an enemy nation? One way the government attempted to reserve even birthright citizenship for "loyal" Americans played out in revised policies for children born to U.S. citizens outside the United States. For example, in October 1940, Congress passed a revised nationality act that for the first time withdrew U.S. citizenship from children born abroad to U.S. citizens unless those children established residency in the United States before they turned twenty-one.[4] In 1943, federal appeals courts ruled again, as they had during World War I, that the United States could revoke the naturalized citizenship of an individual based on evidence that the individual harbored feelings of disloyalty. But during World War II, the courts ruled that the government could legally take away the derivative citizenship of minor children of naturalized citizens on the basis of their parents' alleged disloyalty. Even though the majority of these policies only threatened the citizenship of naturalized citizens against whom the government could produce evidence of disloyalty, it did set a precedent for reexamining the rights and privileges of citizens, even revoking their citizenship, when the political climate shifted or suspicions of disloyalty emerged.[5]

In the context of world war, state definitions of citizenship mimicked contracts that could be terminated if an individual citizen harbored feelings of disloyalty or refused to make the United States his or her permanent home. In 1943, the War Department's registration of Nisei loyalty became a prerequisite for restoring their citizenship rights and responsibilities that the government had taken away based on mere suspicion of disloyalty and misunderstandings regarding Nisei dual citizenship.

The loyalty registration program was also the culmination of War Department's efforts to resolve its questions about dual citizenship. Recall its debates in the House subcommittee regarding the bills it sponsored in 1941. In the context of war, the War Department could stop trying to sponsor broad-based legislation aimed at all Americans who could possibly claim or be claimed by foreign governments as dual citizens. It could instead design a bureaucratic process, following naval intelligence advice, to determine Nisei loyalty and to ask them to go through a quasi-naturalization process by denouncing loyalty to the emperor of Japan and proclaiming not just loyalty to the United States but also a willingness to fight for the country through combat. What was once thought to be an unconstitutional request of the War Department was now going to play out in the form of a loyalty registration process. But this process was little understood. When it was extended beyond just draft-age men to all adults in the camps in an effort to speed up the relocation process for the WRA, it became part of a larger effort to determine Japanese American loyalty and to settle broad-based questions about dual citizenship. The loyalty registration program, then, became one example of a larger trend in U.S. citizenship that, when applied on such a broad scale, produced many unpredicted results.

PROPAGANDA AND RESISTANCE

Before registration was introduced to the Nikkei in the camps, the Office of War Information and the War Department began a propaganda campaign to prevent resistance to registration, particularly resistance from white Americans who might have supported removal and might fear any release of prisoners whom Gen. John L. DeWitt had already declared suspect. The government launched the first phase of this campaign with a statement from President Franklin Roosevelt. He signed a letter to Secretary of War Stimson on February 1, stating most famously:

> No loyal citizen of the United States should be denied the democratic right to exercise the responsibilities of his citizenship, regardless of his ancestry. The principle on which this country was founded and by which it has always been governed is that Americanism is a matter of the mind and heart; Americanism is not, and never was, a matter of race or ancestry. . . . This is a natural and logical step toward the reinstitution of the Selective Service procedures which were temporarily disrupted [for citizens of Japanese ancestry] by the evacuation from the West Coast.[6]

This message defined military service as a political right the government owed its loyal citizens rather than a duty that free citizens were obligated to perform for the state. Conflating the rights and duties of citizenship proved a powerful tool in countering resistance that erupted in Topaz following Stimson's announcement.

The president did not write this letter, though. The Office of War Information's Elmer Davis and WRA Director Dillon Myer worked collaboratively to draft one of Roosevelt's most famous letters, one that offered his conditional support of Nisei loyalty. Davis and Myer were interested in maximizing the propaganda value of the War Department's decision to readmit the Nisei to the military. They believed this decision proved that the United States was not fighting a race war of its own. For the propaganda to work, the government would have to find willing Nisei participants. A strong statement of support from the president, they hoped, would prevent protests that might sabotage the new program for an all-Nisei volunteer combat team.[7]

On the same day Roosevelt signed the letter, the WRA issued instructions to project managers to begin their own internal propaganda campaigns.[8] Topaz administrators and residents had already joined forces to create a positive environment for the registration program. In special editions of the *Topaz Times,* administrators announced that President Roosevelt, Myer, and Project Director Charles Ernst were all very pleased with the program and believed that it was the first step toward a complete restoration of Nisei rights. A smaller side article released the names of those who had recently supported the Japanese American Citizens League (JACL) with monetary contributions, showing the JACL-friendly nature of the official camp newspaper.[9] Local support for voluntary enlistment from JACL members would become one of the most important components in the WRA's and the War Department's efforts to turn widespread resistance into patriotic support for the war effort.

Tsune Baba, chairman of the Community Council, organized an open meeting with administrators. The WRA created Community Councils in all the camps to help maintain order and to manage communication between Japanese Americans and camp administrators. Even though only citizen Nisei could hold office (a requirement that transferred power from Issei fathers to Nisei sons, some of whom were barely adults and had very little political experience), the Community Councils were designed to be democratically elected bodies responsible for representing all the community's concerns, regardless of citizenship.[10] Baba, then, became the most logical person to organize a meeting in which administrators would have to respond to Issei and Nisei questions about registration.

Nisei and their Issei parents were anxious to find out how the program would affect them, to air their grievances, and to ask administrators tough questions. At the meeting, Ernst spoke for a few minutes to explain what residents might encounter during registration, and then he answered questions. Many wanted to know why Stimson was not making an attempt to right "all the wrongs which affected all the individuals through evacuation" rather than asking citizens to make the ultimate sacrifice for the war effort while they still lacked their basic rights. The first question cut to the core of Nikkei concerns about registration: the prospects of Nisei serving in segregated combat teams without first securing a full restoration of their citizenship rights. The crisis from the beginning was not simply a matter of loyalty; it was about Japanese Americans trying to maintain some balance between the rights and duties of Nisei citizenship.[11]

The meeting between administrators and residents crystallized opposition to registration and revealed the Nisei's two main concerns. First, they questioned the segregated nature of the combat team: Why segregate them like "Negro" troops, and why register them only for combat duty? Why not allow the Nisei into all branches of the military? Their second concern was for their families: What would happen to the parents of those who volunteered, especially now that the registration program was being extended to them as well? Would they be forced to leave the camps? Who would support them while their sons were away? Would dependents' benefits be extended to the families of the Nisei even while the WRA still detained them? One Nisei student commented that Stimson's announcement was "like a delayed bombshell exploding in a midst of unsuspecting citizens. . . . Loyal citizens were hoping for some form of recognition from the government enabling them to exercise their full rights of citizenship, but never did they expect to receive their answer in such a way." The Nisei had many serious questions, and the administration had few answers.[12]

Some Nisei felt the government was too late in offering its faith in the Nisei now that they were already behind barbed wire. They accused the government of blatant race discrimination with the formation of what some began calling a "Yellow Battalion." One outspoken, prominent Nisei said when Pearl Harbor was bombed, the Nisei wanted to stand up and to be counted as loyal citizens. At that time, though, "they called us Japs and put us behind barbed wires." The War Department wanted the Nisei to register as loyal citizens and to volunteer for combat, but Nisei said, "It's too late. . . . Why didn't they publicly say we were loyal then when we dearly wanted to be called loyal Americans? . . . I still pledge my loyalty to the U.S. because this is the only country I know, but I shall not bear arms." Speeches like this one had a "surging influence" on the rest of the group, making everyone "consciously alert" to the stakes involved in accepting the government's offers to volunteer for the military. It was clear early on that many Nikkei, not a mere agitating minority, read beyond the government's propaganda of restored rights. They saw a continued pattern of race discrimination in the War Department's disingenuous offer to allow loyal Nisei the opportunity to volunteer for a segregated combat team.[13]

Because the Issei had faced a long history of race-based discrimination, they spoke up early and loudly against the War Department's attempt to recruit volunteers. One Issei asked quite frankly, "Which way are you going to aim the gun?" The Nikkei had been told that they were being evacuated for their own safety, yet when they arrived in camps, they were quick to notice that the guns were pointed inward, as if to prevent the escape of dangerous criminals, not outward in a posture of defense. Why would the military be any different? Where would the deceit end? One Nisei queried the purpose of making enlistment be voluntary. "Our lives will be thrown into a battle of contradicting principles," he said, "and not for the cause of any liberation." The meeting did more than raise two simple questions or create a forum for airing general grievances: It opened up a sophisticated list of concerns that could not easily be answered, because the program had created its own contradictions.[14]

When the War Department's representatives arrived in Topaz, administrators and residents alike hoped they would have the answers that local administrators had been unable to provide, but many of the "answers" they offered were flat-out lies. Lt. William L. Tracey, head of the registration team, presented the program in the most positive light possible, hiding or even denying aspects of the program that might appear distasteful to the Nisei. He said he was not leading a recruiting team, nor did he have a quota to fill. He and his team were merely in Topaz to conduct a loyalty investigation and, as a bonus, to provide the Nisei the chance to volunteer for military service. Tracey observed that, in his opinion, the resistance that was beginning to form at Topaz was not a threat. Instead, it "helped to start the boiling process which would undoubtedly indicate who in Topaz wanted to be loyal citizens of the United States and who preferred to have their citizenship elsewhere." Although Tracey tried to put it nonchalantly, his meaning was clear: Resisting this government loyalty registration program was nearly a treasonous act. Resistance or compliance would separate those who would retain citizenship from those who might lose it.[15]

Some Topaz residents responded critically to Tracey's tactics, arguing that segregation was not compatible with American democratic principles. Segregation was the one aspect of the loyalty program that no amount of propaganda could hide. In an editorial published in the *Topaz Times,* the author wrote on behalf of many Nisei who felt that segregation was "alien to the principles of American democracy." Its form or where it was practiced was irrelevant. The sacrifices of the volunteers might demonstrate Nisei loyalty, but this kind of public relations scheme, the author commented, contradicted the democratic principles for which they would be fighting. The author hoped that the government would instead "remove the onus of segregation from [this] group of American citizens" and allow the Nisei to demonstrate their loyalty in a manner compatible with the American traditions they would be fighting to defend.[16]

As speculation ran rampant among the Nisei and the Issei regarding the possible consequences of registration, local members of the JACL organized to support registration. They held rallies and later organized a media campaign of their own under the title "Volunteers for Victory." Organizers of the JACL rally—Ernie Iiyama, Vernon Ichisaka, Harumi Kawahara, Walter Nakata, Henry Tani, and John Yoshino—hoped that this campaign might encourage other Nisei to join them in embracing the program and in greeting the War Department with willing volunteers, not questions.[17]

While it was only the Nisei who were being accepted for military service, all Nikkei adults had been asked to register their loyalty. A small group of young Issei started to petition for the right to do more than sign a piece of paper to demonstrate their loyalty: They, too, wanted the right to serve in the military. These Issei argued that, despite their formal lack of U.S. citizenship, they wanted to fight as a way of demonstrating that loyalty knew no bounds of citizenship. Citizenship was a mere accident of birth, they said, but loyalty, which they held strongly for the United States, was a matter of the heart. Members of this group declared that they would give up all citizenship ties to align themselves with the global struggle to defend the four freedoms Roosevelt had claimed for all humans. The War Department flatly refused the petition, stating that Japanese nationals would not be accepted at that time.[18] Ironically, the incident furthered local JACL efforts to advertise Nikkei patriotism and highlighted the fact that citizenship alone did not determine loyalty to a nation.

Henry H. Ebihara, a young Issei, wrote an open letter to Secretary of War Stimson and President Roosevelt, protesting the government's decision not to accept Issei volunteers. His letter served JACL efforts to highlight the organization's extraordinary patriotism. Ebihara said that it was unjust for a democratic nation to deny him the right to serve in active combat because of a technicality like birthplace. This was a fight for free men throughout the world, which the president had already said was not a matter of color or race. Why not allow all loyal men, regardless of citizenship, to contribute to the struggle?[19] In response, the War Department assured him that it would make every effort to allow Issei volunteers to enlist at some point in the future but did not say when.

Propaganda supporting enlistment and JACL pronouncements of member loyalty filled the camp newspaper in the days leading up to February 10, the day when registration was to begin. The *Topaz Times* republished Ebihara's open letter to Washington along with an editorial comment that the War Department had promised to consider Ebihara's request. The newspaper also published a complete draft of President Roosevelt's letter to Secretary of War Stimson. The powerful propaganda value of the president's letter cannot be overstated. Some volunteers remember his words to this day as the primary reason they decided to accept military service.[20] Yet as administrators and patriotic supporters of registration would soon find out, a positive propaganda campaign was not enough to thwart resistance in a democratic society, even within a population that was not wholly free.

Unknown to local administrators, a counter-propaganda effort had also been published in the Japanese-language sections of the newspaper. The Japanese-language section of the *Topaz Times* was supposed to offer the Issei a direct translation of the contents of the English section of the paper, but two editors decided to add a pro-Japanese spin to the news, urging readers to declare loyalty to Japan instead of to the United States. Camp administrators did not discover the discrepancy until some members of the Young Democrats in the camps began complaining that the Japanese section had been causing agitation among detainees. Administrators hired translators to analyze the paper for several days. They concluded that "a very deliberate program of misrepresentation was being carried out by these Japanese editors." When community analyst Russell A. Bankson discovered the discrepancy, he asked for the editors' resignations. He found out later that both had provided negative answers to the loyalty question. A similar case appeared in Gila River, when the Japanese-language sections of the newspaper reported events in a more negative light than did the English-language sections.[21] What looked like misinformation to some was a biting criticism of the contradictions of a government program that encouraged racial discrimination against the Nisei and did nothing to repair the damage caused by their forced evacuation from the West Coast.

The most productive debates over registration did not take place in the newspapers but in democratically organized meetings held by Nikkei residents of Topaz. The night before registration was scheduled to begin, block managers met for an independent discussion of the new program. Issei block managers expressed grave concern over the loyalty question, which read: "Will you swear unqualified allegiance to the United States of America and forswear any form of allegiance or obedience to the Japanese Emperor, or to other foreign government, power or organization?" This was meant to establish the loyalty or disloyalty of registrants and to force Nisei dual citizens to choose between their Japanese and U.S. citizenship. But for Issei Japanese nationals, answering this question in the affirmative would leave them stateless.

The Issei organized a committee of nine to present their grievances to the project director and to request that this loyalty question be changed. The committee took a statement to Project Director Ernst's office, which read: "We, the Japanese alien residents of Topaz, hereby resolve that it is absolutely impossible for us to properly answer question No. 28 of the WRA form 126, revised. We, therefore, request the proper authorities of the War Relocation Authority to reconsider the said question."[22] Ernst assured them that although he would take the matter up with WRA headquarters in Washington, D.C., this question was being asked of all residents in all ten camps. He also assured them that they could answer the question in any way they saw fit and should not feel bound to a simple "yes" or "no" response but could qualify their answers in whatever manners best represented their sentiments.[23] Ernst called Washington to inform officials of the petitioners' concerns, and Issei leaders left his office to continue their discussions in private.

Ernst's assurances that every detainee would have to answer the same question did not satisfy Issei representatives in Topaz. The chairman of the Issei committee returned to Ernst's office to reiterate the shock with which they had received the news that they would be asked to forswear allegiance to their emperor as the only means by which they could establish loyalty to the United States. Ernst did not have the power to solve this conflict personally, but he promised that the matter would be resolved and requested that the chairman keep him informed of any further concerns as Issei leaders continued to debate the loyalty question.[24]

On the morning of February 10, registration did not begin as scheduled. Issei leaders had strengthened their stance, refusing to register until administrators could offer them a revised loyalty question that would not deprive them of their Japanese citizenship. Issei collective disobedience forced administrators to respond with action rather than vague assurances. The Issei committee of nine presented Ernst with another, stronger petition: "We, the Japanese nationals, residents of Topaz, do hereby resolve absolutely not to answer question 28 in WRA Form 126, Revised. We, therefore, request the proper authority to delete the whole question No. 28. Signed, Japanese National Residents of Topaz."[25] Ernst immediately responded with a teletype-message to the WRA's Washington offices. The Issei leaders' ultimatum was beyond Ernst's authority to answer, and he needed directions. He wrote:

> Japanese aliens have raised the question concerning number 28 on WRA form 126. . . . To answer an unqualified yes places them in the position of losing such protection as they now have under the Spanish Consul; and because they do not have status of Americans citizens, they consider they will be without the protection of any country with its rights, privileges,

and protection. Japanese aliens feel that they have demonstrated over the past generation that they have wanted to conduct themselves in a manner loyal to the United States and would like to continue to have that reputation without a question being raised which would deprive them of all citizenship.[26]

With the committee still in his office, Ernst placed a call to Myer to follow up. While Ernst was waiting to be connected, he answered a call from the WRA offices in California that were dealing some of the same questions.

The Issei at Topaz were not alone in complaining about the loyalty question that required them to renounce their Japanese citizenship. Ernst received a call from Robert Cozzins at Manzanar to discuss possible alternatives to the Issei loyalty question. They were working on the same problem at Manzanar and had drafted a substitute question: "Are you sympathetic to the United States of America and do you agree to faithfully defend the United States from any and all attacks of foreign enemies on our domestic shores?" Ernst read the amended question to the members of the committee, but they were not quite satisfied with this alternative. They said they still wanted a component that would allow them to express the fact that they had been loyal to the United States for a "great many years and that they wanted to continue to do so," but they would not surrender their only recognized citizenship in the process. Ernst continued to hold for a connection with Myer.[27]

Finally, Ernst reached Myer on the phone. Myer was the only man with the authority to change the language of the loyalty questionnaire, so Myer's staff in Washington began drafting an alternative question.

Issei leaders were pleased not only that their concerns had been taken seriously but also that their resistance had forced the government to change the questionnaire. In response, they requested permission to withdraw their ultimatum to eliminate any impression that they were placing undue pressure on administrators. Ernst, however, refused their request to withdraw the ultimatum. His administrative style had been one of cooperation and compromise whenever possible. Ernst believed that his ability to negotiate provided concrete proof that he would be able to resolve even the most serious of conflicts in camp. "There would be no question of face-saving," Ernst told them. Instead, he requested that Issei leaders continue to inform him whenever they felt a policy had produced "an unnecessary hardship" so they could work on a solution together.[28] Ernst gained a strong reputation for his fair and evenhanded support of democratic principles in Topaz, but democracy came with a price.

Bolstered by the Issei's successful drive for a revised loyalty question, the Nisei began organizing their own resistance, which took shape over the next few days. They insisted that the government fully restore Nisei civil rights before anyone would comply with registration. At first, the Nisei conducted informal "bull sessions" in the showers, bathrooms, and mess halls to discuss their situation. Their list of concerns and questions seemed endless. What should they do? Should they volunteer or wait for the draft? If they waited for the draft, would this label them as disloyal in some way? They had already been told they could demonstrate their loyalty by cooperating with evacuation. What would it take now? Why try to settle this question of loyalty after evacuation anyway, especially when the future seemed so uncertain for themselves and their families?[29] They may have been less organized than the Issei at this point, but at least they were talking.

Successful resistance for the Nisei would be much more difficult to organize, because their complaints and concerns were more diverse and could not be satisfied with a mere bureaucratic revision of the loyalty questionnaire. Their demands required changes that the government was not prepared to grant.

In addition to the Issei and the Nisei, another group was organizing its response to registration: the Kibei. Instead of demanding new questions or requesting civil rights, a group of Kibei voted for a strategy that appeared treasonous to some. On February 11, the Kibei met to discuss the loyalty question as well as the preceding question 27, which asked if they would be willing to serve in combat wherever ordered. They would not draft petitions or present the administration with ultimatums. Instead, they decided they would simply register their lack of confidence in the United States by answering both questions with a simple and defiant "No." Some explained that Japan was their real country, and their only future after the war would be in Japan, not in the United States.[30] They argued that their citizenship in the United States had become farcical and that they would never be afforded equal rights in the United States. Registration would give them a chance to formally register a vote of no confidence in the United States and to declare their allegiance to their ancestral homeland instead.

The day after the Kibei voted to take a hard line against the loyalty and the military service questions, the Issei received word that the War Department had prepared and approved an alternative version of the loyalty question, which read: "Will you swear to abide by the laws of the United States and take no action which would in any way interfere with the war effort of the United States?" The new question still did not offer the Issei an official way to declare their long-standing loyalty to the United States, but at least it did not force them to choose between expressing disloyalty and becoming stateless, and it would have no affect on their citizenship at all. When the committee of nine reported back to the general meeting of Issei leaders with the news, they all agreed that this was a good sign. They voted to take word back to all the blocks that registration could officially begin.[31]

The Issei may have been satisfied with the results of their organized resistance and the Kibei satisfied with their decision to answer "No" and "No," but the Nisei still faced a dizzying list of questions and unresolved concerns. When word spread to Issei leaders that the Nisei had organized their own meeting, they called off their plan to notify all blocks that registration could begin. Instead, they decided to wait until the Nisei had had time to debate their own concerns.[32]

Baba, chairman of the Community Council, called an official "all-citizens' meeting," hoping that citizen Nisei and Kibei could arrive at a consensus as to whether they would register.[33] The Kibei in attendance immediately expressed their resolve to answer "No" to questions 27 and 28, if they registered at all. The Kibei took a hard line, making it impossible for a mixed group of citizens to reach a consensus.[34] Chairman Baba was unsatisfied with the results of this meeting and called another for the following day. Kibei representation dominated the second meeting, too. They read prepared statements pleading with the Nisei to declare loyalty to Japan or at least to refuse to register until their civil rights had been restored. When one Nisei stood with an opposing point of view, he was told to sit down and "shut up." One Kibei tried to mediate. He asked for compromise, calling on the more militant Kibei to think of those who were going to stay in the United States after the war and could not take such a strong stand against the government. The most militant Kibei had been educated in Japan, even though they were born in the United States. They knew that if the United States continued to treat them like second-class citizens on the best days, and like enemy aliens, when push came to shove, they might have a better chance living out the rest of their lives in Japan. But Kibei did not represent the majority of Nisei, who had known only the United States and some of whom could not even speak Japanese. The majority of Nisei knew that their futures lay solidly in the United States, regardless of their current struggles. Finally, a Nisei stood up and asked which it was going to be: Would the citizen Nisei and Kibei register? Or were they really ready to fight for civil rights first? The majority voted to refuse registration until the government restored their civil rights.[35]

Camp administrators were already three days behind schedule and were self-conscious about the fact that Topaz was the only camp out of ten where all detainees had refused to register. Ignoring the results of the most recent Nisei meeting, government administrators set the following morning, February 13, as the tentative start date for registration and hoped for the best. They scheduled blocks 11 and 13 to register first. A handful of individuals did show up to register on Saturday morning, although none appeared from blocks 11 and 13. The number of registrants did not exceed a dozen for the entire day. Administration attempts to force registration failed miserably.

As opposition to registration intensified, Director Ernst feared the worst. On Sunday afternoon, he called the army unit stationed at Fort Douglas, Utah, and asked that the soldiers remain on high alert until Monday, worrying that the trouble brewing in Topaz might require military intervention. The commander at Fort Douglas observed that authority had broken down at Topaz.

By Monday morning, word of the resistance at Topaz spread to upper levels of the War Department and to the Western Defense Command headed by Gen. DeWitt. Even though resistance was spreading at all the camps, military leaders agreed that Topaz represented the "only major trouble."[36] Col. Karl Bendetsen reported to DeWitt with some surprise that the entire population had forced the War Department to delay registration for several days. Far less organized resistance had also arisen at Manzanar. Instead of stalling registration as a whole, 45 percent of each block at Manzanar had requested repatriation or expatriation to Japan rather than registering loyalty to the United States. When Bendetsen finished reporting on the situations at each camp, he declared, "Isn't that amazing?" He had predicted that the program would cause trouble and even expose contradictions in government policy that might destroy any legal basis the government once had for the entire program of evacuation. Historians Roger Daniels and Klancy Clark de Nevers note that Bendetsen was deeply concerned about the loyalty registration program. The forced evacuation of Japanese from the West Coast had been based on the claim that loyal and disloyal Japanese could not be distinguished. He feared that a loyalty registration program at this late date would eventually expose the program of forced removal as unconstitutional and might force the government to accept responsibility for a grave injustice. Yet he and DeWitt appeared surprised at the range of resistance the Nikkei had mustered against registration, particularly the well-organized campwide protest at Topaz.[37]

The WRA responded to the crisis in Topaz by sending Dr. John Embree to help administrators resolve the situation. Embree was the director of a new division within the WRA called the Community Analysis Section (CAS). The CAS had been created to help reduce conflicts between the incarcerated population of Japanese Americans and the WRA administration.[38] Embree was sent to oversee the situation at Topaz personally, and he was determined to resolve the conflict before letting it grow to the point of a major crisis.

When Embree arrived in Topaz on Sunday afternoon, February 14, 1943, another citizens' meeting was scheduled to begin. He met briefly with Ernst beforehand and suggested ways that Ernst might regain control over the situation at Topaz without military intervention.[39] When Nisei representatives gathered on Sunday night to present the results of the campwide vote, Ernst took control of the meeting and declared that all citizens who refused registration would be in violation of the Espionage Act. Ernst read the Espionage Act to the audience and explained that as American citizens instructed by their government to register, they could and would be prosecuted for obstructing the government in its attempt to raise an army if they refused to comply. Embree reported that if a vote had been taken at that Sunday afternoon meeting of the representatives, the majority probably would have voted not to register at all. His intervention had a pivotal effect on the outcome of registration at Topaz.[40]

The Nisei representatives did not give up right away. They tried to go over Ernst's head with a set of resolutions and an ultimatum they prepared for Secretary of War Stimson. The Nisei organized their own representative body to carry their complaints to the administration. Similar to the Issei committee of nine, the Nisei organized a committee of thirty-three, from which a smaller committee of nine was selected to draft the first set of resolutions. They went to work immediately, foregoing dinner and finally presenting their draft for ratification by the larger representative body of Nisei at 9:45 P.M. A general meeting was called in every block at 10:00 P.M. to consider the resolution, and at 11:30 P.M. the committee of nine reported back to Ernst with the results of their collaborative efforts.

Representatives met in Director Ernst's apartment and requested that their set of resolutions be sent to Secretary of War Stimson. The committee continued to make registration contingent upon a restoration of rights, so Ernst refused to send the letter. Ernst warned them that they would have to take out any references to registration in their demands for civil rights or no government official would pay attention to any of their resolutions.[41] More important, Ernst told them that it was not Stimson's job to deal with civil rights, so they would have to choose a different audience. Only the secretary of state or the president himself could address citizens' rights; Stimson's job was to raise an army. With a weakened set of resolutions, the committee still insisted that its demand for civil rights be forwarded to Secretary of War Stimson. Stimson may not have been in charge of civil rights, but his department was the one asking the Nisei to give service in the absence of their most basic rights.

Ernst agreed to send the citizens' petition if all references to withholding military service were removed. He assured the representatives that he would send their modified petition to Secretary of War Stimson and WRA Director Myer first thing in the morning. The meeting disbanded well after 2:00 A.M.[42] As Embree later observed, Ernst had averted a crisis of major proportions. Ernst's shift in tactics was successful, even though the Nisei continued to agitate for civil rights.

When Myer received the resolutions drafted by the committee of nine and signed by the committee of thirty-three, he dismissed them as petty and unimportant, responding that this was "not the time to quibble or bargain." He said that registration was a crucial test to be taken seriously and that the very demands made by the committee of thirty-three might be obtained if they would take this first step toward restoring their own citizenship. Stimson had made this policy change in "good faith," Myer said, and until the residents of Topaz demonstrated their willingness to comply, Stimson would not be able to consider any further action on their behalf. "It is my hope and my belief," Myer concluded, "that they will not fail this crucial test."

As administrators and Washington officials took a hard line with the Nisei, Issei leaders brought a new grievance to Ernst: a problem with the title of the questionnaire. Filling out a form titled "Application for Leave Clearance," particularly in a program touted as a demonstration of loyalty and an opportunity to contribute to the war effort, caused great concern for those Issei who intended to return to Japan after the war. They did not want it to appear as if they had requested this questionnaire. Ernst agreed to rename the form simply

"Questionnaire." The demands of the Issei continued to be easier for Ernst to satisfy than those of citizens.[43]

Once the Issei had satisfactorily resolved their own complaints, some Issei began to speak out on behalf of the Nisei. They argued that the Nisei should not voluntarily enlist when they lacked their basic rights. They based this new set of concerns on the basis of their own experiences with race discrimination and broken promises during World War I. One Issei pointed out that during war, promises are sometimes made that cannot or will not be kept: "During the last war, India was promised independence, but that was not given." He raised his concern that the volunteer service of the Nisei may become futile. "They are expected to do their duty as citizens of the United States," he said, "but at the same time, they may not be given the freedom" their citizenship implied. He requested on behalf of the Nisei that their future standing in the United States and citizenship must be clarified now.[44]

Issei parents knew from experience that the United States had fought to make the world safe for democracy in the past but had not in practice kept all its promises. Issei soldiers who volunteered to fight during World War I with the promise of citizenship had to fight for more than fifteen years to get their reward. Some Issei veterans did, in the end, get U.S. citizenship in 1935, but without mounting a sustained struggle, they knew that the government would not have voluntarily given this status to veterans who under any other circumstances would have been ineligible for citizenship. The Issei warned younger Nisei, who lacked these personal memories of broken promises, to be cautious of the government's offer of restored citizenship rights in return for voluntary combat duty.[45]

In response to Issei warnings that the Nisei may never get a full restoration of their rights, even if they served in the military, Ernst repeated his warning of criminal prosecution for any who refused to comply with registration. "The War Department has nothing to do with civil rights," he said. The War Department "is not engaged in anything but war now." To this declaration, someone asked whether the Nisei would or would not be prosecuted under the Espionage Act if they did not register on the scheduled date. Ernst responded that the Espionage Act would be in force against "anyone who willingly obstructs and hurts a country."[46] This was not a very precise answer, but it maintained Ernst's threat of prosecution for any further resistance against registration, whether from the Nisei or from the Issei.

As the administration killed the momentum and effectiveness of Nisei resistance to registration, a new movement took its place that worked hand-in-hand with the response of the government. This movement was organized by those in camp anxious to demonstrate their patriotism and to distance themselves from those who had challenged the government's absolute authority during wartime. In the early hours of Wednesday, February 17, a new committee approached Embree for assistance with their own petition. They took exception to the resolution drafted by the committee of thirty-three and wanted to formalize their dissent with a counter-resolution. With Embree's help, they wrote:

> We feel that loyalty to our country is something to be expressed without reference to past grievances or wrongs. We feel that in according us the right to the second article of the Bill of Rights that it is the right of every man to bear arms in the defense of his country the War Department has in good faith started the first step to restore us all rights as citizens of the United States. We feel that the issue of expressing our loyalty has been confused. We believe in fighting for our country and our ideals is [sic] the most important thing when our country is at war trying to uphold those ideals for which we stand. We shall register, we are loyal, we shall fight for the United States. Signed, other residents of Topaz.[47]

The committee of thirty-three's smaller subcommittee of nine became incensed when they heard about this petition. They had been democratically elected and felt that this unofficial resolution undermined their authority. They complained to Ernst that they should be the only group allowed to speak for the Nisei of Topaz. Ernst replied that they would have to lodge a complaint with the Community Council.[48] Embree encouraged the smaller group's efforts to project their patriotism and to skirt the democratic process. By combining threats of criminal prosecution while stimulating patriotism, Embree demonstrated the power of these two coercive powers in ending the registration crisis at Topaz.

Resistance against registration ended dramatically when members of Block 5 flooded into administration offices on Wednesday, February 17, to register their loyalty. A large number of leading pro-U.S. Issei and pro-JACL Nisei lived in Block 5, so their turnout was not a complete surprise. For the first time, registration seemed to be gaining momentum. Word spread throughout the camps that registration had begun. After this massive response from one block, those who had resisted in the past began showing up for their own turns to register.[49]

Ken Yoshida registered on February 18, 1943. The form was entitled, "Statement of United States Citizen of Japanese Ancestry." A U.S. Selective Service symbol was at the top of the form, and a statement at the end warned that any who gave false information would be in violation of Selective Service laws. This was no simple form, and most Nisei understood so when they appeared for registration.[50]

The questionnaire began simply, asking for basic biographical information, but the questions became progressively more complicated. The questionnaire first asked for the registrant's former place of residence, names of Caucasian acquaintances, family members, occupations, and voter registration status. The form asked for information about education, employment, foreign travel, and relatives living in Japan. It also asked for details about language skills, sports and hobbies, foreign investments, clubs, organizations, magazine subscriptions, and so on. Yoshida's record demonstrated little connection with Japan: He boasted an American education, and his employment history was lengthy. His responses did not seem unusual or problematic.[51]

Unknown to detainees, the military evaluated the answers to most questions on a point scale depending on how "Japanese" or how "American" registrants seemed based on the simple facts of their lives.[52] For example, if a registrant marked that he or she was Christian, he or she earned 2 points, but if a registrant marked that he or she was Buddhist, 1 point was deducted. Any registrants who identified themselves as Shintoists were automatically classified as disloyal. Registrants even earned or lost points by association. Those with relatives in the U.S. military earned 1 point, but those whose fathers had been interned in Department of Justice camps lost 3 points. If registrants were members of a judo or kendo club, they lost 3 points, but members of the JACL earned 1 point. Registrants earned 3 points if they were members of the YMCA, the Masons, the Rotary Club, or the Boy Scouts of America.

Yoshida had been falsely identified as a member of the JACL, which gave him 1 positive point, but this mistake was also indicative of the possibility that forms did not always reflect the registrants' answers with 100 percent accuracy.[53] Yoshida's form also indicated that he donated money to the Red Cross occasionally, which may have counted positively on his behalf. One of his pastimes, though, was judo, possibly deducting 3 points from his loyalty score. Had the Federal Bureau of Investigation (FBI) found his father, a high-ranking judo instructor, following Pearl Harbor as the agency had intended, Ken's score would have been at least 5 points in the negative even before he answered the loyalty questions.[54] Judo instructors had been among those community leaders picked up by the FBI and sent to Department of Justice camps in the first weeks of the war. Yoshida's father had been on that list, but the family had moved around so frequently that the FBI could not find him. In an ironic twist, by complying with the orders for forced removal and by becoming a part of the massive bureaucratic WRA system, he became lost in the system but luckily was able to stay with his family in Topaz.

The infamous final two questions on loyalty and military service caused the Nisei lasting concern. Question 27 asked whether individuals would be willing to serve in the armed forces wherever called. Many balked at this question, because it seemed like an underhanded way of getting people to volunteer for the military. Question 28 asked registrants to declare their unqualified allegiance to the United States and to forswear allegiance to the emperor of Japan. The Issei had already agitated for a replacement question, but the Nisei were still required to answer this question, as it had been removed from only the Issei questionnaire, and it implied that Nisei, even those born after 1924 who had no legal ties to Japan at all, had once been loyal to Japan. Yoshida answered "Yes" to both questions, even though he personally did not believe it was necessary to disavow allegiance to the emperor. He had been born and raised in the United States. It was the only country he knew and the only country he claimed as a citizen.

Questions 27 and 28 received the most attention during the war and from historians after the war, but one additional question also deserves closer scrutiny: the dual citizenship question. Question 25 asked, "To the best of your knowledge was your birth ever registered with any Japanese government agency for the purpose of establishing a claim to Japanese citizenship? If so, have you applied for cancellation of such registration?" Together, these questions functioned as a method to resolve once and for all the citizenship status of Japanese Americans. Congress killed two attempts to pass legislation forcing dual citizens to renounce one of their allegiances. This registration form supplanted the failed congressional legislation and could be applied specifically to Japanese Americans, eliminating the problems associated with judging German and Italian Americans against a law that was designed to address fears of Japanese disloyalty.

Yoshida indicated that his birth had not been reported to the Japanese government. He was not a dual citizen in any demonstrable way. To Yoshida, he had but one country: the United States. Even so, the government wanted more proof of Nisei renunciation of Japanese citizenship, whether it was a mere technicality or a hypothetical possibility. By answering "Yes" to question 28, as far as the U.S. government was concerned, Yoshida had renounced any allegiance he may have held, knowingly or not, to the emperor of Japan and any possibility of holding dual citizenship no longer had any bearing on his obligations to the U.S. military.

Yoshida's name was forwarded on for further processing by the Selective Service as a potential candidate for the draft if and when it would be reinstated for the Nisei, but he and his family made other plans. Many families responded to the bitterness they felt at the end of the registration crisis by filing for repatriation to Japan for the parents and expatriation from the United States for the children. The principle goal of most families in choosing this option was keeping the family together at all costs. Yoshida's father was not content to wait to see what the future would bring to him and his wife, his five sons, and his two daughters, so he instructed the family to file for repatriation and expatriation to Japan after the program of registration was complete. He had been active in camp politics before registration and believed that the United States had demonstrated quite clearly that it would not defend even the rights of his citizen children. He held some property in Japan, according to the FBI, and in an apparent effort to protect his family's financial welfare and to keep the family together, the Yoshidas all filed for repatriation or expatriation.

The Yoshida family does not appear on any of the official lists of those requesting re- or expatriation from Topaz, so it may be the case that at some point Yoshida's father rescinded the request on behalf of the entire family. People requesting re- or expatriation were interviewed to ensure that they did not hold any reservations about their requests and to see if anyone wanted to change his or her mind. It was not uncommon for individuals and families, who at times filed their initial requests out of anger, fear, or protest, to reexamine their motivations and to rethink the difficulties they might face if they were actually sent to Japan. Families made difficult decisions to stay together, regardless of how they appeared in the context of very strict wartime definitions of loyalty to the United States or loyalty to the enemy.[55]

The Yoshida family was not alone in its request for re- and expatriation. After registration, the number of requests increased from little more than a thousand at the end of 1942 to nearly five times that many by the end of 1943. Unlike the requests in 1942 that came almost entirely from the Issei, the requests in 1943 came from the Issei and the Nisei as entire families made the choice to seek their fortunes in Japan after the war, where they hoped to find greater economic security and full citizenship.

THE END OF THE REGISTRATION CRISIS AT TOPAZ

On February 19, the official representative body of Topaz Nisei received a response from the Secretary of War to its petition. The response came from the War Department's Office of Assistant Secretary and had been written by Col. William P. Scobey:

> Public pronouncement has already been made by the President of the United States and by the Secretary of War. It is only by mutual confidence and cooperation that the loyal Japanese Americans can be restored to their civil rights. The present program [the loyalty registration program along with the drive for Nisei voluntary military service] is not complete rehabilitation but is the first step in that direction. The United States government has evidenced its faith in the loyal Japanese Americans giving them the opportunity to serve their country. This is their opportunity to demonstrate to the American people that they have faith in America.[56]

The government's position was not new to residents, but at least the demands of the Nikkei had been noticed when they presented the government with a petition that had been written through a democratic process. The government responded by listening to their concerns, even though officials did not acquiesce. Individual citizens had been able to appeal to a high-ranking government official—Secretary of War Stimson—and had received a response and assurances that the restoration of more civil rights would come.

Some detainees whose expectations for a positive government response had all but evaporated welcomed this small victory. One observer wrote, "Word quickly flashed through the center that the answer had come. . . . That night pans were banged and gongs were rung in almost every block of the center, calling people to listen to the announcement of the committee that the Secretary of War had answered their questions and that now everyone should register." This observer concluded that from his point of view, a very important civil right had been restored: the right of citizens to make themselves heard and to get a response directly from one of the "highest ranking government officials, which gave them the assurance they needed." He added, "That was democracy at work."[57]

For others, this version of democracy—where the government responded only to rebuke its subjects for wanting full citizenship in the face of the War Department's request for soldiers—was far from perfect and not to be celebrated. The official response had done nothing to restore real rights but instead had pacified some grievances and had suppressed attempts to agitate for real democratic change. A few may have welcomed Stimson's response as evidence that their petition was heard, but many more probably realized that no matter how organized their resistance, their citizenship rights and obligations would remain out of balance, likely for the duration of the war.[58]

It is reasonable to believe that the majority of the Nikkei in Topaz were not as overjoyed by the government's lack of responsiveness to their demands for a full restoration of their rights as camp administrators indicated in official reports. Topaz ranked fourth among the camps in numbers of Nisei who requested expatriation and fourth overall in numbers of Nisei who renounced their citizenship following the registration crisis. The Nikkei in all the camps may not have been able to organize effectively against the government, but individual families and individual Nikkei continued to assert their wills against that of the government by refusing to pledge their loyalty to the United States, by renouncing their citizenship, or by requesting repatriation. The resistance continued and could not be stopped completely, but it could be reshaped through the lens of criminalization and patriotic propaganda.

The committee of thirty-three responded in its own way to Stimson's letter by announcing that it was time for all the residents of Topaz to register. The registration crisis at Topaz had officially come to an end.

Stimson's letter did little more than reiterate the propaganda that the War Department used to launch registration in the first place. This was a first step in restoring the responsibilities of citizens, but it was no guarantee that rights would follow. The organized resistance at Topaz demonstrated that citizens lacked the ability to force specific change because of their citizenship. They were required as citizens to comply with Selective Service procedures under penalty of the Espionage Act. Unless they were willing to move their protests from dissent to civil disobedience, their only recourse was to petition for a promise that someday their rights would be restored.

UNEXPECTED RESULTS OF REGISTRATION

By February 27, all adults in Topaz had registered, but only about 3 percent of Nisei and Kibei young men who were eligible had volunteered for military service. This number would continue to rise in response to aggressive recruiting campaigns, but the initial response was so weak, it became clear that the protest had not ended. Nisei and Kibei efforts to use noncompliance with registration as a tool to leverage a restoration of their citizenship rights had only resulted in threats of criminal prosecution and War Department promises that their citizenship rights would be restored, eventually. Citizens at Topaz may have been willing to comply with registration, but no more than that in the majority of cases.

The few who had volunteered organized a grassroots effort to recruit their peers, and their efforts paid off when twenty more Nisei volunteered. They increased their efforts by holding open meetings. Some volunteers shared their enthusiasm for the war effort with women who were considering volunteering for the Women's Auxiliary Army Corps (WAACs). On March 6, volunteers organized a formal committee designed to recruit even more enlistees and called it the Resident Council for Japanese American Civil Rights. They prepared a pamphlet explaining to male citizens reasons why they should volunteer for service. On March 7, with the help of a growing number of enthusiastic women supporters, the committee organized a group called the Volunteers for Victory and held a large banquet and dance. The Committee of Future WAACs hosted the event and invited one hundred thirty "guests" from within the camp whom they hoped they could persuade to volunteer for military service. In just three days following the dance and banquet, 112 additional Nisei men volunteered, meeting the final March 10 deadline for voluntary recruitment for the new combat team.[59]

The Topaz Volunteers for Victory turned their recruiting effort into a propaganda campaign of Nisei loyalty in an attempt to change public opinion about the Nisei. They met with political, ecclesiastical, and business leaders of the State of Utah and sent their own Volunteers for Victory pamphlet to members of Congress, ministers, educators, and JACL leaders nationwide. Most recipients of the pamphlet wrote back to congratulate the group on its support of the war effort, and some even pointed out how well it had used propaganda for their own purposes. The JACL requested that the Volunteers for Victory let them use portions of their pamphlet for JACL's national image campaign, which shows that they were not just puppets of the organization. Instead, this was a genuine grassroots effort adopted by the JACL and then disseminated to a broader audience. The Volunteers for Victory may have supported the stated goals of the JACL, but this was propaganda from the bottom up.

As a result of the vigorous national campaign of the Volunteers for Victory and the ultimate failure of Topaz Nisei to force any concrete changes in government policy regarding their citizenship rights, by the end of 1943, few remembered the trouble that registration had initially caused at Topaz. The efforts of individual Nisei to promote patriotism in combination with government threats of criminal prosecution to crush the resistance turned the perception of registration at Topaz from that of one of the most organized sites of resistance to one of the most patriotic of the camps. The organized resistance to registration at Topaz remains absent not only from surveys of the registration crisis but also, most remarkably, from those books that focus exclusively on Topaz.[60]

The registration program and the loyalty questionnaire provoked the first widespread resistance to the War Department's decision to restore Nisei obligations of military service without first restoring their rights. Topaz led this early resistance as the only camp to stall registration for an entire week.[61] Even though residents of Topaz eventually lost their fight to delay registration permanently until Nisei rights were restored, some continued the resistance in more personal ways, such as answering "No" to questions 27 and 28 or registering for re- or expatriation. Most important, just because registration finally got underway and all draft-age Nisei men in Topaz complied with registration— 1,450 in all—this cooperation did not mean that all were satisfied with the results of their resistance. Of all adults who registered, 83 percent responded positively to the loyalty question, 12 percent answered "No," and fewer than 5 percent simply left the answer blank.[62] For some, this was only the beginning of their continued fight for a full restoration of civil rights.

Only 1,208 people, fewer than 6 percent of eligible Nisei, enlisted in the military voluntarily from the camps as a whole. This number fell far short of the quota the War Department had set for itself, starting with 2,500 Nisei volunteers from inside the camps and later reducing the goal to 2,000. Seventeen percent of all registrants and approximately 20 percent of all Nisei answered loyalty questions in the negative. Most shocking to WRA administrators was the sharp rise in applications for re- and expatriation. The previous year, only 2,255 individuals had requested repatriation, and most of these were Issei. By 1943, this number surpassed nine thousand, and most new applicants were citizens. The trend continued into 1944, when the number of requests topped out at nearly twenty thousand, or 16 percent of the total evacuated population. Of 19,963 Nisei of military age, 6 percent volunteered (1,181); approximately 800 of the 1,181 volunteers passed loyalty tests and their physical examinations and were inducted into the original 442nd. By contrast, 24 percent answered "No" to question 28, or a total of 4,783. An astonishingly high 50 percent answered "No" at Manzanar. By contrast, only 2 percent answered "No" at Minidoka. Overall, 6,700 answered "No" to question 28, and an additional 2,000 qualified their answers. Sixty-five thousand responded with an unqualified "Yes."[63]

The WRA, the FBI, the War Department, and even a special Senate committee all tried to explain the results of registration. WRA social scientists argued emphatically that negative responses to the loyalty questions served as a final means of protest against evacuation. Negative responses did not, in their eyes, constitute any concrete proof of disloyalty.[64]

Registration produced many unexpected problems and revealed frustrations and anger among the Nikkei population that could not easily be contained by state repression or by the propaganda of patriotism. The War Department had initially planned to house all those who fell into the "disloyal" category in a small isolation facility located in southern Utah. It became clear that this plan would not work after three thousand individuals at Tule Lake refused to register and the registration process fell apart in that camp. As a result, Tule Lake became the new segregation center. The camp became overcrowded and could not accommodate all those who filed for expatriation and repatriation over the coming year. Six thousand of the original residents of Tule Lake remained in the camp once it became a segregation facility to house "disloyal" Nikkei. More than eleven thousand individuals were sent to Tule Lake from other camps, bringing the "disloyal" population up to a total of eighteen thousand. The pressures of overcrowding and the lack of tolerance exhibited by administrators led to rioting and eventually to military repression and control of the camp.[65] But this "disloyal" label is misleading and remains a point of contention and divisiveness today. Some preferred to cast their lot with Japan. Some gave up on the United States. Anger, frustration, and dissatisfaction with the results of organized attempts to force the government to restore Nisei rights led some to lash out against the U.S. government in whatever ways they could. The simplistic categories of "loyal" or "disloyal" used during the war are not adequate to explain the varied motivations of individuals who ended up at Tule Lake.

Congress conducted its own investigation of the results of registration and responded by passing the first wartime law that allowed citizens to renounce their citizenship. Many had already accused the WRA of incompetence at the end of 1943, after major disturbances at Poston and Manzanar (discussed in Chapter 2) had weakened congressional confidence in the WRA's ability to manage the camps. After the registration crisis unfolded in the first months of 1943, Congress interpreted resistance on the part of detainees as proof that large numbers of Japanese Americans were loyal to Japan. On July 1, 1944, the president signed Public Law 78-405, otherwise known as the Denaturalization Act of 1944, which allowed citizens to renounce their citizenship. In October 1944, instructions were sent to all the camps to help facilitate the process.[66]

President Roosevelt was equally concerned about the disastrous and unexpected results of registration and asked an old friend, Milton Eisenhower (the original director of the WRA), for his reaction. Eisenhower replied that the negative response should not have been unexpected. After all, nothing in the democratic training of young Nisei prepared them for the conditions and decisions they faced in the camps. He wrote in a letter to President Roosevelt:

> Persons in this group find themselves living in a situation for which their public school and democratic teachings have not prepared them. It is hard for them to escape a conviction that their plight is due more to racial discrimination, economic motivations and wartime prejudices than any real necessity from the military point of view for evacuation from the West Coast.[67]

Eisenhower wisely noted that a young person schooled in democracy may very well balk at the idea of being treated like an enemy alien, but perhaps Eisenhower misinterpreted one point: It is likely that the democratic training of children in the public schools prepared them very well for the problems they encountered in the camps. They learned to respond with dissent, petitions, noncompliance, and creative forms of resistance, sometimes even choosing the least desirable and most costly form of protest: civil disobedience.

One of the most damaging results of registration was the artificial division of the Nisei into "loyal" and "disloyal."[68] One Nisei student related a saying in response: "The army, being the cowboys, and us Japs (that's what they call us and I don't like it) as cattle, rounded up and sent to a place where they will be separated from the good ones and the bad ones (loyal and disloyal ones) and slaughter the good ones and leave the old ones to die."[69] The divisions that were created did not represent "loyalty" and "disloyalty." Instead, they came as a result of a rare opportunity for individuals to face their government and to voice their dissent. The loyalty questionnaire was presented to individuals at a time when many were desperate for a way to have a voice and to declare their unhappiness with their undemocratic, unconstitutional treatment. But the labels stuck, and Japanese Americans are still talking about how to stop using the same artificial wartime classifications of loyal and disloyal that the government imposed upon them and their ancestors. The "loyal" young men, were, in effect, selected to risk their lives for their country, while the "disloyal" were sent to more permanent detention facilities and further traumatized by their lack of due process. The elderly Issei, caught in the middle, remained deeply uncertain of where their futures lay and what would become of their children's futures in America.

CHAPTER 4

Gordon Hirabayashi in the Tucson Federal Prison Camp

ॐ৩ ৎৎ৩

WHEN GORDON HIRABAYASHI was sentenced after losing his initial court case in October 1942, he knew that he might have to serve prison time for his decision to refuse the government's exclusion order, but he did not want to spend any more time inside an institution like the King County Jail. He had spent months confined in this short-term facility waiting for his trial and months more waiting for some acceptable form of parole while lawyers worked on his appeals. He could not bear serving his official sentence in a "walled institution." He preferred the freedom of a road camp. In a humorous end to what Hirabayashi described as a trial that was not so much a trial as a demonstration of "how much unbalance can be caused by fear and hysteria," he asked for a longer sentence. This request ended up costing him in a way he did not expect. The judge had given him two short consecutive sentences for failure to obey curfew and for failure to obey the exclusion order. But to be admitted to a road camp, Hirabayashi needed at least a ninety-day sentence. Judge Lloyd Black agreed and gave Hirabayashi two ninety-day sentences, set to run concurrently at Dupont, Washington. But Hirabayashi never made it to Dupont, because it was inside the exclusion zone. He would have to serve his sentence elsewhere.[1]

Judge Black's decision to replace Hirabayashi's original consecutive sentences with concurrent sentences allowed the Supreme Court to choose which of the two charges it would address. The justices chose the issue of curfew and delayed ruling on the exclusion order until the Fred Korematsu case came before them a year later. In a unanimous decision, the court upheld Hirabayashi's curfew conviction. Supreme Court Justice Frank Murphy had intended to dissent in this case, but the rest of the Court pressured him to change his dissent to a concurring opinion. This was a time of national crisis, the justices told him, when the country needed the Court to demonstrate its undivided support of the government's wartime powers to defend the country.[2]

The majority opinion, written by Chief Justice Harlan F. Stone, detailed the threat the country was facing at the very time that Hirabayashi was demanding that all Americans be subject to curfew laws or that none be subject to them. In actuality, Hirabayashi was just barely formulating his own position of conscience when he decided to disobey curfew: He had meant to challenge the exclusion order. Nevertheless, in choosing curfew as the Court's main focus, Chief Justice Stone wrote that in a time when war was spreading throughout Europe and the Pacific; when German sympathizers had aided Germany's invasion of western European countries; and when, he suggested—based on falsified and inaccurate evidence, unbeknownst to him—Japanese Americans had aided in the successful attack on Pearl Harbor, the country could not take any chances in allowing freedoms for individuals who might be harboring feelings of disloyalty. Stone's majority opinion recited the most-repeated racial assumptions prevalent at the time: Japanese Americans demonstrated race-based loyalties, an unwillingness to assimilate, and the problem of dual citizenship. The Supreme Court not only perpetuated racial stereotypes in its representation of Japanese Americans as a group but also declared that in a time of war, the Court could not second-guess the military's judgment, even if this meant excluding from service an entire population on the basis of race and on the assumption that some among them *may* commit acts of sabotage at some point in the future.[3] The broad powers that this decision gave to the military in the name of national defense ended up causing a split decision a year later in the case of Korematsu, who also challenged the exclusion order.

The Supreme Court case involving Hirabayashi and the associated cases of Minoru Yasui and Korematsu are the subjects of numerous studies on the ways in which the Court acquiesced to the military in the context of war and how civil rights lawyers and activists found sufficient evidence to exonerate these individuals in federal courts in the 1980s. Lawyers and the various individuals who resisted and who supported their causes hoped that their wartime cases would clarify the constitutional limits of state powers to proscribe citizens' rights on the basis of race, even during war. But when the Court handed down its ruling and upheld the military's authority to exclude individuals from military zones, the consequences of the criminal aspects of the cases applied to only the individuals involved. Chief Justice Stone announced the Court's rulings on the Hirabayashi and Yasui curfew cases on June 21, 1943. Korematsu was still awaiting his trial, free on bail and working in Salt Lake City. Yasui was brought back to Portland, Oregon, from Minidoka, Idaho, for resentencing, but the judge ruled that he had served his time while awaiting trial in county jail, so he returned to Minidoka. Hirabayashi was the only defendant sent to prison, because Judge Black specified that he could not count his time in jail toward his final sentence.[4]

For the purposes of this book, the outcome of Hirabayashi's Supreme Court case represents a personal disappointment and an important milestone in the life of a conscientious objector (CO). Hirabayashi's ultimate conviction sent him to Tucson, Arizona, where he served his prison sentence. In Tucson, he became acquainted with many different types of resisters, and he came to see himself as a part of a much larger battle for social justice and an advocate for the Christian principles of peace and pacifism.

HONOR CAMPS AS PRISONS

Because this book focuses on the prison where Hirabayashi and the Tucsonians were sent after committing acts of civil disobedience, this chapter positions the history of Japanese Americans' removal and wartime confinement within the historic context of a reformed, expanding federal prison system. Hirabayashi requested that he be sent to the road camp at a time when progressive penology had reformed much of the prison system in America.

Even though prison reform was uneven across the country, western states had been on the cutting edge of progressive penology since the 1910s and 1920s. Arizona and Colorado were the first states to give special treatment to the mentally ill, and Colorado was the first to combine the "honor camp" concept, a minimum-security facility for those with demonstrated good behavior and short sentences, with meaningful work and early parole for prisoners working road construction or repair projects.[5] Others followed Colorado's lead and established road camps of their own. The Catalina road camp, established in the mountains above Tucson, Arizona, was exactly this kind of honor camp. Prisoners with short sentences who were trustees, meaning those prisoners who had been awarded trustee status because of their good behavior, were selected to work on the highway. Hirabayashi had already been living in the trustee ward of the King County Jail while awaiting trial. This status allowed him to be selected to serve his sentence in an honor camp, where he was allowed a great deal of freedom as long as he remained worthy of trustee status.

The core values of "constructive penology"—an emphasis on job training, early parole for good behavior, and citizenship rehabilitation—guided management of the Catalina road camp. It made the prison environment ironically similar in many ways to the War Relocation Authority (WRA) camps, where inmates were offered a type of parole if they passed the loyalty tests. The experiences the Tucsonians endured living under a variety of forms of confinement highlight the ways in which the confinement of Japanese Americans, the bureaucratic process of sorting out individuals for segregation or early leave clearance, and even the offer of early leave and full "rehabilitation" of citizenship through voluntary induction into the military paralleled standard methods of processing convicted felons. The WRA and the Federal Bureau of Prisons were a part of a massive, growing federal system designed to protect the public from potential threats; only the military and prisons promised to rehabilitate citizens.

HIRABAYASHI'S JOURNEY TO TUCSON

When the Supreme Court handed down its ruling, Hirabayashi was still living in Spokane, Washington, working with the American Friends Service Committee on matters related to Japanese American relocation from the camps. Several weeks later, during the summer of 1943, Hirabayashi was busy mowing the lawn at the home of the Suzuki family when a couple of agents drove up, parked, got out of the car, and approached Hirabayashi, announcing that they were sent to bring him in. Hirabayashi responded, "Well I was expecting you. What took you so long?" After Hirabayashi changed into some clean clothes, the agents took him to speak with District Attorney Edward Connelly, who announced to Hirabayashi that it was time for him to serve his ninety days. He said he would send him over to the federal tank of the Spokane County Jail so Hirabayashi could get started.[6]

Hirabayashi was quick to correct the district attorney, who obviously did not understand the deal made with Judge Black, which allowed Hirabayashi to serve his sentence in a road camp. He said, "Oh, wait a minute now. I could have gotten sixty days, if I'm going to do it in a county jail. I asked for ninety days . . . so that I could be outside [in] a road camp somewhere."[7] District Attorney Connelly replied, "Well, we can't send you to a road camp, because the nearest road camp is outside of Tacoma, and that's in the restricted area. We can't send you there. The only other one that I know of is in Tucson, Arizona—outside of Tucson, Arizona—on the mountains there. That's 1,600 miles away, and we don't have travel funds to send you there." (Neither Connelly nor Hirabayashi realized that Tucson was also in the restricted zone.) Hirabayashi started thinking creatively. He would not agree to serve the longer sentence he had requested if he would have to do so in a county jail. "Well, if you can't send me there," Hirabayashi said, "what if I just take the transportation on my own?" Connelly replied that if Hirabayashi wanted to travel at his own expense, he would write him a letter granting permission so he would not get "pestered along the way." Hirabayashi would have to travel to Tucson in the most inexpensive way possible, so he decided to hitchhike.[8]

Hirabayashi took several weeks to reach Tucson. He had hitchhiked only once before, when he left for leadership training in New York during that monumental summer of 1940. He had hitchhiked halfway across the western United States before he finally found a car that was going all the way to New York. But he did not take into account war rations—with strict rations on gasoline, people were not driving as far or as frequently as they had in the past, making hitchhiking more difficult—or the desolate areas of southern Utah, Nevada, and Arizona that he would have to traverse this time, so he took his time. He stopped to visit his parents in Weiser, Idaho, and then he rested for a couple of days in Salt Lake City, where he stopped by the offices of the Japanese American Citizens League and had a friendly visit with *Pacific Citizen* newspaper editor Larry Tajiri. He sent a postcard to Eleanor Ring from Cedar

City, Utah, on September 15, 1943: "Am getting closer to my winter vacation resort," he wrote, adding, "So far, have had good luck on my thumb."[9] He dealt with only one minor incident that ended up being more humorous than anything. He caught a ride from a Utah state highway patrolman who was happy to take him as far south as his route extended. But when he asked Hirabayashi where he was headed and Hirabayashi said prison, he stomped on the brakes. Hirabayashi offered him the letter Connelly had written to vouch for his story. The patrolman read it, and Hirabayashi recalled, "I could see his mind operating." "He was wondering," Hirabayashi assumed, "'What should I do? Should I take him in? Should I do something official?'" He finally decided to take Hirabayashi was far as he was going and then let him go on his way.[10]

When Hirabayashi finally reached Tucson and walked into the federal marshal's office, he was hot and exhausted. He had hitchhiked 1,600 miles, a trek that took an entire month to get from Spokane, Washington, to Tucson, Arizona. After sleeping in ditches along the way to save money and taking any ride he could get, no matter how short, Hirabayashi finally paid for a bus ticket in Las Vegas so he could finish the journey and get on with the business of serving his prison term. But when Hirabayashi finally made it to Tucson, the marshal's office was not expecting him.[11] Hirabayashi showed the marshal the letter from Spokane District Attorney Connelly, stating that he was to report to Tucson to serve a short sentence at the road camp.

The marshal was confused and dumbfounded that Hirabayashi had appeared alone and seemingly without the proper paperwork, because this was not the way prisoners normally arrived. The marshal told Hirabayashi, "You might as well turn around and go home," but Hirabayashi was not about to leave after he had worked so hard to get there. Hirabayashi replied, "Well I would gladly do that, but you're going to find those papers some time, then I would have to interrupt what I'm doing, and come back again." "So," he said, "you had better find it. And if you can't find it after looking carefully, you could call the judge in Seattle." Hirabayashi also gave him the name and phone number of the Spokane district attorney. In addition, Hirabayashi recommended that the office call the U.S. Bureau of Prisons to see if it had any record of his sentence. The marshal agreed to investigate the matter further. Because it was the latter part of the afternoon and still hot outside, he said, "Why don't you go to an air-conditioned movie, and then go to an air-conditioned restaurant and then come here about 7:00 P.M. and we'll see what we have?" Hirabayashi did what the marshal recommended. When he came back, the marshal said, "We found your papers. We're ready and we have a car here." One of the officers drove Hirabayashi to the camp thirty miles away. Hirabayashi's long trek was finally over, and his prison sentence began.[12]

Fifty-five years later, Hirabayashi recalled that he did realize that while he was waiting for the federal marshal to find his paperwork, he had been allowed, even encouraged, to roam freely through the streets of Tucson, a town that all Japanese Americans were forbidden to enter by the same exclusion order he had refused to obey in the first place. Hirabayashi was being sent to prison because he had violated this very law. Hirabayashi said that he would have experienced a greater degree of satisfaction had he known that, even though the courts had ruled that his ancestry made him a dangerous threat to national security, he had been allowed to hitchhike back into the exclusion zone and to enjoy dinner and a movie before he began his prison sentence. The contradictions that his story represents are symbolic of the many contradictions that this book seeks to unravel.

THE TUCSON FEDERAL PRISON CAMP

The "camp" that Hirabayashi would spend the next ninety days working at was the Tucson Federal Prison Camp, a minimum-security honor camp built to house trustee-level felons. Prisoners provided cheap labor for the construction of a twenty-four-mile highway from Gibbons' Ranch, on the outskirts of Tucson, near the Catalina National Forest boundary, to Soldier Camp. The completed highway crests at more than 8,000 feet above sea level, gaining more than 5,200 feet in elevation from beginning to end. The highway quickly climbs through transitional vegetation zones that would be the equivalent of

Cutting out road for the construction of Hitchcock Highway. In this picture, an excavator is removing rock to build the highway. Even though heavy equipment was used during construction, prisoners broke rocks manually with sledgehammers and jackhammers to build the road bed. (*Courtesy of the National Archives.*)

"From Saguaros to Pines in 60 minutes." Capturing the scenic view of the highway from Windy Point, which remains a popular turnout for tourists, this postcard advertises the benefits of the new highway, which allowed tourists to drive from the heat of the saguaro desert floor to the cool of the pine-covered mountaintop in just an hour. (*Courtesy of the National Archives.*)

driving from the deserts of Mexico to the alpine forests of Canada. An agreement was reached between the Bureau of Prisons, the Bureau of Public Roads, and the Arizona Highway Commission to use prison labor to build the new highway. Prisoners began building the road during the summer of 1933. Initially, prisoners were housed in tents near an existing Boy Scout camp. (The Boy Scouts agreed to hold their summer camp elsewhere that summer.) The Bureau of Prisons selected a permanent camp site in the Vail Corral Basin, but the site was accessible only by pack trail. The permanent camp was opened in 1939, after prisoners had built more than seven miles of road through solid rock, making the new site accessible for motor vehicles. Highway construction was completed in 1951. While building the highway, prisoners busted rocks, hauled pipes, shoveled gravel, and cut this road through an impressively rugged mountainous terrain.[13]

The road the prisoners built is called the General Hitchcock Highway. It is now a scenic highway, and millions of tourists and local residents use it every year to enjoy the alpine climate and its welcome reprieve from the desert heat of Tucson. The road provides stunning views of the valley floor and of impressive geologic formations. The General Hitchcock Highway has been widened, so much of the prisoners' original construction has been replaced. However, the road follows the same route as the original highway, and it still gives visitors the feel of a remote and treacherous mountain road.

Aerial view of Tucson Federal Prison Camp, ca. 1944. *(Courtesy of Coronado National Forest.)*

The prison camp itself was located seven miles up the highway at a comfortable five-thousand-foot elevation. The food was good, the environment was beautiful, and the guards were kind. When compared with other sites of wartime confinement, prisoners have referred to their time at this prison as "summer camp."

The Tucson Federal Prison Camp was hardly a traditional prison. It had no iron bars and no fences. Rows of painted rocks marked the boundaries of the prison. The prisoners housed at the camp had been convicted of federal crimes ranging from immigration-law violations to tax evasion and bank robbery.

During World War II, prisoners began arriving who had resisted the draft, including Jehovah's Witnesses (JWs), Hopi, and Japanese Americans. Hirabayashi described the four main types of prisoners in his own way: "J.W.s (about 50), Bow and Arrows (selling liquor to Indian—about 100), Border Jumpers (about 30), C.O.s (about 20)." The rest, he said, were miscellaneous "crooks." Of the twenty COs, about "a dozen were FOR [Fellowship of Reconciliation] type," and the rest were Pentecostals, Mennonites, Molican Brethren, and Independents. Nearly ten had walked out of the Civilian Public Service (CPS) camps, having been assigned there as COs for alternative service. Some "walked out" of these camps, frustrated by the experience and perhaps morally objecting to being placed in the CPS camps. Some would not accept their Selective Service classifications of I-A when they were COs or objected to the war on intellectual grounds. They were sent to Tucson after they had failed to appear for induction.[14]

Within hours of Hirabayashi's arrival at the Tucson prison camp, the Hopi invited Hirabayashi to their hillside ramada for tea. They explained that they had been stopped and searched by law enforcement officers around their homes in northern Arizona after the war began, because they looked Japanese. When they saw Hirabayashi, they told him that they shared a common ancestral heritage, a common root language, and a common history of racial oppression.

The Hopi COs had been sentenced to serve several years in the road camp for refusing to register with the Selective Service. They were members of a religious order of Hopi priests, who had all taken vows never to take up arms against another nation. But that was not the basis for their conviction. They had also taken a vow of secrecy and could not reveal their status as priests to anyone. They appeared before the courts with no defense, and some were sentenced to prison for several years for their conscientious resistance.[15]

As a final ceremonial welcome into the Hopi family, the Hopi resisters washed Hirabayashi's hair in soapweed to honor him as their brother. This ceremony is usually used for Hopi weddings. Hirabayashi recalled, "'You are a brother,' they said. And more than that, they told me their symbol is the sun." They told Hirabayashi that his ancestors had probably been left behind on their migration to Arizona, that they were probably the "lost tribe of Israel." They would ask Hirabayashi to say Japanese words until they found words that sounded familiar. "They'd hop on that and they'd say, 'See, we're brothers!'" Consequently, as Hirabayashi recalled, he "had a very good friendship with them."[16] When I was conducting research for this book, the last living Hopi resister would consent to an interview only if Hirabayashi conducted it. I was fortunate to be asked to remain in the room as an observer. The special bond that the Hopi resisters felt with Hirabayashi lasted for the rest of their lives.

SEGREGATION AND DESEGREGATION

The Tucson prison segregated its inmates by race, as did most federal prisons during World War II, but it was one of the last prisons to become segregated. In 1939, when most federal prisons already segregated inmates by race, particularly separating Caucasian inmates from African American inmates, the Tucson prison made no such distinctions in its living quarters or its eating facilities. The racial makeup of inmates at Tucson was not merely divided between "white" and "black," and therefore prison officials may not have seen a justification for racial segregation, but inmates did. Caucasian inmates began agitating for segregated housing and dining in 1939, complaining that theirs was the only federal prison that remained integrated. Their chief complaint was that immigration violators from Mexico did not share their standards of cleanliness and personal hygiene. They complained bitterly about the smell and offensive habits that made eating together with the inmates from Mexico so foul that it ruined their appetites for the day. Inmates petitioned to have the prison segregated, and they won. R. H. Armstrong, supervisor of Prison Camps, wrote to Superintendent C. B. Mead in Tucson:

> There never has been any segregation of colored and Mexicans at the Tucson Prison camp. If the inmates actually want segregation, I see no objection to assigning colored, Mexicans and whites to separate sections of dormitories and assigning separate tables to each of the groups. The Superintendent has been instructed to make the segregation.[17]

But this was just the first stage of segregation in Tucson.

Between 1939 and 1942, the Tucson prison camp remained racially segregated, keeping Caucasian inmates mostly separate from other inmates, but when wartime prisoners started arriving, another segregation crisis emerged. The two main wartime groups that began filling the prison in Tucson were COs and JWs. The COs in Tucson were there either because they refused to comply with the Selective Service entirely, regardless of their option of noncombat service, or they were not granted CO status in the first place and were therefore forced to resist the draft entirely to avoid active military service.

JWs were distinct from COs in that they did not object to combat per se but instead had requested Selective Service deferments on the basis that they were all ministers and therefore should not be subject to the draft. The courts did not agree that all members of the church could be classified as members of the ministry and therefore refused to grant them deferments. As a result, many JWs served federal prison sentences during World War II.

When COs and JWs came to Tucson, conflicts sometimes arose, because they did not necessarily share the same values even though they were technically convicted of the same crimes. One incident threatened real violence.[18] On January 7, 1944, around 9:15 P.M., Officer King Murphy heard some commotion coming from inside one of the barracks and found two inmates engaged in a scuffle. They had started fighting over a piece of glass that each claimed was his: The disagreement began verbally, but it quickly became more serious. One of the inmates involved in the argument was a JW. When a fellow JW stepped in to defend his "brother," religiously speaking, the trouble spread. Officer Murphy tried to break up the fight as other JWs started coming out of Barrack "C" to see what was causing the commotion. Two among the JWs were overheard talking about ending the trouble then and there with more violence.

The entire camp became tense and verged on violence as JWs from Barrack "C" stormed the hospital to take out their anger on the inmate they believed had unfairly attacked one of their "brothers." An orderly in the hospital acted fast and locked the door, preventing an escalation of the violence. Officers were able to bring the chaos under control eventually, but this incident exposed underlying tensions between the JWs and the COs that prison guards would have to address.[19]

For weeks before the fight, prison guards had been hearing rumors that individuals among the different factions of COs and JWs were secretly arming themselves with "homemade knives, clubs, and various other weapons." After the fight broke out January 7, Superintendent Mead ordered guards to begin searching for weapons. Guards first searched the inmates as they left the dining hall and found approximately a dozen knives, "ranging in size from a small pen knife to a homemade knife with a blade approximately two inches in length." Then they confined the prisoners to the bathrooms while officers searched the barracks thoroughly, uncovering approximately twenty more knives, "the most dangerous one being a knife with about a two and one-half inch blade and a homemade wooden handle." All weapons were confiscated, and the guards agreed that they would conduct searches like this more often. As Superintendent Mead noted, it was not uncommon for prisoners to collect such items, but the numbers could be controlled via more regular searches.[20]

Superintendent Mead decided to segregate the JWs by giving them their own barracks. When seeking permission for this move from Armstrong, supervisor of Prison Camps, in Washington, D.C., Mead argued that this separation would quiet conflicts and prevent further violence. Armstrong agreed that separate barracks might be a good idea.[21]

Segregating JWs from COs might have resolved some conflicts, but as far as the COs were concerned, racial segregation at the prison was intolerable. They immediately started agitating to end the separation. Superintendent Mead complained that the COs were relentless in their efforts to goad the few African Americans in the prison into some sort of protest. In January 1944, the African American prisoners signed a petition requesting simply that the dining hall be desegregated, but this brought no immediate change. Then, an African American prisoner referred to only as "Tully" decided to go on a hunger strike to press the issue and to force prison officials to desegregate the dining hall. He drank only water as he continued to work. As a result of his protest, he lost a lot of weight. Prison officials finally gave in and desegregated the dining facilities, but the segregated barracks remained unchanged.[22]

When Hirabayashi arrived in 1943, he noticed that the lines of segregation were a bit mixed up in Tucson. He wrote to Ring that she could put this example in her book of oddities: "It was because of my ancestry that I was in prison," he wrote, "yet in Tucson there were 3 barracks—one entirely for white; one Negroes, Mexicans and Indians; one for Mexican border jumpers and leftover whites; and I was placed in the all white barracks." Hirabayashi commented that this was "very wise" on the part of prison officials, because they were dealing with a prison full of COs. Fellow COs were closely watched in the camp. Had Hirabayashi been placed in the "colored barracks," he said, the other COs would "all demand colored barracks or strike." Hirabayashi felt a little uncomfortable about this level of solidarity. "Personally," he wrote, "I feel that the same sense of protest ought to exist whether it was me or a Negro who was sent to the colored barracks, but I can understand how much easier it is to act for a friend." Despite the convoluted systems of segregation based on race and types of wartime resistance, Hirabayashi concluded that the "race situation" in Tucson was much better than it was at other institutions.[23]

REHABILITATING CITIZENS

Most aspects of life in Tucson epitomized the latest trends in federal prison reform and expansion. In 1930, the Department of Justice formed the Federal Bureau of Prisons to manage and to regulate the growing number of federal prisons.[24] By 1940, on the eve of World War II, the number of federal penal facilities increased from eleven to twenty-four. One of these new prison facilities was the Tucson Federal Prison Camp, created in 1933.[25]

The number and scope of federal prisons and detention facilities exploded after the United States entered the war. Suspect citizens and enemy aliens were housed in Department of Justice internment facilities, in some cases county jails were converted into temporary federal housing until more federal facilities could be constructed, and old Civilian Conservation Corps (CCC) camps were converted into temporary holding facilities for the Department of Justice and the WRA. The WRA even used an old Indian boarding school in Leupp, Arizona, to hold "troublesome" Nisei after the Manzanar riot. Added to this early process of converting existing facilities into holding cells for Issei community leaders was a massive program to evacuate and to incarcerate Japanese Americans from the West Coast and lower portion of Arizona. The WRA may not have called these camps "prisons," but they epitomized the massive expansion of the federal government's involvement in creating and managing facilities used to detain or to imprison civilians.[26]

The Tucson road camp also epitomized changes in the prison system that had evolved over the first few decades of the twentieth century because it was a minimum-security prison designed to hold only the most minor, nonviolent offenders. Prisons had become multitiered and diverse in their purposes, and their treatment of prisoners provided a wide array of choices depending on the nature of the individual's crime. Judges gained more discretion over sentencing so they could better respond to convicted criminals' individual circumstances, providing some with heavy sentences and others with extremely light sentences.[27]

Perhaps no prison epitomized constructive penology more than the Tucson Federal Prison Camp, because here prisoners performed work with a clear purpose. The Federal Bureau of Prisons worked hard to rehabilitate citizens through job training and meaningful work. In Tucson, this meant building a road from the outskirts of town to the top of Mt. Lemmon to provide local residents with quick and reliable access to this cool summertime retreat from the oppressive heat of the desert valley floor. Some of the work prisoners performed was pure drudgery. Joe Norikane, who would end up in Tucson the following year, commented that he thought prisoners busted rocks only in cartoons, but when he got to Tucson, it was his job to do just that—bust rocks with a sledgehammer to create gravel for the highway. Others enjoyed work that was a little more exciting. Ken Yoshida, who was also sent to Tucson a year after Hirabayashi, was thrilled when he received orders to work on the blasting crew. He had always been interested in engineering, and now he had a chance to use explosives to break up difficult sections of the road.[28]

Prison reformers, especially those in charge of the Tucson Federal Prison Camp, believed that it was important to give prisoners opportunities to perform what they called "meaningful work." Building a road instead of merely moving rocks from one pile to another and then back again was one example of work with a purpose. They believed prisoners would develop a sense of accomplishment through hard labor and become better citizens. The "Good Roads" movement and the proliferation of road camps gave prisoners a stronger purpose for their work and an opportunity to learn real skills.[29] In Tucson, administrators deliberately trained prisoners in skills that might lead to employment once they were released.[30]

In wartime, the most "meaningful" work, according to penologists, was military service.[31] Every month, prison officials gave inmates the chance to commute their sentences if they would join the military. For the first time in its history, the War Department agreed to grant all nonviolent offenders early parole from prison if they would enlist. Although no Nisei sent to Tucson ever accepted this offer, many other prisoners did. When the military began accepting convicted felons for induction, it assumed the prisons' role of rehabilitating citizens, blurring the boundary between the purpose of prisons and of the military during wartime.[32]

Hirabayashi started out busting rocks and shoveling gravel until he discovered that he was doing this work just to fill in the floor for a welding building. He had an interview with the superintendent to request a new position and was switched over to the athletic department in a job created just for him. He was made the athletic director and put in charge of fixing up the fields, improving home plate, and so forth. But this was a boring job, and it was hard to stay busy.[33] This assignment lasted for about three weeks, until Hirabayashi appealed to the chief steward over the kitchen. Hirabayashi had sent him a letter thanking him for the good food, and the steward was shocked, because he had never received anything but complaints in the past. When Hirabayashi asked if he could be reassigned to the kitchen, the steward agreed. Hirabayashi enjoyed this new job: "It was fun throwing dough around and baking various delicacies. . . . Also, being in the kitchen, I was slightly better fed than the rest of the hungry horde." Being able to serve pies and cakes to fellow inmates also made him "one of the most popular guys in camp."[34]

HIRABAYASHI'S LESSONS IN PRISON

Hirabayashi was relieved to be in the road camp and called it a tremendous improvement over the walled institution he had spent months confined to in Seattle. The living quarters were set up like CCC camps, with inmates sleeping in bunks and eating in a dining hall. The facility even included a ball field for recreation. However, "Mentally and psychologically the typical prison atmosphere prevails," Hirabayashi wrote. "Very strict censorship of mail (I was called on the floor several times for vociferous reporting), counts taken every hour, raising hands to be excused from dining room after eating, ordered out of bed in the morning, ordered to bed in the evenings, 'good time' being used as a weapon to keep inmates in line, race segregation, starch predominated meals." It may have been called a road camp, but it was still a prison.[35]

Even though Tucson was supposed to epitomize the best kind of "rehabilitation camps," this goal did not necessarily apply to COs. Hirabayashi wrote that in private conversations with the prison superintendent, he would tell COs that this was not a "rehabilitation camp" for them. He told them this because he had never really wanted to start accepting COs at his prison. Each CO, as Hirabayashi remembered the Superintendent saying, "[had] the peculiar tendency of protesting one way or another every injustice he sees." Hirabayashi shared, "In the course of one of these injustice protests the superintendent said, 'If you think C.O.s are the only ones who want this war ended, you are crazy.'" He also wished the war were over so he "could settle down to some good, old bank robbers." Many prisoners at the Tucson road camp were not passive recipients of job training and citizenship rehabilitation; they agitated to transform the prison to more closely reflect their values.[36]

Hirabayashi enjoyed discussions he had with other COs. Often these discussions were about the Selective Service and the CPS. The war had made many change their minds about their positions relative to the Selective Service and alternative service. Even "those church-ordered Mennonite C.O.s," Hirabayashi wrote, "have come to see the weakness of C.P.S." and have rejected it in their stand against war, "even though it is safe and more popular than prisons." In the minds of a growing number of pacifists, the CPS camps were still a part of the war-making mechanism of the state. To work in a CPS camp would be akin to participating in the war itself, something absolute pacifists rejected. They even turned down parole offers when those offers meant they would be sent straight to CPS camps. They would accept parole only if it were free of any form of conscription, or they would remain in prison to serve out their full terms.[37] Hirabayashi came to remarkably similar conclusions when faced with his own conscription into a CPS camp just a few months after leaving Tucson.

Hirabayashi also enjoyed the diversity of personalities that were joined together in prison. One inmate was a "liberal son of a N.Y. state Methodist minister." "Another," Hirabayashi mused, "is a gay songbird and poet—boy, we had fun with him." Another resister was a co-op farm enthusiast, and yet another was a Catholic intellectual, "as intellectually brilliant as they make them," Hirabayashi wrote. "I was in a truly inspiring atmosphere, and experienced quite a bit of growth. I was sad to leave them."[38] Hirabayashi expected to keep many of the people he met in prison as lifelong friends. He, like other Tucsonians, found prison to be a largely memorable, bonding experience.

After serving his ninety-day sentence, Hirabayashi was released and found that traveling home from prison was a bit easier than getting to Tucson had been. He received the standard parting gifts: a new suit, a bus ticket, and a bit of pocket money for the journey. Just like during his trip to Tucson, he was traveling in a restricted zone, except this time he could enjoy the small thrill he got from *knowing* that he was in the exclusion zone. His bus went into Needles, California, and stayed in California for several miles before entering Nevada and continuing to Las Vegas. "So, I was in the restricted area again," he said, and "while we were going through there, I got a little extra thrill out of that part of the ride." Hirabayashi enjoyed the ride back to Spokane, where he resumed his relocation duties with the Quakers. But his return would not be uneventful. Within a few weeks, his confrontation with the government would begin again.

CHAPTER 5

The Obligations of Citizenship

⎯⎯⎯

Therefore, we should devote ourselves . . . to make every man under-
stand that unless he in good faith performs his duties he is not entitled
to any rights at all.

—Theodore Roosevelt, speech, October 1915

O N JANUARY 20, 1944, Secretary of War Henry Stimson announced
that the Selective Service had restored Nisei eligibility for the draft.
Stimson declared that the draft gave Nisei the chance to restore their
citizenship and to repair their public image as loyal Americans. The government had demonstrated its faith in Nisei, Stimson said, and now it was time
for Nisei to demonstrate their faith in America.[1]

On February 22, fifty-three Nisei men were scheduled to take the train
from Amache to Denver for their preinduction physicals, but five refused to go.
They became the first Nisei to resist the draft, but they were not the first to
protest. In Topaz and Amache, as in other camps, residents organized against
the draft much as they had against the loyalty registration program the year
before. Groups held meetings, filed petitions, sent letters, and tried to negotiate for a full restoration of Nisei rights before they could be drafted.

Japanese Americans protested against the draft in diverse ways, including
civil disobedience. Most detainees could see that the draft did little to restore
Nisei rights directly when it was applied to an incarcerated population of citizens. Vague promises of a future restoration of rights did not sit well with
those who knew the U.S. government had promised citizenship to Issei in
exchange for military service during World War I, only to force Issei to battle
for almost two decades to make the government fulfill that promise. Those
who refused to comply with the draft represented the remnants of a broad-
based attempt to force the government to restore citizenship rights along with
responsibilities.

In an attempt to squelch resistance, government officials, the Japanese
American Citizens League (JACL), and individual Nikkei marginalized the
resisters with accusations of criminality, disloyalty, and even unmanly cowardice while promoting patriotic compliance as the only appropriate response to
the draft.

THE DECISION TO REINSTATE
SELECTIVE SERVICE FOR NISEI

The decision to reinstate Selective Service for Nisei had been made on some levels as early as the end of 1942, but the decision was not formalized until a vote was taken on the matter at the end of 1943. The vote involved representation from G-1 (personnel), G-2 (intelligence), G-3 (operations and training), the Provost Marshal General (PMG) and the Military Personnel Division (MPD)/Air Force (ASF). They voted unanimously to reinstate the Selective Service for Nisei; to assign inductees to the segregated 442nd Regimental Combat Team rather than distributing them generally throughout the army, to say nothing of the other branches of the military; and, for now, not to admit Issei, even on a volunteer basis. Aliens would not be allowed to volunteer until September 11, 1944.[2]

The decision to reinstitute the "non-voluntary induction of loyal Japanese Americans" would require a strong publicity campaign to encourage compliance and discourage resistance. Lt. Col. Harrison A. Gerhardt, of the Office of the Assistant Secretary of War, wrote that the success of this program would "depend largely upon the hype of publicity which is given it and the method in which this publicity is handled." The reason was the timing of this change. Recently, the 100th Battalion had suffered extensive casualties. Gerhardt warned that, combined with major unrest at Tule Lake over the issue of segregation and mistreatment of Nikkei segregated there, some might conclude "that the reinstitution of selective service was designed as an 'exterminating measure' for Japanese Americans." He recommended that in light of the probable backlash against the draft, a conference should be held with representatives from the Bureau of Public Relations, G-1, G-2, the War Relocation Authority (WRA), the Selective Service, and the Office of the Assistant Secretary of War to design an effective information campaign that would encourage compliance with the draft and discourage dissent.[3]

The matter of segregation was likely to become a problem, as it had been raised immediately during the registration crisis of 1943. Nisei had asked why they were being segregated like "Negro" troops and why they were being assigned to only combat duty.[4] The War Department and the WRA claimed publicly that Nisei would be segregated to highlight their achievements and to spotlight their heroism.

One of the reasons for keeping Japanese Americans segregated was not shared publicly. Certainly some believed that Nisei heroism would be less visible if Nisei were distributed throughout the army. Their service, some said, would be "diluted" and would not have the same propaganda value. But a November 1942 internal, confidential memo from the provost marshal general's office raised another larger issue: upholding the policy for continued segregation of African Americans. "Despite my belief that the great majority of Americans of Japanese descent are loyal to the United States," Maj. Gen. and

Provost Marshal Gen. Allen W. Gullion wrote, "I recommend against their general assignment and favor their assignment to certain specified units." He explained:

> Although it is true that colored enlisted men have always in our service been segregated into colored units while the few Japanese who have served in the Army, prior to this war, were the subject of general assignment, the fact of colored segregation would be emphasized by the re-adoption of general assignment of Japanese-Americans. In view of the fact that the colored people and their friends have, since the beginning of this war, been increasingly bitter in their protests against segregation of colored people, no one short of the Commander-in-Chief should order the general assignment of Japanese-Americans with its resulting emphasis on colored segregation.[5]

President Franklin Roosevelt had already stressed the fact that he preferred that Japanese Americans be kept under tight control and supervision in specific units because of his general reservations about Japanese American loyalty and because of the propaganda value that an all-Nisei unit would provide. Instead of moving away from the policy of segregation for Nisei, Japanese Americans already serving in the army were to be transferred as replacements for the 442nd, meaning that segregation of Japanese Americans in the military was actually being strengthened as the draft was reinstated, not dismantled.

The primary reason for reinstating the draft was to provide replacements for Japanese American combat units. Early recruitment of volunteers had fallen short of projected quotas. Far fewer Nisei had volunteered than were estimated, and far fewer had volunteered than were deemed "eligible" for service. Only 5.3 percent of the total number of Nisei men deemed eligible for the draft, inside or outside the camps, had volunteered. In some camps, the number of volunteers was higher. In Minidoka, 18.6 percent of eligible Nisei men volunteered, and in Gila River, 10.3 percent volunteered. Other camps fell well below the average. Only 2.1 percent of eligible Nisei men volunteered for service from Jerome and Rohwer, and only 2.3 percent volunteered from Heart Mountain (see Table 5.1). According to military analysts, a pool of 22,353 Nisei remained from which to draw replacements for the 442nd combat team, but it would take more than an aggressive recruiting campaign to entice them to volunteer. They would have to be compelled to serve.[6]

Drafting and inducting 23,606 was unrealistic due to a variety of issues. Analysts estimated that of the 19,506 draft-age detainees in the camps (setting aside for the moment the estimated 4,000 draft-age Nisei outside the camps), 6,856 would be rejected due to their negative answers to question 28 on the loyalty questionnaire, 2,550 would be rejected for other "loyalty" related concerns, 1,632 would probably be given agricultural deferments, and 1,885 would likely be rejected for physical reasons. This meant that the draft might bring in only an additional 6,683 inductees from the camps. When analysts

TABLE 5.1 Citizens eligible for military service and numbers of volunteers, March 29, 1943

WRA camps	Citizen males 18–37, inclusive	Volunteers	%
Central Utah (Topaz)	1,475	111	7.5
Colorado River (Poston)	3,405	228	6.7
Gila River	2,210	114	10.3
Granada (Amache)	1,580	121	7.7
Heart Mountain	1,970	45	2.3
Jerome	1,578	33	2.1
Manzanar	1,809	97	5.4
Minidoka	1,601	298	18.6
Rohwer	1,608	34	2.1
Tule Lake	2,270	57	2.5
Total inside camps	19,506	1,138	5.8
Outside camps	4,000	119	3.0
Totals	23,506	1,253	5.6

Source: Memorandum, John Lansdale, Maj., Field Artillery, Chief, Review Branch, CIG, MIS, to Col. Gibson, March 29, 1943, Office of the Secretary of War, College Park, Maryland, RG 107, Box 15, Folder "Loyalty Investigation."

performed similar calculations for Nisei outside the camps, they concluded that at most 1,665 might be drafted.[7]

Analysts tried to predict the numbers the War Department could expect to be able to draft, while such people as Maj. Gen. Gullion tried to explain the lack of volunteers. Thousands of Nisei had qualified their answers to question 27 ("Are you willing to serve in the armed forces of the United States on combat duty, wherever ordered?") by responding, "Yes, if drafted." Gullion said he took these statements at face value. "In many cases," he wrote, "that was probably a sincere answer on the part of the registrant who was torn between strong family opposition on the one hand and a desire to serve his country on the other." He also suggested that others were "physically able and probably loyal in the broader sense" but did not "wish to serve in the Army for personal and selfish reasons." He said quite frankly that these individuals "should be compelled to do so through the reinstitution of Selective Service." His lack of sensitivity was echoed throughout the War Department.[8]

Maj. Gen. Gullion offered another reason for reinstituting the draft that revealed the ongoing concern that some War Department officials had about the loyalty of Nisei and security outside the camps. He commented that the younger Nisei preferred to relocate to urban areas, such as Chicago and Cincinnati. They had not been as interested in relocating to rural areas and performing agricultural work. Gullion wrote, "It is more difficult to keep those suspected of disloyalty under surveillance in communities thickly populated with Japanese-Americans, and the reinstitution of Selective Service would relieve that situation." Oddly, it is not clear whether this meant that Nisei who were suspected of disloyalty would be inducted and then kept under close surveillance in the military or that the loyal Nisei would be inducted, leaving only those suspected of disloyalty free to roam the metropolitan areas. Either way, the suggestion was made that the draft would thin out Nisei populations outside the camps, too, making the drafting of Nisei a priority inside and outside the camps.[9]

Finally, reinstituting the draft, Gullion believed, would resolve the complaints that Nisei had been unfairly and unjustifiably classified as "enemy aliens" by the Selective Service: "The professed loyal Japanese-Americans had strongly resented the fact that they are classified 4-C in the Selective Service process, and that they are treated in a manner different from other American citizens." He was not the only one who believed that reinstituting the Selective Service and reclassifying Nisei as 1-A (citizens available for service) would "remove one cause of dissatisfaction among these people."[10] Little did he realize that another change in status would draw criticism from those who resented being labeled an enemy alien one year and then being restored to citizen status just for the purpose of being drafted into segregated combat units in the army the following year.[11]

The message sent publicly to Japanese Americans was that the restoration of the draft would provide an opportunity for Nisei to prove their loyalty and to reassure Americans that they were contributing to the war effort as the sons of other American families were. Americans would respect them for their service, they were told, and would recognize their sacrifices. But underneath the publicity was a more complicated set of priorities: replenishing and reinforcing the segregated all-Nisei combat units so African Americans in the military would not be the only ones segregated on the basis of race, thinning out populations of young Nisei in urban areas, forcing able-bodied men to serve despite their reluctance to do so, providing the justification for men who wanted to serve but were pressured by their families and communities not to volunteer, and correcting the fiasco that IV-C classifications had caused. The justifications for reinstating the draft were complex and varied, as would be Japanese Americans' response to the news.

RESPONSE TO THE DRAFT AT AMACHE

Some in Amache proposed that if the entire Nisei population resisted the draft, none of them could be prosecuted. This sentiment had a very popular following. The Community Council requested that the entire camp vote on how it should respond to the draft, especially whether detainees would threaten mass resistance. Five blocks voted to withhold Nisei service entirely. Some blocks declined to vote on the issue at all. Others voted by an overwhelming majority to avoid making threats against the government. All twenty-nine blocks agreed unanimously to send some sort of resolutions to Washington protesting the draft, but they could not unanimously support withholding Nisei service in an attempt to create leverage in their drive for a total restoration of civil rights. Those who chose to resist the draft would have to act individually.[12]

The idea of total resistance to the draft may not have won the support of the majority of detainees at Amache, but it is still significant that the camp took the idea under consideration. It shows that far more considered the possibility of civil disobedience than ultimately faced criminal prosecution. It also demonstrated to WRA administrators that if they did nothing to counter the growing unrest, they could have another crisis on their hands.

Administrators did not understand detainees' objections to the draft, so they looked to John A. Rademaker, their resident community analyst, for answers. Rademaker described his position while working in Amache: To Nikkei, his job was to explain administrative rules and regulations. To administrators, his role was to explain Nikkei reactions.[13] The draft crisis was one of those times when administrators and Nikkei needed whatever mediation services someone like Rademaker might provide. His observations were not without their biases and flaws, but, as a nonadministrator charged with the task of working to understand the mind-set of incarcerated Japanese Americans, he did his best to use his outsider position to bring empathy and reason to his observations. Initially, his reports appeared decidedly sympathetic to those who objected to Nisei's being drafted into segregated units without first securing a full restoration of their rights. But in the end, Rademaker supported JACL and administration efforts to squelch outright civil disobedience to the draft.

Rademaker wrote a lengthy report to Edward Spicer, his supervisor in Washington, explaining Nikkei reactions. Nikkei had many legitimate reasons to withhold support for the draft. These reasons included a long history of race discrimination, the extraordinary risks Nisei faced on the battlefield due to the fact that their units not only were confined to combat duty but also were assigned the most dangerous missions, and a seeming absence of democracy in the camps.

First, Rademaker explained the Issei point of view: They still harbored resentment from World War I. Alien volunteers were promised citizenship in exchange for military service, but the government had not given citizenship to Issei. They had to lobby Congress for more than fifteen years to get the citizenship they were promised. Issei warned Nisei that if they accepted military service without first demanding their full citizenship, they, too, might be "left holding the bag" when the war was over. Rademaker wrote that it was more Issei than Nisei who "were not in sympathy with the idea of the draft-age Nisei going into service until their citizenship rights were restored along with their duties and responsibilities." Feelings had become so "acrimonious" that any who supported the draft might be accused of being an administrative "stooge or *inu*."[14]

Nisei responses to racial discrimination varied greatly. Very few Nisei had attended segregated schools. More experienced racial segregation and discrimination in other ways. Some could not swim in public pools or patronize the same beaches or golf courses as white Americans. Others just learned the unwritten rules of race-based social segregation. For example, most professional occupations were not open to Japanese Americans. Some responded to these experiences with resentment or resistance, but others, Rademaker observed, responded with "excessive patriotic zeal" by becoming "belligerent" in their loyalty.

Interestingly, Rademaker predicted one of the most important dynamics of the draft crisis. The self-proclaimed patriotic Nisei would become the most hostile critics of the resisters, yet the resisters and the self-proclaimed patriots responded to wartime conditions based on prewar lessons in race and discrimination.[15] It is important to recognize that those who proclaimed extraordinary loyalty *and* those who committed acts of civil disobedience were engaged in a dialogue with the state about the meaning of their own citizenship. Their responses were shaped by prewar understandings of the rights of citizens and the limits of social and legal equality in the United States, the country in which they were born.

Another reason Nisei were reluctant to embrace the draft enthusiastically was the unusually high casualty rate of the all-Nisei combat team. During the summer months of 1943, the 442nd combat team suffered heavy losses: 1,272, or 25 percent of the unit's total size. In addition, rumors abounded that the Nisei combat team regularly received the most dangerous missions. Rademaker wrote that nobody celebrated the draft, not even outside the camps. Citizens accepted it as an unpleasant duty not a privilege. For those in the camps, especially those who believed the army was drafting Nisei as replacement cannon fodder, Rademaker implied that it would be unreasonable to expect anything less than resistance.[16]

Rademaker concluded that, in his opinion, the opponents of the draft were "probably justified." Many had begun calling America "a benevolent dictatorship under the guise of a democracy." Rademaker sympathized—patriotism is hard to feel from inside a relocation center. "Democracy," he wrote, no longer functioned "as we were taught and as we believed." "It is small wonder," Rademaker continued, "that few Nisei dare to raise their heads now and say, 'we're loyal and we're willing to fight for the U.S.' even though many of them feel that way." Rademaker explained that the reluctance on the part of the majority to express their patriotism in the face of their treatment in the camps was why what he called "a veritable flood of resolutions, requests, demands and ultimatums [had been] floating around."[17]

Rademaker made an important point when he concluded that few Nisei dared to raise their heads to declare their willingness to fight due to the overwhelming climate of resentment against the draft. It appears that the majority in the camps believed that the draft was an unfair demand on citizens who had been stripped of their rights and freedoms. Many employed conventional forms of protest, including questions, resolutions, and letters requesting a revised policy, and some threatened to withhold service if their rights were not restored, but few followed through by committing acts of civil disobedience when these forms of protest seemed to fall on deaf ears.

FORMS OF RESISTANCE TO THE DRAFT

As with organized resistance to registration, Topaz's Nikkei were among the first to send Washington a list of questions regarding the draft. Topaz's draft-age Nisei wanted to know why they had been classified IV-C in the first place. Could those honorably discharged regain the right to travel freely anywhere in the United States, including California? Why would they be drafted into only combat teams in the army and not other branches of the military? Was this draft merely a publicity stunt? These were questions that many shared, not just Nisei in Topaz. Asking questions demonstrated that Nisei believed some dialogue should take place if the government was ready to change the way it categorized them. The restoration of the draft represented a fundamental shift in policy and in Nisei citizenship. No longer treated as if they were potentially disloyal unless specifically proven trustworthy (and in these cases, always treated as though this trust were tenuous), Nisei were now being moved incrementally over to the category of partial citizens—worthy of sacrificing their lives for their country but not yet trustworthy enough to return home to the West Coast. This disparity raised important questions that would have to be answered for Nisei to understand what interpretation of citizenship they were agreeing to through their military service.

Some organized groups to demonstrate solidarity and strength in numbers and wrote letters requesting that the government rethink this partial restoration of citizenship obligations without any restoration of rights. The best-known group to form in opposition to the draft was the Heart Mountain Fair Play Committee, led by Kiyoshi Okamoto, who started out as the Fair Play Committee of One. He was joined by others, such as Frank Emi, who were concerned that Nisei rights had been violated on a constitutional level. The organization became "galvanized" on January 20, 1944, when Secretary of War Stimson announced that the draft had been reinstated.[18] On February 25, 1944, Okamoto wrote:

> Our legal status in these concentration camps have not been cleared. We are herded within barbed wire fences and, guarded against freedom by soldiers, bullets and bayonets. We exist as Citizens without a Country. In truth, all the guarantees of the Constitution are denied us. Under these conditions, what are we? Are we American Citizens? Are we Enemy Aliens? Or, are we . . . what? This absence of clarification of our status and rights is the keystone of our indecision towards any proper orientation of attitude towards the draft.[19]

Okamoto's ideas and leadership attracted 275 "dues-paying members" to the Fair Play Committee. The committee's primary argument was that if members' rights were first restored, they would gladly perform their duties. With additional members paying dues, the group had enough money to consult with an attorney about organizing a test case that would challenge the way the Selective Service applied to citizens who were incarcerated and lacked their basic freedoms. The committee then petitioned President Roosevelt to request clarification of members' citizenship status. The Fair Play Committee did not end its efforts with petitions: It went on to resist the draft by refusing to appear for preinduction physicals. Sixty-three committee members ended up being tried as the largest single group of resisters and Wyoming's largest mass trial; each was convicted and sentenced to three years in a federal penitentiary. The committee's six leaders, including Okamoto and Emi, were tried separately, and after conviction, each was given a two-year prison sentence.[20]

A group calling itself Topaz Citizens for the Principles of American Democracy also formed in response to the reinstatement of the draft. Topaz residents had been extremely well organized in their response to registration and protested on a campwide basis under the direction of Issei, who successfully achieved their goals of forcing the WRA to offer them a revised questionnaire. When it came to the draft the following year, Nisei were on their own. The Topaz Citizens was one of the first groups to approach the War Department directly with its concerns. Its members wrote to Washington, insisting that the principles of American democracy were incompatible with segregated units. The committee recommended that the president and the War Department not use Nisei draftees as replacements for the all-Nisei combat team that had been created with the volunteers recruited through the loyalty registration program of 1943. Instead, draftees should be assigned to units throughout the U.S. military branches. Finally, the citizens of Topaz reminded the president that Nisei had a stake in two wars: the war against fascism abroad and the war against prejudice at home. Friendships made on the battlefield, regardless of race or ancestry, would translate into better race relations after the war. The citizens of Topaz requested a "redress of grievances prior to their being inducted into service."[21] They wanted the government to restore their citizenship fully before they would be willing to enter into military service.[22] This argument was quite popular. The volunteers had already proven Nisei heroism and trustworthiness, so now it was time to integrate Nisei servicemen throughout the armed forces so they could truly serve on the same basis as other Americans.

Members of the Topaz Citizens were joined by their mothers in their protest. The Mothers of Topaz sent resolutions and recommendations to the president, Dillon Myer, Brig. Gen. Robert H. Dunlop, and Eleanor Roosevelt. When the Mothers of Topaz met to draft its resolutions, some women proposed that they withhold their sons' service unless their children's rights were first restored. When the women considered the details of their petition, most thought such an ultimatum would go too far. The final resolution contained no ultimatum but still demanded that something be done to rectify the undemocratic circumstances under which their sons would be drafted. The petition, signed by 1,141 women, stated:

> We mothers of American citizens of Japanese descent have fully cooperated for years with the American educational system so that our children would be worthy American citizens. We have taught our children to affirm their loyalty especially in time of a National emergency. This ideal is in keeping with the traditional spirit of Japanese mothers. As you may know, before the evacuation we did not in one instance oppose the drafting of our sons, but willingly sent them with our encouragement.[23]

How could these mothers send their sons into battle so willingly under the present circumstances? Until the War Department restored citizens' rights to free travel and to serve in all branches of the military, these Japanese mothers wrote, they could not in good faith send their sons into harm's way. They would do so only under protest, and they were not alone. Women from other camps also submitted letters on behalf of their Nisei children, including the Blue Star Mothers and the Women's Federation of Amache, who filed a joint resolution, drafted by Kay Sugahara (a male JACL leader), calling for the restoration of Nisei citizenship rights.[24]

In response to the Mothers of Topaz's petition, Brig. Gen. Dunlop reminded the mothers that they had no right to dictate military decisions. It had long been the policy of the War Department to assign inductees where they were most needed to win the war, wrote Dunlop, and the War Department needed replacements for Nisei units. He appreciated the mothers' desire to see fair treatment for their children and promised that every effort would be made to eliminate inequities in policies affecting their sons.[25]

Myer responded to the Mothers of Topaz with sympathy and a warning that they avoid any appearance of "espionage." He wrote that he appreciated the mothers' devotion to democratic principles, but in their devotion they needed to be aware of the time necessary to make important changes, such as what they were demanding. Myer urged the mothers to see the draft as a first step in the gradual restoration of their children's citizenship. He also conveyed a stern warning when he wrote, "I am certain that you want to take no step which would interfere with the progress toward complete restoration of civil rights and the recognition of your children as loyal American citizens." His corrective tone prevailed in official responses to all forms of resistance, particularly those that hinted at an ultimatum.[26]

Early attempts to resist a restoration of Nisei obligations to serve in a segregated military represented a broad cross-section of the Nikkei population and a continuation of strategies that had enjoyed some success against registration. Petitions came in from various camps written by Nisei themselves, their Issei mothers, Community Councils, and sympathetic individuals. Some hinted that they would refuse to comply with the draft until their rights were restored, but others hesitated to threaten civil disobedience—they did not want to draw further suspicion of disloyalty. Civility dominated these early forms of resistance, but this trait did not make them ineffective. Instead, resisters forced the WRA to revise its definition of loyalty to prevent mass draft evasion by those who had previously maintained their loyalty but might be willing to accept labels of "disloyalty" to avoid the draft. Early resistance also forced the War Department to clarify its role vis-à-vis Nisei citizenship and civil rights: Its job was to raise an army, and it had nothing to do with civil rights. Although this limitation should have raised even more serious concerns that military service might not actually lead to a full restoration of Nisei citizenship, it instead diffused dissent, as complaints about citizenship and civil rights were directed to a different branch of the government than were complaints about segregation in military service. The only way to retain a cohesive argument about Nisei citizenship was for individuals to refuse the draft entirely and to address their grievances in federal court. But retaining authority over their citizenship came with a heavy price.

A DEVELOPING CRISIS IN AMACHE

Administrators turned to Rademaker and other social scientists to explain Nikkei behavior as protest against the draft grew, while detainees looked to attorneys to explain their legal rights and obligations. Each camp had its own resident attorney to assist detainees with assorted legal needs that arose while they were in the camps and to assist the WRA in its administration of the camps. Amache's attorney was Donald T. Horn. Horn met several times with the Community Council during the first weeks of February, when turmoil and confusion were at their peak. From a legal perspective, he told detainees, the draft and Nisei rights were two separate issues, and under no circumstances should they make their acceptance of the draft contingent on a full restoration of their rights.

Persuaded by Horn that the grievances of evacuation and the duty of citizens to submit to the draft could not be connected legally, the members of the Community Council sent a letter to Washington, accepting the draft as a duty and a right of citizenship. This letter, however, did not represent unanimous support for the draft.[27]

At the same time that Horn was urging the council to accept the draft, one hundred fifty requests for repatriation and expatriation came flooding into Camp Director James G. Lindley's office over a two-day period following the announcement that the draft would be reopened for Nisei. Only fifteen of the one hundred fifty requests came from draft-age Nisei, but because of their timing, camp administrators feared they represented another attempt to avoid the draft. Lindley responded by declaring he would no longer accept any applications for expatriation or repatriation. Myer likewise announced that no more detainees would be transferred to Tule Lake.[28]

In an ironic twist, once the draft was in place, those requesting to leave the United States would no longer automatically be classified as disloyal or even be exempt from the Selective Service. Just two years earlier, government officials and private individuals had debated one vexing question: Would Japanese Americans be loyal to the United States or to Japan? No matter how hard Nisei tried to prove their loyalty, the Selective Service reclassified all persons of Japanese descent as enemy aliens. All those living in the restricted West Coast were forced to report for removal and incarcerated, along with their enemy alien parents, on the presumption that they might be disloyal. Now it seemed that loyalty was no longer a prerequisite for military service.

The resistance Hirabayashi had hoped for verged on fruition as Nisei faced the possibility of refusing to comply with the draft as a legitimate form of protest against the draft. It was unlikely that only a handful of individuals would have been willing to risk imprisonment for their civil disobedience after two years of confinement. As Hirabayashi noted while in King County Jail, it was far easier to transition from the camps to jail than it was to go from free society to jail. In camp, the detainees had already become accustomed to the confinement, the lack of privacy, and, to some extent, even the stigma of incarceration.

On February 21, Myer sent instructions to all camp administrators on how they should handle the growing threat of an outright draft-resistance movement. He listed a variety of problems all camps should expect. The first would be petitions. Myer reminded camp directors of the right of every citizen to petition the state. If they received any of these documents, they were to forward them directly to his office for his inspection. At the same time, directors were to explain that the draft remained independent of other complaints. "No real or fancied grievances can be allowed to interfere with its operation," Myer warned. Second, young men who chose to file for expatriation were to be allowed to do so as long as they were warned that such action would not "preclude or delay a call for induction." Requests for expatriation, Myer declared, did not provide "conclusive evidence of disloyalty." Third, some Nisei were already declaring their intention to ignore their calls for preinduction physicals. These Nisei were to receive the strongest warning of all. Camp administrators were instructed to tell Nisei that they would be guilty of Selective Service violations and subject to the criminal penalties of draft evasion. Moreover, Myer told camp authorities to provide local draft boards their full cooperation in apprehending and prosecuting any detainees who carried through with their plans to resist the draft.[29]

Even as Myer gave instructions regarding how camp administrators were to handle potential resisters, he cautioned that a simple declaration of *intent* to refuse the draft was not a criminal act. He maintained that widespread draft resistance could be avoided if handled properly. In a teletype to the camp directors, he wrote, "The wiser heads among the evacuees may want to talk to such young men, to their parents, and help them realize the serious consequences to the young man . . . and to the whole group." Accepting the draft, after all, represented a "major step toward the restoration of the rights of American citizens of Japanese ancestry and if properly accepted can lead to the restoration of many other rights which evacuees feel they should have." Any act to resist this opportunity, wrote Myer, would create a "serious detriment of the whole evacuee community." Myer concluded with the hope that Nikkei leaders within the camps would do whatever they could to "avoid the drastic effect which might come from the unthinking actions of a few prospective or actual draft dodgers." The personal penalties draft resisters would suffer by law—$10,000 in fines, twenty years in prison, or both—would pale in comparison to the overall harm that the resistance would cause the entire evacuee population.[30]

Director Lindley decided that, for his part, he would make most of Myer's recommendations public by way of an all-camp announcement. He drew up a list of items to be read in every dining hall throughout camp, declaring that no more Nisei of draft age would be sent to Tule Lake and that the five who had been sent already were on their way back to camp. He told block managers, "Please advise your young men of military age that a request for expatriation will not in itself preclude or delay a call for induction." He warned, "It cannot fail to have a serious effect on their future in the United States and indirectly on the future of the whole evacuee population." In reviewing the instructions from Myer, the threat of fines and prison were the least Nisei had to worry about: The future of the entire evacuee population was at stake.

Significantly, Lindley's announcement met with resistance of an unexpected sort. Two out of five mess halls failed to read portions of his letter, and none of the mess halls read the letter in English. This lack of translation bothered Lindley the most: Reading the notice only in Japanese meant that the target audience was Issei, but he was trying to avert Nisei resistance to the draft. Why not give the information to Nisei in English so they, too, could understand the seriousness of the situation? Lindley was baffled and upset that Nisei, many of whom could not understand Japanese, did not get the message firsthand.[31] It is unclear why the announcement was read in Japanese. Perhaps those reading it believed that parents still retained enough authority in their households to pressure would-be resisters into compliance, or it might have been a warning to Issei that those who had warned Nisei that they were not given their citizenship after serving in World War I should not discourage Nisei from serving in this war. In any case, the message, according to Lindley, had been misdirected, despite the possible reasons the messengers had for targeting Issei.

Other staff members at Amache tried their hand at encouraging Nisei to accept the draft and to dissuade those who were contemplating resistance. Amache Superintendent of Education Paul Terry reminded Nisei, who had "been educated in the institutions of the West Coast," that they had already benefited immensely from their free education in the United States at great expense to taxpayers, and they continued to benefit from education in the camps ("What would they say about the one-third of a million dollars being spent for the Amache school buildings?"). It was imperative, according to Superintendent Terry, that Nisei give back in the form of military service. "If this program proves successful," Terry said, "then the public will immediately recognize your loyalty. But if it should prove a failure," Terry warned, "then they will say, 'I told you so. . . . They belong right where they are.' The responsibility lies with each of you."[32]

Despite camp administrators' best efforts to prevent any direct disobedience to the draft, some Nisei had already made up their minds and could not be dissuaded. When the first group of Nisei received orders to appear in Denver on February 22, 1944, for their preinduction physicals, administrators organized a banquet to honor these young men, and the entire camp was invited to join in the celebration. Attendance was disappointingly low. Only twenty-eight draft-age Nisei attended the event, some of whom were not even among the fifty-three being honored. They were joined by thirty staff members, thirty-six members of the girls' glee club, and sixteen members of the high school band.

Organizers were surprised by the utter lack of interest in the banquet and seeming lack of support for the inductees, but Nisei staff working under Rademaker had predicted that few would attend. The prevailing attitude, he wrote, could be summed up in just a few words: "Why get enthusiastic about going out and fighting unless there is something for us to fight *for*? If we get the benefits of citizenship, we are willing to take the responsibilities."

Administration staff did not understand the difference between the benefits and responsibilities of citizenship. In private, they told Rademaker that Nisei complained that they could not enlist, yet once that privilege had been restored, few had volunteered. Then Nisei complained that they did not like being classified IV-C. If they were given back their citizenship status and drafted like anybody else, they would go. Unsympathetic staff concluded that now the draft had been reinstated, Nisei were simply making up more excuses. Rademaker tried to explain the Nisei side of the argument:

> Now that the draft is reinstated, there are many who honestly resent being asked to die for the "goddamn bastards in California who kicked us out and enriched themselves at our expense," while the same Californians strongly oppose giving even the Nisei any of their civil rights or the privileges accruing to citizenship.[33]

Nisei and their parents would not rest until their rights were restored along with their responsibilities. Not only were these Nisei justified, Rademaker wrote, but they would also make far better soldiers if their demands were met.[34]

On the morning of February 22, when five Nisei refused to go to Denver for their physicals, administrators knew they had not defeated antidraft sentiments in Amache. An article about the draft resisters at Amache appeared that day in the *Topaz Times,* in which several of the resisters explained why they did not feel obligated to obey the draft. One eighteen-year-old said, "I don't think I

owe the United States anything after the way they have been treating us, and I
don't see my future in the United States." Another young man said:

> I asked for repatriation before. I feel no loyalty to the United States. When
> we came to the center we lost all civil rights. The Constitution says that in
> the United States all men are created equal, regardless of color, race or
> creed. I don't call this democracy.

Among the oldest of the resisters, a twenty-five-year-old said his actions were
to protest segregation and the fact that Nisei were being drafted exclusively
into combat teams. He said, "I would like to have all the services open to Japanese just as they are to Caucasians."[35] Each resister's reason was slightly different and quite personal, much as Hirabayashi had expressed when he wrote
down his reasons for refusing to obey the exclusion order. He did not just
write about constitutional principles. He spoke of the humiliation of living
conditions in the "assembly centers" as one of the reasons for his resistance,
and draft resisters responded to their segregation into combat teams with a
similarly broad point of view. Each had responded within the context of his
own life and personal experience, and each expressed the need to fight for
something. It was not easy to fight and to possibly die in defense of home
when that home was in a "concentration camp." But some found comfort in
fighting for the right to keep their citizenship intact. Either they were enemy
aliens or they should be restored to full citizenship, but this partial restoration
of only the obligation of military service was something that some Nisei ultimately could not accept.

Initially, the Amache resisters lacked organization when compared with
the Fair Play Committee. They immediately came under attack from critics,
some of whom supported the idea of resistance but accused these first resisters
of being reckless in their statements. James Omura, editor of the English section of the *Rocky Shimpo* newspaper in Denver, Colorado, feared the message
of disloyalty the resisters from Amache had sent. He responded with an editorial called, "Let Us Not Be Rash." "We are in full sympathy with the general
context of the petitions forwarded to Washington by the Amache Community
Council and the Topaz Citizens Committee," Omura wrote, but he urged cau-
tion. "The Nisei are well within their rights in petitioning the government for
a redress of grievances," but any actions beyond that, he continued, "would be
treading on unsure footing." "We must not forget we are at war," he cautioned,
adding, "those who are resisting the draft are too few, too unorganized and
basically unsound in their viewpoints."[36]

In looking at the first cases of resistance coming out of Amache, Omura
criticized the young men for what he called foolish statements of disloyalty
just because democracy seemed to have failed this time. Instead, although the
suggestion was carefully guarded, Omura wrote that only organized resistance
could accomplish anything substantial. He urged all Nikkei to stand up for

their rights and to let their voices be heard, but he advised that any actions against the draft should be deliberate and well-planned.[37]

Unlike Omura, camp administrators did not differentiate between organized and disorganized resistance. They took immediate measures to deter anyone else who was contemplating draft resistance. In a letter to Solicitor General Phillip Glick of the Justice Department, attorney Horn explained that five Nisei had resisted the draft so far at Amache. Although the general meetings held throughout the camps were a "good way to divert the emotional feelings" in the camp, he suggested that those planning draft resistance were a constant source of irritation and should not be allowed to remain in camp. He vaguely added, "I believe the contemplated action against the five boys who did not appear will have a salutary effect." What was this "contemplated action?"[38]

The first five resisters were sent straight to the penitentiary. The authorities picked up Susumu Yenokida along with four other resisters and took them to a county jail in Pueblo, Colorado, to spend the night. The next day, the five young men were transferred to the Federal Correctional Institute (FCI) Englewood, in Littleton, Colorado, where they stayed for three months. No other resisters reported being sent directly to a federal prison before trial; most followed the normal procedures of waiting for their trials in county jail.

While the five were incarcerated in Englewood, they received letters pressuring them to give up their fight. Administrators encouraged parents to write to their sons, asking them to reconsider their positions. Director Lindley sent letters to the resisters advising them of the cost of their decisions.[39] If they would agree to be inducted, all charges against them would be dropped.[40] Although the War Department had described the reinstatement of the draft in terms of "involuntary" inductions, they could not truly involuntarily induct individuals who refused to comply. As Hirabayashi found out during a discussion with Capt. Michael Rivisto, it was not legal for the army to literally force him to obey the exclusion orders. In a civil society, citizens had to choose to obey the law, and each had the right to refuse to obey so long as he or she was prepared to accept the consequences of civil disobedience.

Joe Grant Masaoka and Min Yasui, national leaders of the JACL, put the real pressure on the resisters at Englewood.[41] They asked prison officials to place the resisters in solitary confinement for a few days, at the end of which time they would personally interview each one. Yenokida remembered that they asked whether he would consider changing his mind, but we refused. He did not believe that telling them his plans would accomplish anything, so he simply kept his mouth shut. Even though Masaoka and Yasui were not able to persuade Yenokida to accept the draft, they did convince two others. George Satoshi Marumoto, age twenty-five, and Mitsuye Oshita, eighteen, were released from Englewood after agreeing to join the army.[42]

Masaoka's appearance was not a surprise. He was in a position of national leadership within the JACL, and the JACL had petitioned the War Department in 1942 to restore what the JACL considered normal Selective Service proceedings for Nisei in the camps. But Yasui's participation caught the resisters off guard. This man had himself refused to obey an unjust law, yet now he was trying to tell these resisters that they had no right to resist. How could this be? The JACL had labeled him a "self-styled martyr" for challenging the curfew law, but during the draft crisis, Yasui closed ranks with the JACL as it turned its accusation of self-interested martyrdom on the draft resisters. Many resisters mentioned feeling that Yasui had been a hero to them but had betrayed them when he joined the JACL and attacked what they believed were battles for civil rights not unlike Yasui's test case.[43]

Prison officials eventually released the resisters who refused to change their minds, including Yenokida, from Englewood and sent them to Denver County Jail to join the growing number of resisters awaiting trial. The experiment had been unevenly successful. Two had given in to the pressure to join the military, but three remained firm in their convictions. By mid-June, twenty-seven Nisei from Amache were being held in Denver, where the pressure to give up the fight never dissipated. Government officials welcomed virtually all efforts to persuade the resisters to change their minds and to accept military service. In their eyes, even a few resisters posed a serious threat to the overall success of the draft efforts in the camps.[44]

Even though Rademaker wrote openly in support of those who petitioned and spoke out against the draft, he urged detainees to think realistically about the consequences of their actions. He warned that Americans understood nothing of the injustices Nikkei had suffered during evacuation and would never understand the real causes of their resistance. If Nisei continued to resist the draft, their actions would most certainly be used against them in the press without fair explanation of their motives. Bad publicity would only make resettlement more difficult for all Nikkei. Rademaker explained that white parents with sons serving in the military would have a hard time understanding Nisei demands for greater rights. Rademaker concluded, "Friends and foes alike will feel that the protestations of loyalty and patriotism which the Nisei have so often made are just so much propaganda and hog-wash."[45] It would hardly be realistic to expect the press to give the real story behind any resistance, Rademaker suggested, and he was right. Even the JACL presented the resisters' case only as seditious behavior, writing that the selfish acts of a few put all Japanese Americans at risk.

Rademaker suggested ways that administrators could reduce or even eliminate resistance by using modern psychological techniques to "penetrate the defense mechanisms" of detainees. The first technique Rademaker suggested was what he called "shock treatment." A potential resister would be isolated or perhaps called before the Community Council, where a trained professional could break down the facts for him and explain why his actions would harm the entire community. The second method Rademaker suggested was positive reinforcement. If the Community Council organized a banquet or a dance in honor of those who accepted their call for induction, not only would the event reward those Nisei who accepted the draft, but it would also encourage positive feelings in others about the draft.[46]

Following Rademaker's recommendations, a small group of local JACL leaders brought six Nisei men they suspected of intending to evade the draft before an ad hoc council. On March 3, Kay Sugahara, former president of the Los Angeles chapter of the JACL, Robin Kanedo, Robert Tashima, Andrew Noda, Masao Satow, Brush Arai, and Jimmy Makimoto decided that something needed to be done to prevent more Nisei from resisting the draft. Arai ordered a WRA car and rounded up each of the six suspects to bring them before the group. Sugahara and the others explained to the men that if they refused the draft, they may be putting the future of all Japanese Americans at risk and that under no circumstances should they follow through with their intentions to disobey the law. Five of the six thanked the committee "very carefully, and expressed their appreciation for the efforts of the committee in helping them with this information."[47] The sixth was not so deferential.

When the self-proclaimed committee of community leaders interviewed the sixth unnamed Nisei in an attempt to forestall any plans he had to resist the draft, their attempts backfired. Arai began the conversation, but when the young man asked what Arai thought he should do, Arai replied that he thought the young man should go into the army. This kicked off a heated argument between the two, and when the interview ended without resolution, the young man and his father left "pretty well wound up." Rademaker reported of the incident, "The boy and his father, residents of 6H block, I believe, were pretty well incensed."[48] After the conflict was over, the committee decided that in the future it would ask a block manager or councilman first what a suspect's attitude might be so that they could be better prepared. Instead of calling someone who might be "hardheaded" in before a formal hearing, they would seek out a friend who might be more successful at getting him "to see reason in the matter."[49] As Rademaker suggested, when "shock treatment" would not work, a more indirect method of persuasion was needed.

The official Community Council took great exception to the actions of this group, not to mention the members' audacity in calling themselves "community leaders" with no authority to do so. The Community Council created its own committee similar to the one Sugahara, Satow, Arai, and others had formed, but this official committee's tactics would be a bit more restrained. The council hoped to help Nisei avoid the "unnecessary hardships of going to jail" and save everyone else "the injurious effects upon American public opinion occasioned by much publicized refusals to answer the call for physical examination." They would not "indulge in persuasion," though. This new committee was led by Rokuro Okubo, manager of Block 7 (a block from which at least nine resisters came). He declared:

> Some think they are serving the cause by making martyrs of themselves by going to jail for 20 years, whereas the fact is that such refusal casts a large shadow of doubt on the loyalty of all Japanese-Americans who had been found loyal. . . . This should be told to each draft-age Nisei.[50]

The committee agreed that the issue was much larger than the personal choices of individual Nisei. Even though the committee itself would not "indulge in persuasion," its report concluded that it "might be a good thing for someone to get out and do some real persuading."[51]

While the Community Council took on the role of educating Nisei on the greater consequences of draft resistance, the camp administration tightened up its control over public meetings. The camp director issued orders that all those wishing to hold public meetings must first obtain a permit from Internal Security. Residents feared that this new policy may have stripped them of yet more basic rights, including the right to assemble and freedom of speech.

When Internal Security broke up an unauthorized meeting of Nisei, someone sent word to Omura. Even though Omura publicly admonished the first five resisters from Amache for being rash and unorganized, he wrote a letter of protest to Amache's Chief of Internal Security Harlowe Tomlinson. In this letter, Omura insisted Nikkei must retain their basic First Amendment rights of assembly and free speech. Tomlinson forwarded the letter to Myer, and Myer replied to Omura:

> I agree with you completely as to the importance of preserving, in the relocation centers as well as outside of them, all the privileges which are guaranteed by the Bill of Rights and I am extremely anxious that the administration of the centers be conducted in such a manner that no serious question can arise concerning the preservation of these rights. At once after receiving your letter, I checked with the Project Director of the Granada Relocation Center, Mr. James Lindley, to discover what the situation was.[52]

Myer explained that Lindley had merely implemented a security measure allowing police to be present at all authorized meetings, thus ensuring the physical safety of those present. Myer wrote, "This is a type of regulation which is not unusual in ordinary American communities and, of course, involves no violation of constitutional rights." He continued, "It simply affords a reasonable assurance that disturbances will not break out at times when the authorities have had no opportunity for advance preparation to guard against them." Myer assured Omura that his concern over the constitutional rights of those at Amache being violated was unfounded.[53] What Myer did not say was that the mere presence of law enforcement at any authorized meetings would create an intimidating environment, possibly squelching further support for draft resistance.

While Omura wrote letters defending detainees' rights of assembly, the national leadership of the JACL openly attacked Omura for his sympathy for the resisters. JACL President Saburo Kido declared in an open letter to Omura, "I have a slight suspicion and fear that anyone who follows your theories most likely will land in jail or face the firing squad." He accused Omura of misleading the Heart Mountain group and said that Omura had "sold them down the river." Kido concluded that Omura simply did not know what he was writing about and yet pretended that he did. He was putting young men in danger by filling their heads with the hope that, through their violations of the draft law, they might be able to challenge internment. Kido suggested they would not generate a test case. Instead, they might lose their lives as traitors rather than heroes.[54]

Roger Baldwin, president of the American Civil Liberties Union (ACLU), agreed with Kido that the draft resisters would not be able to generate a test case for internment as a whole as some hoped. In fact, he wrote that the resisters had no legal case at all—only a moral one. In an open letter to Okamoto, leader of the Heart Mountain Fair Play Committee, Baldwin wrote that anyone had the legal right to refuse the draft, but he would have to accept the consequences of his actions, such as serving a prison sentence, paying a fine, or both (not facing the firing squad, as Kido suggested). Baldwin wrote this not from purely a legal perspective but as a former resister himself. He had refused to comply with the Selective Service during World War I and went to prison for civil disobedience. His experience led him to found the ACLU to defend the rights of others. But Baldwin warned that individuals who advised others to refuse the draft, as he had also seen during World War I, were not within their rights. He supported the Heart Mountain group's cause but urged realism in its methods, cautioning that the "only possible way such a small minority can get its rights is through the orderly process of the courts in test cases brought under the most favorable circumstance." Baldwin concluded, "We appreciate your feeling, but we do not think you can stand solely upon logic or justice if you are to get results."[55]

Resisters from Amache were not organized into a single group as were the resisters from Heart Mountain. For the resisters from Amache, the only result some sought was to honor their own consciences, not to change the rule of law. Honoring their consciences meant relying on justice. Justice meant not being forced to accept partial citizenship. For those resisters who grew up believing in the Constitution and the value of their citizenship, accepting the government's partial restoration of their citizenship would have violated their sense of justice. Drawing a hard line against second-class citizenship and partial citizenship was the only way to remain true to their understanding of the principles for which America was supposed to stand.

In addition, some resisters acted out of duty to their parents and their families. The war and a long history of racially prejudiced citizenship laws had divided families. It was unclear what would happen to Issei after the war. Most had lost their entire life savings, their businesses, and their homes, and they were too old to start over. What would happen to them when the war was over, and when the camps closed? Many knew they would be the only ones their parents could turn to for support after the war. They could not risk dying in a war that had already cost them and their families so much. Many resisters chose to maintain loyalty to their families, knowing that they risked being accused of disloyalty to their country.

When Yenokida went before the judge, he presented yet another justification for resisting the draft, based on his belief that as a dual citizen he could choose which nation deserved his loyalty and service. Yenokida's lawyer explained to the judge that he had "renounced his citizenship and applied for expatriation to Japan after the tragic evacuation." Yenokida "felt his rights had been taken from him and he had been deprived the liberties to which he was supposed to be loyal." Instead of using arguments based on full citizenship rights and due process of law, Yenokida outlined all the reasons why he should have been ineligible for the draft. Like so many resisters concerned about their duty to their families, Yenokida explained that if he were killed or maimed as a result of military service, his family would suffer a severe financial loss from which it would not be able to recover.[56]

In court, Yenokida found that neither the long string of abuses he and his family had suffered nor the steps he took to renounce his loyalty to the United States would be factors in determining his guilt or innocence. The prosecution called a variety of witnesses for its case, focusing simply on the issue of induction. Elizabeth Ford, clerk for the Lamar, Colorado, draft board; Bennie C. Garren, special agent for the FBI; and Tomlinson, chief of Internal Security, all testified against Yenokida. According to the judge, these witnesses established that Yenokida had been notified properly of his duty to report for a preinduction physical and for induction itself. The judge concluded that "the whole thing arises from the defendant's default on the pre-induction notice and he must accept the consequences." Yenokida and Kenji Akita were convicted on the same day. Both were found guilty of two felony counts of Selective Service violations and sentenced to one year in prison.[57]

By the time Yoshi Kubo was arrested for refusing to appear for his preinduction physical in May 1944, he had become one of twenty-two who had resisted the draft at Amache. His brother, Shizuma Kubo, wrote a letter with Tsugimo Heya and Michitaka Nakaguma seeking legal representation for their family members Yoshi Kubo, James K. Heya, and Yoshitatsu Nakaguma. They first approached the renowned Hugh E. Macbeth, an African American attorney from Los Angeles, California, known for his long-time defense of civil rights and his wartime defense of Japanese Americans.[58] In 1944, he traveled to Amache to speak with family members of the resisters. He was shocked to hear of some resisters who did not explain their cases in terms of race discrimination. Shizuma Kubo, Tsugimo Heya, and Michitaka Nakaguma were equally concerned and detailed the thinking of another group of resisters who justified their actions in terms of civil rights and race discrimination.

In a letter to Macbeth, Shizuma Kubo, Tsugimo Heya, and Michitaka Nakaguma explained that they had engaged in a long conversation with Yoshi Kubo, James K. Heya, and Yoshitatsu Nakaguma before they were taken to jail. They were not opposed to military service, and they were not opposed to the draft. They insisted that they had been and remained loyal law-abiding citizens. But the conditions under which they were being drafted, they argued, were contrary to the principles of American democracy. The Selective Service, as it was being applied to Japanese Americans, was racially biased and discriminatory. In addition to protesting military service in the absence of basic citizenship rights, these resisters also protested the segregation of Japanese Americans in combat teams. They were not interested in bargaining with the government but insisted on a full restoration of the rights that should have been theirs from the beginning of the war. They requested respectfully that Macbeth consider representing their family members and the rest of the Amache resisters in court.[59]

Macbeth did not end up representing the resisters, but he did consult with them, and the resisters retained another civil rights lawyer to represent them. They also organized a defense fund to ensure that all who remained in jail would be represented equally well. The resisters retained the services of Samuel D. Menin, a civil rights lawyer from Denver. Menin had a long career fighting in defense of civil rights, not unlike Macbeth, and was especially well known for taking unpopular causes. He had accepted cases involving the rights of Japanese Americans as early as 1941. After the war was over, he was branded a Communist for defending clients who were accused of disloyalty during the postwar Red scare.[60]

It is one thing to find a lawyer willing to take the case, but lawyers cost money, and the resisters had limited access to funds. So they pooled their resources and worked together. Yoshi Kubo kept a notebook tracking their legal expenses and the contributions of resisters and their family members to the joint legal defense fund. Each resister was supposed to contribute $120, and whether he paid that sum all at once or in installments, his individual contribution gave him adequate money to pay not only for Menin's services but also docket fees, a court reporter, telephone and telegram costs, and other miscellaneous expenses. By collecting $120 from each of eighteen resisters, the men raised $2,160 for their defense, which in the end was only $7.20 more than they needed.[61] The Amache resisters may not have been organized when the draft was first announced and may have drawn criticism for being "rash" and unwise in their statements of disloyalty, but by the end of the summer, eighteen of the Amache resisters had organized themselves, shared a lawyer, raised a substantial defense fund, and clarified their reasons for refusing the draft based on principles of equal citizenship and their constitutional rights.

The Amache resisters were not the only ones seeking Menin's representation. Menin had been asked to defend the draft resisters of the Heart Mountain Fair Play Committee, the largest organized group of draft resisters in U.S.
history. Menin agreed to take on both cases, but to do so, he requested that
the judge push back the trials of the Amache resisters while he attended to the
cases in Wyoming. Menin lost these cases, but he learned from defending the
Heart Mountain resisters. He used similar arguments to defend both groups,
but in Denver, he gradually adopted strategies that earned this second group
of resisters shorter prison sentences.[62]

AMACHE RESISTERS IN COURT

After losing his cases in Wyoming, Menin came to Colorado to defend the
Amache resisters in a different court and under a different judge. As Eric
Muller found in his investigation into the draft resisters, which judge heard
the case made all the difference.[63] To prepare for court, Menin went to Denver
to meet with the resisters. He asked each to write his own case history for
him so he could have in a consolidated form their personal details—who they
were, where they came from, and why they resisted the draft. As Kubo sat in
his Denver County Jail cell, pen and paper in hand, he contemplated what he
had been asked to do. Where should he begin? Kubo picked up his pen and
began to write. Kubo presented historians with a different way of looking at
the draft resisters that defies simple definitions of patriotism based solely upon
military service; despite his brother's eloquent explanation of his motivations
earlier in the summer, Kubo had another way of explaining his actions when
asked by his lawyer to write his own case history. Kubo owned a farm and had
worked to make that farm extremely productive since he had graduated from
high school. When he first had to register for the Selective Service, he sent a
letter to his draft board requesting that his classification be changed to an
agricultural deferment. Farmers serve a critical role in the nation during wartime by continuing to work their land. When he was forced to leave his farm
in 1942, Kubo resented the fact that he was left with no choice but to leave his
farm in the hands of a less-experienced overseer. And when he was classified
IV-C, or enemy alien, in 1943, the message seemed clear. His government had
virtually disowned him and denied him his most basic standing in the nation.
When in 1944 his classification had changed yet again to 1-A, draft-eligible
citizen, Kubo formulated a response that he recommended to other farm-
owning Nisei: He wrote that as a farm owner, he should not be classified 1-A
but should be given an agricultural deferment and returned to his farm in
California so he could provide service to the nation as a citizen farm owner.
This basis for refusing the draft defied simple definitions of loyalty or disloyalty, but when he sent this request to his draft board, it refused to grant his
request for a change in status or deferment.[64]

Kubo's justification for resisting the draft was indicative of the highly personal nature of resisters' explanations for their actions and became part of Menin's defense strategy at first. These men did not resist in a vacuum. They responded to the draft as it fit into the context of their lives, their experiences growing up, their positions within their families, their identities as farmers and land owners (as applicable), and their wartime treatment.

Nisei were not reintroduced to the Selective Service on the same basis as other Americans. They were processed only as combat soldiers and could not claim agricultural deferments to work on their own farms in the exclusion zone of California. This choice was not acceptable to people like Kubo, who knew that this was unequal treatment.

Menin argued again that the government had exercised excessive power in applying Selective Service laws to individuals who were confined in WRA camps, and he filed a motion to quash the case entirely. The government had taken away his clients' rights of citizenship and their property, yet it demanded that they fight "to uphold the principles of democracy."[65] He asked the judge where the government got the authority to evacuate Nisei, to detain them in camps, and then to draft them into the military.

In Menin's motion to quash, which he presented on behalf of each of the first Amache resisters facing trial, he provided the judge with three main arguments: (1) "that at the time of the commission of the offense and at the time of the presentment of the indictment, defendant was and is deprived of his liberty without due process of law"; (2) "that at all times during this proceeding and at the time of the arraignment and entry of plea by the Court, defendant was and is deprived of his liberty without due process of law and by reason thereof, defendant's plea is not and cannot be voluntary because of defendant's restraint and fear, due to his confinement"; and (3) "that defendant was not lawfully subject to registration under the Selective Training and Service Act." Menin cited Section 611.4 of the Selective Training and Service Act.[66] The first argument did little for the resisters' case. Even ACLU President Baldwin wrote: "We do not think you can stand solely upon logic or justice if you are to get results." The second argument provided the basis for another judge to dismiss the charges against another group of resisters entirely. Judge Louis E. Goodman heard the trial against the resisters from Tule Lake, and he stood alone as the only judge to dismiss a case against Nisei resisters, because, as he told the court, their case was shocking to the conscience.[67] He argued that as prisoners in a WRA detention facility, they could not enter a plea, as Menin argued, and therefore they could not be tried as free citizens. Menin could not convince Judge John F. Symes to dismiss the case before him on these grounds. Finally, as historian and civil rights activist William Hohri discovered, according to the Selective Training and Service Act of 1940, Nisei detained in the camps could not be drafted legally. Even though Menin made this same point in defense of the resisters from Amache, Judge Symes refused to consider anything but the facts of the case. Just as the judge had instructed the jury in Hirabayashi's trial, the judge in this case ruled only on the basis of the following questions: Did the defendants appear for their preinduction physicals, and did the defendants report for induction? No other facts in the case seemed material in Symes's court. Because the resisters did not contest the facts of the case, only the constitutionality of their treatment and the legality of being subjected to the Selective Service under the circumstances, they were convicted and sentenced to serve time in prison for their "crimes" of civil disobedience.

Judge Symes would not grant Menin's request to quash the case against the Amache resisters, but he did provide at least one response to Menin's arguments, citing *Korematsu v. United States*. Fred Korematsu had been arrested for failing to comply with the exclusion order. He never intended to create a test case as Hirabayashi had, but lawyers used his case as the main test case against exclusion nonetheless. The Supreme Court handed down its ruling in time for Judge Symes to use it in his opinion. In a split decision, the Court cited the precedent of the Hirabayashi case. It was reasonable, although regrettable, that in times of war, even the rights of citizens might be proscribed to protect the national security of the country as a whole. The "government's authority" to exclude "any class of people for military security" had already been upheld by the Supreme Court, Judge Symes reported. Furthermore, Symes declared, "fairness" of exclusion would not be allowed as a consideration in the case of the draft.[68]

Menin did not win any cases for the Amache resisters, but his clients received shorter and shorter sentences as Menin presented each of their cases, because he finally realized that by changing his clients' pleas to *nolo contendere,* he could at least help his clients reduce their sentences from twenty-two to eight or even six months (in the case of Kubo) by begging for the mercy of the court rather having his clients enter pleas of "not guilty." As Baldwin had suggested, their cases could not be won on the basis of justice alone. They had to demonstrate some level of deference to the court and to the federal government's demands for their service by begging for mercy. The court was not the venue for them to explain their reasoning or a place where they would achieve any understanding. Between September 12, when the first group of resisters received their sentences of twenty-two months, and October 31, when the last resisters represented by Menin changed their pleas at the last possible moment and received eight-month sentences, it appeared as though Menin resigned himself to losing his idealistic arguments in court and instead set his sights on winning the shortest sentences possible for his clients.[69]

Some resisters escaped sentencing entirely by agreeing to give up their cases and to join the military. Chikara Kunisaka was one who changed his mind in court. When he indicated to the judge his "desire to enter the army," he was acquitted immediately.[70] Ironically, though, when he appeared for his physical, he did not pass. Project attorney Horn commented that "he could have prevented serving about four months in jail if he had reported the first time he was called."[71]

HIRABAYASHI'S DRAFT-RESISTANCE CASE

As Nisei draft resisters were navigating their way through the courts, Hirabayashi was engaging in yet another legal scuffle, this time over the loyalty questionnaire and the Selective Service system. Kubo was right to complain that the Selective Service system had failed him and that it was not being applied to Nisei and other Americans on the same basis, despite the claims of government and JACL propaganda. The War Department admitted this discrepancy, too, albeit in an internal memo rather than in public. Nisei were being inducted "involuntarily" and not on the same basis as other Americans.[72] They were required to undergo loyalty screenings not required of any other American group, and they were still being treated like suspect citizens, even though, as John McCloy wrote, "We have now assembled about as complete a set of records on Japanese-Americans as has ever been gathered together for any segment of our population, sufficiently so that loyalty can be determined pretty accurately."[73] Each and every male of draft age was still subjected to more rigid scrutiny and bureaucratic processing than other Americans.

Hirabayashi had recently returned to Spokane, Washington, after being released from the Tucson road camp when he received his "loyalty" questionnaire in the mail. His local draft board had sent to him Selective Service Form 304A, "The Statement of United States Citizens of Japanese Ancestry." Immediately, he became alarmed. He had dealt with his local draft board before, when he petitioned to be shifted from I-D, deferred student eligible for service, to I-E, CO. The questionnaire's title told him this was a bureaucratic layer added only to the Selective Service process for Japanese Americans because of their race and ancestry.

Based on his previous decisions to disobey curfew and the exclusion order, Hirabayashi sent the form back to his draft board with a letter explaining why he could not answer its questions:

> This questionnaire, which I am returning to you unfilled, is an outright violation of both the Christian and American principles of justice and democracy. The form, entitled, "The Statement of United States Citizens of Japanese Ancestry," is a form based purely on the ground of ancestry. As I understand it, no other persons have been required to fill in a further statement because of their ancestry. I believe that if I were to fill in this form, I would be cooperating with a policy of race discrimination. I cannot conscientiously do so.[74]

When the draft board received his letter and blank questionnaire, it requested instructions from the War Department. The War Department in turn sent a letter on April 7, 1944, authorizing the draft board to waive the necessity of Hirabayashi's voluntarily completing Form 304A. With the support of the War Department, the draft board moved forward with the Selective Service process and ordered Hirabayashi to appear for a preinduction physical.[75]

The War Department had given the Selective Service instructions to administer Form 304A to all Japanese Americans to determine their loyalty before they could be inducted into the military, but the department also sent the questionnaire to Nisei already in the military to resolve questions about their loyalty. Some soldiers responded as Hirabayashi did and refused to complete the questionnaire. Some were so angry that they requested expatriation for what seemed like an extreme insult from the very government they were already serving.[76] Other soldiers answered the loyalty questions negatively as a form of protest. They wanted to know why they were being asked to reaffirm their loyalty through the same questionnaire given to detainees in the WRA camps. Had they suddenly become suspected of committing future acts of sabotage?

Just as detainees labeled "disloyal" after registration were transferred to isolation facilities, such as Tule Lake, Nisei soldiers who resisted during the loyalty registration process were also transferred to a special unit at Fort Leavenworth. Stationed right next to one of the highest-security federal prisons, this unit was kept under constant surveillance. The unit was eventually used to repair bridges and roads in the upper-middle South, but the men never escaped the feeling that they were being guarded as if they were criminals. After the war was over, the army gave most of these young men "blue" discharges, a distinction as ambiguous as their status in the military. A blue, or "not honorable," discharge had a very negative effect. It prevented discharged soldiers from attaining civil service jobs, just as if they had been dishonorably discharged. Nisei who challenged the government from within the military may not have been punished with prison terms, but they carried the stigma of "blue" discharges for the rest of their lives.[77]

When Hirabayashi received his notice that he was required to appear for a preinduction physical, he had to make another decision. Refusing to fill out the questionnaire had just been a formality on both ends, apparently. But now he had to decide how he felt about the entire Selective Service process. It had certainly singled him out on the basis of his race by asking him to fill out a questionnaire that in its title indicated it was meant only for Japanese Americans. But it also supported the larger purposes of the state's efforts to make war. While in prison in Tucson, Hirabayashi had discussions with other COs who objected to their assignment to alternative service camps. In some resisters' minds, allowing themselves to be drafted to work in CPS camps still meant that they were supporting militarism. Hirabayashi finally came to the same conclusion himself. In a letter to Eleanor Ring, he explained:

Douglas Steere objected to the Friends continuing administration of CPS. . . . It is militarily controlled in the final analysis and therefore it prohibits a more constructive and more immediately essential work for the COs. However, my objection to CPS goes a little further. . . . It is a matter of principle. To me CPS is a part of military conscription which is basic to war. Therefore, even if CPS were the huge success, which it is not, I could still not accept it without changing my beliefs. The most consistent place for one like me to draw the line is at the point of registration (as far as registration is concerned) but having come to this view after I had registered, I can only act where action is forced upon me. I seek no trouble, and would not raise a "stink" if given a fair choice. . . . National and world service should come from free men if it is to be true service, not from conscripted men. There is all the difference in the world between voluntary work camp and compulsory work camp. There is all the difference in the world between forced labor and free labor, free men and slaves. Please stop me before I envelope you with my hot air.[78]

On the basis that he could not cooperate with any aspect of the Selective Service, Hirabayashi engaged in another wartime act of civil disobedience. When ordered to report for "work of national importance" at one of the CPS camps, he refused to go. He later found out that a crowd gathered at the CPS camp the morning that he was scheduled to arrive at the train station. When he did not get off the train, a cheer erupted from the crowd. He was becoming something of a national hero for his continued willingness to go to prison rather than to cooperate with a government program that contradicted his principles. Some of the COs assigned to the camp were so pleased that Hirabayashi had taken this stand that they followed his example and left. They were already at McNeil Island federal penitentiary when Hirabayashi arrived after being sentenced to a yearlong prison term for resisting the Selective Service.[79]

When Hirabayashi was brought to trial, this time he decided to defend himself. He felt quite secure in his ability to explain his reasoning to the judge and did not care to do so through an intermediary. Besides, in this case, he would not have a team of interested supporters willing to raise funds for his defense. This case did not offer hope of resolving questions over the wartime constitutional rights of all Nisei, as supporters believed his first case did. This case represented Hirabayashi's own personal understanding of his Christian principles, pacifism, and right as a citizen to refuse obedience to an unjust law. He attended court on several occasions before his trial to study the proceedings and to prepare himself for his own hearing. When he finally appeared before the judge, as he recalled, the judge was very kind, explaining each step of the process so Hirabayashi would have a chance to understand everything that was happening despite his decision to forego legal representation. Hirabayashi recalled that despite his moral grounding, he expected to receive the maximum sentence. But much to his surprise, the judge declared that because Hirabayashi was a Quaker, and because this helped the judge understand the basis for his resistance, he was sentenced to just one year in the McNeil Island penitentiary.[80]

At McNeil Island, Hirabayashi continued to act deliberately in response to his understanding of his rights as a citizen and the rights of others to be treated fairly and without racial prejudice. When he witnessed what he believed to be clear race discrimination in the way prison officials transitioned prisoners from the temporary holding tank into more permanent cell assignments, he refused to accept his own permanent assignment until the prison superintendent invited him to his office and assured him that the problem would be corrected. Hirabayashi was prepared at that time to start a hunger strike if his first efforts were not successful. It was not just in Tucson that prison officials realized that housing resisters created unexpected problems with disobedience to their own rules. And it was through Hirabayashi's various prison experiences that he realized that he felt most alive and most engaged as a citizen when he made a deliberate decision each time he obeyed a law or an order—not because he was in the mere habit of obeying but because his compliance with the law coincided with his own understanding of justice and moral living.[81]

CREATING HEROES:
THE PROPAGANDA OF PATRIOTISM

The forms and reasons why Nisei refused to comply with the draft varied widely from camp to camp and outside the camps. Each resister responded to a different set of personal experiences and a different concept of their own principles. One thing was clear: If people who served as role models for young people who were undecided how they might respond continued to resist, new cases of resistance would develop. Just as Hirabayashi inspired COs who had already been working at a CPS camp to go to prison rather than to continue cooperating with their alternative service assignment, Nisei continued to refuse to appear for their preinduction physicals. To stem the tide of resistance completely, the government would need a strong propaganda campaign that would outweigh the appeal of civil disobedience.

At Topaz, except for the exceptionally well-organized resistance to registration, resistance to the draft did not go far beyond the petitions and letters filed by the Topaz Citizens and the Mothers of Topaz. Only seven individuals refused to appear for their preinduction physicals, compared with more than thirty from Amache; hundreds from Tule Lake, Minidoka, and Heart Mountain; and only one from Jerome, Arkansas. It is nearly impossible to say with any certainty why more individuals resisted the draft at some camps than at others, but one might conclude that at Topaz, resistance started early and ended early. Topaz detainees organized a campwide resistance to registration a year before the draft had been reinstated, and this early organized resistance drew out those who might have resisted the draft but who registered their discontent in other ways, such as answering "No" to the loyalty questions or requesting expatriation. Many of Topaz's would-be resisters had already been transferred to Tule Lake by the time the draft was reinstated. When Secretary of War Stimson announced the draft, those who remained in Topaz protested but never really crossed the line of obedience except in seven individual cases.

Instead of organizing direct resistance to the draft, Topaz leaders called on a prominent civil rights lawyer, Abraham Lincoln (A. L.) Wirin, for counsel. When Wirin accepted their invitation, he quickly learned that neither the WRA nor the Justice Department wanted him to go.

Solicitor General Glick wrote to Wirin and suggested that he postpone his trip. Glick wrote that the situation in Topaz was "tense" after the "re-extension of Selective Service":

> Some of the evacuees, who are subject to induction under the Selective Service Act, have mistakenly thought that they could demand the immediate reopening of the evacuated area as a condition to their submitting to induction under the Selective Service Act. Your discussion of the constitutional rights of evacuees may indirectly serve to increase resentment. In the present excited state of opinion, it may be difficult for the evacuees to draw careful distinctions, and you will in all probability be misunderstood and misquoted.[82]

Glick wrote that he and Myer agreed that Wirin should put off his visit for at least two months.[83]

Wirin refused to postpone his trip and wrote a letter to Glick to explain. First, he had already accepted the invitation from Roy Takagi, chairman of the legal committee of the Topaz Community Council, and he could not cancel his acceptance. Second, he wrote that he was "not persuaded" that his visit or his intention to discuss the constitutional rights of American citizens of Japanese ancestry would increase tensions. Instead, he wrote, "If such a tension exists I propose to do everything I can to relieve the tension, at least by stating my position clearly and unequivocally—a position which both Mr. Baldwin and I have heretofore expressed distinctly to persons at Topaz and elsewhere— namely, that wholehearted and complete compliance with Selective Service on the part of all, including American citizens of Japanese ancestry is both expected and desirable." Wirin assured Myer and Glick that they had no need to worry.[84]

Glick agreed to allow Wirin to visit Topaz, but only if he would agree to certain stipulations. First, he was not to address large or general audiences. He could counsel only those leaders of the Community Council who had extended the original invitation—no one else. Second, he was not to interview any prospective clients unless he had their names before he arrived at the center. To this second stipulation, Wirin pointed out that he was already on the road and could not get names in advance. Still, Glick insisted that any new interviews would be grounds for postponing Wirin's visit.[85]

With all the stipulations in place, Wirin's visit was overshadowed by a hastily arranged visit from a Nisei war hero. The WRA, the War Department, and the JACL all worked together to bring Sgt. Ben Kuroki to Topaz. His visit would not be limited to a small exclusive audience. Instead, sponsors brought

Kuroki to Topaz and to other camps to highlight the accomplishments of Nisei in uniform and to overshadow the efforts of those still working to disrupt the War Department's recruiting efforts by agitating for greater restorations of Nisei rights. In the case of Topaz, the timing of Kuroki's visit just days after ACLU lawyer Wirin came to consult with clients was more than coincidental: It was a staged attempt to create greater enthusiasm for Nisei war heroes than a lawyer could generate for legal battles over technicalities of rights and the Constitution.

Sgt. Kuroki was received by a near-capacity crowd at Topaz just days after Wirin made his visit. In a letter to the Japanese American unit of the USO, Executive Assistant to the Secretary of War Lt. Col. Gerhardt wrote that Kuroki was a top turret gunner on a bomber that had recently returned from "a very hazardous tour of duty over Europe." Although this was just one war hero whom the War Department was prepared to send on a tour of the camps, he noted that a more extensive program was "being given consideration." The assumption was that Nisei needed heroes whom they could admire and role models for what the War Department hoped would be many more combatants to follow in Kuroki's footsteps of heroism.[86] Kuroki told the audience of his experiences as part of a bomber crew over Europe and Africa. He grew up in Nebraska and had been inducted into the military before Japan attacked Pearl Harbor. He was exceptional for not having experienced the trauma of exclusion from the West Coast and was one of the few Nisei allowed to remain in the U.S. Army Air Corps instead of being transferred to the 100th infantry battalion or the 442nd. He became a gunner in missions over North Africa and Italy and returned home a war hero. He toured the camps to discuss his experiences and to encourage young Nisei to follow him into service. But his reception was mixed at the camps he visited, including such camps as Topaz and Heart Mountain, because some realized that he did not share the experiences of loss and restricted rights that the majority of Nisei had already faced and would continue to face in a segregated military.[87]

At Topaz, Kuroki visited the high school and the USO and appeared at several luncheons and banquets. A camp analyst reported that he was received with enthusiasm, writing: "Young and old Nisei ganged up on Sgt. Ben Kuroki to get his signature in typical hero worship, American style." "With heartwarming modesty," the analyst continued, "he asked the Reception Committee not to encourage autograph seekers, because he was near to getting writer's cramps." Kuroki insisted that "he was not so important as to have so many people make a fuss over him." He was a reluctant hero, openly expressing his bitterness over having to leave his family in Nebraska for yet another camp appearance. He did mention in a speech at one of the many banquets held in his honor that he had been so warmly received at Topaz that his initial resentment quickly vanished. The community analyst credited the hard work and enthusiasm of the Selective Service Committee, members of the Community

Council, the Topaz Citizens Committee, the Topaz USO, the Girl Reserves, and the Boy Scouts for the success of Kuroki's visit.[88]

Administrators were delighted to report of the success of Kuroki's visit. It seemed that young Nisei boys admired how easily Kuroki seemed to warm up to the young ladies in camp. "One boy was heard to say," an observer noted, "'Ever since evacuation I and another fellow tried to date Miss _____ [sic] without success. . . . Ben has been here little over 24 hours and he's walking that girl home already and I know for a fact that he doesn't know her from Adam.'"[89] Kuroki gave young men a model for how to win respect and the girl. The analyst predicted that of those who awaited draft notices or had already been inducted but were waiting for their call to serve, "many would like to duplicate Ben's success story as a fighting man for Uncle Sam."[90] He had demonstrated enviable traits as a Nisei and as an American, but most of all, as a man.

Although Issei appreciated learning firsthand what their sons were experiencing or would likely experience once called up for service, they were far more reluctant to accept Kuroki as a hero. Many Issei remarked that Kuroki's patriotism was natural for a young man born a citizen and never subjected to the humiliation and discrimination of evacuation. According to some Issei, Kuroki was not "too well acquainted with the Japanese and with the post–Pearl Harbor experiences in America." The analyst reporting on his visit remarked that "some think that his position would have been much more effective in his visit to Topaz had he been evacuated and had he later served in a combat unit on the Italian front." His experiences did not compare with Nisei from the camps, because he was spared the evacuation experience. Issei made it clear that they respected Kuorki, but their experience and that of their sons had been and would continue to be unique.[91]

Taking war heroes on tour helped local administrators promote patriotism and quell dissent. As Rademaker suggested in the first weeks of the draft, Nisei were asking what they were fighting for. When such heroes as Kuroki came to visit, they saw firsthand at least one answer: a hero's welcome. The deliberate timing of Kuroki's visit to overshadow that of Wirin gave his presence in Topaz the desired effect. He represented a role model young men could admire. He was just an ordinary guy who had joined the military and become a war hero. He had risked everything for his country and had gotten the girl, too.

With a pamphlet titled, "Nisei in the War against Japan," the WRA promoted stories of other Nisei heroes across the country, and, most importantly, to Nisei in all the camps. This pamphlet contained newspaper articles that came from Baltimore, Chicago, Sacramento, Salt Lake City, Seattle, New York, and Oregon, all praising Nisei for their heroism and outstanding service records. Articles told of unequaled valor when a "Seattle Nisei" had saved his entire platoon.[92] Nisei soldiers were Americans first, articles boasted, and some were even willing to fight the Japanese, calling them the "Nips."[93] Camp residents who read this pamphlet saw that entire families had volunteered to serve, with one family sacrificing seven sons to fight for "Uncle Sam."[94] A photo showed a Nisei soldier bending down to show his little brother his Purple Heart, becoming the greatest war hero in his little brother's eyes. The message seemed clear: The sacrifices of soldiers were already paying off in greater acceptance, and even praise, for Japanese American war heroes.[95]

HEROES IN DEATH:
MEMORIALIZING FALLEN SOLDIERS

Wherever there were heroes, there were also casualties, and the rate at which Nisei soldiers were dying was shocking to those who remained in the camps. Topaz attorney Horn wrote, "All the members of the staff were stunned this week at the number of casualties reported by the War Department involving servicemen from this Center. For the most part these boys volunteered from this Center and all of us know at least some of them."[96] The report came as increasing numbers of young men were receiving draft notices, leaving virtually no family untouched by the brutality of war.

At Topaz, many Issei were not sure if they should be consoling each other for their losses or congratulating each other for their great sacrifice to the nation. In December 1944, a memorial service became a turning point for the community. The memorial service was well attended, primarily by Issei, but as one observer wrote, those in attendance were "impressively quiet—more so than usual." This was not a celebration, as some memorial services had appeared to be earlier in the year. "One could not help but feel that this was the beginning of a new era at Topaz," the analyst concluded. Until recently, the camp had been deeply divided by those who supported the United States and those who still had feelings for Japan or who at least were quite vocal and organized in their attempts to petition the government in response to the growing list of insults and abuses from which they were suffering. But as time marched on, and as more and more young men returned in coffins, having made the ultimate wartime sacrifice, the author of this report indicated that "interest had veered toward a narrower aspect of the struggle . . . , namely, their own flesh and blood or their close friends—the Nisei soldiers." Nearly every resident of the camp had been directly affected by this side of the war: "A son, a brother, a husband, or a close friend is either at the battlefront, in training camps, or waiting to be inducted."[97] Regardless of whether they wanted to remain neutral, the effects of war could not be escaped.

The loss of loved ones closed the door on collective resistance. Topaz had become, in community analyst Oscar F. Hoffman's words, "atomized." Each family became less concerned about the collective rights of Nisei and more concerned about their own sons, their own parents, and what each individual family might face after the war. This refocus translated into an individualized response to the draft, too. It was unusual for Nisei to organize against the draft: Heart Mountain's Fair Play Committee stood out as an exception. Most resisted on an individual basis, not knowing for sure how many might join him. Families and individuals had to decide for themselves whether to demonstrate criminalized acts of civil disobedience. Would-be resisters risked prison, but as casualties mounted, they also risked drawing the same sort of accusations from Japanese Americans in the camps that the government had warned they would be subject to from non–Japanese Americans. Mothers of the resisters were chastised by other women whose sons were in the service. Do not hold your head so high, they were told, because your sons are in prison, not serving their country.[98]

Even in death, the JACL and the WRA saw opportunities to advance a public-image campaign of "loyal" Japanese Americans to the general American population and to help grieving families view their own sacrifices in a positive, patriotic light. The JACL used the growing list of Nisei casualties for its own publicity purposes, sending the names to the servicemen's hometown newspapers for publication. They encouraged families to send letters to their own papers in California telling of their sons' sacrifices. The idea was that by publicizing Nisei casualties, racists on the West Coast would be encouraged to reconsider their opposition to reopening the restricted zone to Nikkei resettlement.[99]

Chaplain Masao Yamada of the all-Nisei 442nd combat team criticized the JACL for its self-serving publication of the sacrifices of Nisei while ignoring the needs of the soldiers themselves. He saw the JACL working for its own interests more than its professed goal of repairing Nisei status. JACL National President Kido replied that the Pacific Citizen had "played up" the casualties and "feats" of the 100th battalion because they had been given little space or notice by West Coast newspapers, and the JACL wanted to "show that the Nisei were fighting for America and dying, too."[100]

In the camps, the JACL and other patriotic organizations, such as the USOs and the Boy Scouts, joined with the WRA administration to organize memorial services and other symbolic displays of sacrifice and service. Camps created honor rolls. Service flags were put on display containing one star for each individual from camp serving in the military. The purpose of these tributes, particularly memorial services, was to remind detainees that all who served in the military were patriotic heroes deserving of honor and respect. The idea that patriotism must be taught abounds in the literature on loyalty, Americanization, and patriotism. Merle Curti's Roots of American Loyalty argues that high-minded patriotism does not come naturally to soldiers in the field, and it certainly does not come naturally to those family members who risk losing their loved ones in a war. The memorial service was just one of many rituals of patriotism that played an essential role in shaping outward attitudes toward military service and definitions of patriotism.[101]

When Topaz first held its memorial services, the events seemed like celebrations, attracting huge crowds and elaborately demonstrating ritualized patriotism. Each service boasted a flag ceremony, the band playing the "Star-Spangled

Banner," and a traditional Japanese floral arrangement replicating the American flag made by Issei women. Buddhists and Christians contributed to the event, and detainees and administrators offered speeches to honor the veterans. Each service ended with a military salute. After one such service, attorney Horn suggested that a newsreel showing a memorial service, such as the one he had observed at Topaz, might effectively counter the claims of West Coast racists who continued to charge that Japanese Americans were not true Americans.[102] He clearly had a sense that this ritualized patriotism represented much more than honoring the dead—it was a performance of Americanism.

Even though memorial services provided good propaganda against race-based attacks on Japanese American loyalty outside the camps, for those detainees who attended the services, they brought a nationalistic meaning to a young person's death and encouraged family members to support the war through patriotic remembrance. Just as the tours of such heroes as Kuroki were meant to encourage young men to emulate them, even in death, memorial services elevated young Nisei to a new status of manhood in a way that was meant to encourage continued support for the war effort despite the tragic personal costs. In a memorial service honoring Nobuo Kajiwara, killed in Italy on July 11, 1944, his former pastor relayed a conversation he had with the young man shortly before he volunteered for service. Kajiwara had been greatly troubled in his attempt to decide whether to volunteer or to wait for the draft, but he had finally concluded that it was his duty to volunteer. He explained that he had been talking to friends who had already volunteered, but he was there waiting for the draft. They were going to sacrifice all they had, even their lives, for the future of all Japanese Americans, without a thought for themselves. Kajiwara explained, "When I saw their manly attitude, I felt very much ashamed. It seemed to me that it is not good to wait until I'm drafted; it would be cowardly. I've never sacrificed myself for a noble cause; I'm disgusted with myself. Now is the chance for me to be born again as a man." Just as the resisters refused simplistic definitions of their civil disobedience, Kajiwara conflated patriotic sacrifice, including the possibility of death, with Christian metaphors of death and rebirth as well as the emergence of his own manhood. No side of the debate could be confined by simplistic definitions of loyalty and disloyalty anymore.

CHAPTER 6

Prison and Punishment

WHEN U.S. DEPUTY MARSHALL Alf G. Gunn drove his car into
Topaz on May 16, 1944, he was surprised by the living conditions in
this isolated camp in the middle of the Utah desert. Deputy Marshall
Gunn had come to arrest Ken Yoshida for refusing to appear for his preinduction physical exam and failing to appear for military induction. Dust filled the
air, making it difficult to see and even more difficult to breathe. Finding his
way to Block 11, Barrack 3, Apartment C, Deputy Gunn knocked on the door,
hoping to find Yoshida at home but also hoping to escape the unpleasant conditions outside. Yoshida needed a minute to get his things together. As Deputy
Gunn waited, he looked around. Dust had seeped into the tiny apartment
through every crack and crevice. He asked, "Is it always this dusty? Is it always
this bad?" When Yoshida replied that indeed it was, Gunn declared in sympathy, "I don't blame you for not going in [the army]!" Yoshida thought to himself, "I'm not going to have a problem with this guy," and he did not.[1]

When Yoshida was sent to the Tucson Federal Prison Camp for refusing to
obey the draft, he found that prison, compared with life in Topaz, was "paradise." For two years, Yoshida had lived in a place euphemistically called the
"Central Utah Relocation Center," otherwise known as Topaz, where detainees
suffered from low-quality food, inadequate nutrition, and poorly constructed
housing. They suffered from extreme heat and dust storms in the summer
and freezing temperatures and snow in the winter. And they were confined in
a place that defied all legal classification. It was not a prison, not a formal
Department of Justice internment camp, and not a voluntary relocation camp.
He was held without due process of law, and his status as a citizen was unclear.
After he was convicted of violating Selective Service laws, Yoshida was sent to
a work camp in the mountains just north of Tucson, Arizona, where he and
the other inmates labored to build a highway to the top of Mount Lemmon
as prison administrators worked to "rehabilitate" their citizenship. This was a

Central Utah War Relocation Authority Center, Topaz. The desert winters here were cold, the summers were hot, and the wind easily picked up the powderlike dust. The blowing dust was an annoyance and a health hazard and intensified at times into blinding storms that inhibited any form of outdoor activity. (*Courtesy of the National Archives.*)

federal prison, where due process applied and the prisoners' status was quite clear, and yet it had no fence and no wall. The only barrier between prisoners and the outside world was a line of painted rocks marking the perimeter of the property. Living conditions were good, and Yoshida's time there had already been set by a judge. No ambiguity confused when or how he might be released, and, as with all other prisoners, with good behavior and with monthly offers to volunteer for the military, his sentence might even get shorter. Yoshida and the rest of the resisters called it "summer camp."[2]

For those who decided to resist the draft and were sent to the mountains east of Tucson for hard work and "rehabilitation," prison was the least punishing of all their confinement experiences. The Federal Bureau of Prisons stated that the purpose of the Tucson Federal Prison Camp was to put prisoners to work, to teach them skills, and to rehabilitate them into productive citizens. Those Nisei who came to the Tucson road camp learned a different lesson: that the choices each one of them had made as individuals to stand up for their rights had brought them to the same place and created among them a lasting bond of friendship.[3]

FROM COUNTY JAIL TO
THE TUCSON FEDERAL PRISON CAMP

Yoshida's first stop after his arrest (and a brief overnight stay in a county jail in Fillmore, Utah) was the Salt Lake City County Jail. This jail was where he would await his trial, which in his case would be a period of nearly six months. Most resisters remember their time in county jails as the worst of all of their confinement experiences. These facilities relied on local funding and were not well regulated. As a result, county jails became well known for their problems with underfunding, poor sanitation, inadequate food, and overcrowding. When resisters arrived, they found that the blankets were dirty, mattresses reeked of urine and vomit, and rats and fleas were abundant. In some cases, they received only two meals a day of barely edible food. Many resisters waited for up to six months under these conditions for a grand jury to hear their cases. It was under these conditions that resisters started paying for their "crimes" even before getting court hearings.[4]

When Yoshida was booked in the Salt Lake County Jail on May 17, 1944, the grand jury had just finished hearing its last case and would not reconvene again for six months. Yoshida was ordered to pay a bond of $1,000 for release, but this was not possible. Yoshida worked as an ambulance driver in Topaz for only $16 a month. He had no choice but to await his trial in county jail.[5]

Forcing resisters to await trial in county jail had the affect of removing potential agitators from camps, but in Poston, the Arizona court did not retain resisters in jail until trial. Instead, the court allowed resisters to remain in War Relocation Authority (WRA) custody until the grand jury could hear their cases. In those instances, Poston administrators complained bitterly that leaving the resisters in camp caused problems for administrators and for the overall morale of draftees. Poston's project attorney wrote to U.S. Solicitor Gen. Philip Glick to complain. Those who obeyed the law risked losing their lives in the war, he argued, while those who disobeyed were safe in camp and causing him endless troubles. He complained in vain. The resisters from Poston remained in the custody of the WRA until the grand jury could convene to hear their cases more than a year later. Poston's attorney feared, with good reason, that this lack of instant punishment sent the wrong message to young men facing the draft. If a man accepted his country's call to duty, he might die in battle, but if he refused, he remained in camp, idle and miserable perhaps, but in the short term without even so much as a slap on the wrist.[6]

Other administrators who complained about the resisters in camp received more favorable responses to their requests that they be jailed immediately. In Minidoka, Idaho, administrators convinced the courts to raise the bail so high that it was impossible for resisters to leave. They even made arrangements with the local draft board to rid the camp of suspected resisters. Administrators handed over lists of those they believed were planning to resist, and the draft board would move those names to the top of its list for induction. When some did refuse the draft, they were identified and taken to the jail, removing them as potential agitators within the camp.[7]

In the case of resisters from Topaz, it does not appear as though unusual pressures were placed on the resisters to remain in county jail other than the simple fact that the resisters could not pay for their own release and were therefore held in miserable conditions by default. However, the first five resisters from Amache were sent directly to the Federal Correction Institute (FCI) Englewood in Littleton, Colorado, when they failed to appear for their physical examinations and for induction. As discussed in the previous chapter, these first resisters bypassed local jails and were sent straight to the penitentiary with the express purpose of coercing them into accepting the draft. But even after being transferred to the Denver County Jail and joining the growing numbers of resisters there, the resisters from Amache shared the displeasure most resisters experienced of rigid confinement and fairly bad conditions in the jails. Regardless of intent, all the resisters from Topaz and Amache were confined for months until their court hearings were completed and their sentences set, always while under pressure to give up their fight.[8]

While Yoshida waited in jail for the grand jury to hear his case, he did what he could to improve conditions there. He fixed an old washing machine in the basement and began washing his friends' blankets. Soon, the warden started delivering blankets from all the floors for Yoshida to wash. His repairs on the machine held out until he had washed the last blanket, and then it broke down for good. He also asked for chemicals to kill rodents and pests. The warden was happy to comply and provided all that he needed to eradicate the problem. His reward was a cleaner place to live and trustee status. For good behavior, he and his friends enjoyed one pouch of tobacco per person every week. As Yoshida remembered, they had lots of fun, particularly once he had cleaned up the place and made it more comfortable.[9]

Mac Yoshida did not share his older brother's positive experience improving his conditions in jail. He suffered greatly from being confined in yet another kind of prison. Masimitsu ("Mac") Yoshida was arrested with Ken on May 16, 1944, and their brother Sakaye ("Sock") was arrested by U.S. Deputy Marshal George M. Baker four months later, on September 26, 1944. The entire family had made a choice after the registration crisis to stay together at all costs. All filed for repatriation or expatriation at the request of their father, and all three draft-age sons refused to appear for their physicals. Ken explained that the decision to refuse the draft was his own, based on his belief that as an American citizen his confinement in Topaz was unconstitutional and that the army's demand for military service only added insult to injury. This was not the way an American citizen should be treated, so he refused to cooperate.

Because he was the oldest son of the family, Ken said, his brothers may have felt somewhat compelled to follow his lead. Ken and Sock continued on to prison, but Mac found jail so unbearably confining that he was desperate not to remain in prison any longer. According to U.S. Attorney Dan B. Shields, Utah District Judge Tillman D. Johnson offered Mac a deal: "Upon arraignment and plea of guilty the Judge gave this boy [Mac] an opportunity to submit for voluntary induction into the Army and on November 18, 1944 he was inducted and is now serving in the armed forces."[10] Mac accepted this chance to get out of jail by submitting to what the judge ironically called "voluntary" induction into the army, but he did not rest easy, as his other brothers continued on to federal prison and his parents and younger siblings remained confined in Topaz.[11]

Mac Yoshida went into the army, where he served in the United States for the duration of the war. With two brothers serving federal prison sentences for Selective Service violations and parents who had requested repatriation, Mac Yoshida became suspect. Once he was in the army, the government kept him under close surveillance, even though he appeared to be serving as a free citizen.[12]

The terrible conditions detainees suffered in the camps, followed by the squalor of county jail and persistent threats of long sentences in federal prisons (where some feared they might even face a firing squad), deterred many young men from challenging the draft. Interviews with resisters reveal that many feared the conditions and treatment they would face in prison, including possible retaliation from other inmates in prison for their draft resistance or, more likely, for being Japanese. Frank Emi and his cohorts put on a judo demonstration when they arrived in Leavenworth. They arranged for a very small guy to throw a large guy to the mat to show their expertise in the sport, and, Emi said, they never had a problem with other inmates after that.[13]

If prison was supposed to function as a deterrent, how effective was it? Some Nisei indicated that it was very effective for them. They explained that they went into the army in the first place not out of loyalty or duty but from a fear of ending up in yet another prison. An anonymous Nisei in Poston, Arizona, said, "Although I don't especially see any reason to fight for the United States, I'd choose the army to another camp because I don't think that I can stand another couple of years in jail or a camp."[14] The WRA camps became an integral part of the penal system even though they were never officially classified as prisons. As one social scientist noted, by the time the draft had been reinstated, the conditions in the WRA camps had become so bad that some Nisei accepted the draft and some volunteered for military service just to escape the worsening conditions of their confinement.[15]

JOURNEY TO TUCSON

Ken and Sock Yoshida did not join the military and instead became felons, sentenced by a federal judge to serve nine months in prison for violating Selective Service laws. After they were sentenced, authorities transferred the Yoshida brothers by car to the Tucson prison camp. They traveled in relative comfort. Ken remembered that the officer transporting them asked them to wear cuffs only when they stopped to eat or approached a jail where they would stay overnight. Once they got back in the car, the cuffs and came off and they could relax.[16]

The resisters from Denver had a very different experience on their journey to Tucson. First, there were more of them, and their trials were spread out
over the summer and fall of 1944. The first group to be taken left on July 12.
As Yoshi Kubo wrote in his diary:

> Eleven boys were notified that they were to leave at 6:40 P.M. this evening
> for Tucson, Arizona to serve their time. They got ready putting belongings
> away in their suitcase. . . . They left here in a panel like squad or riot car.
> Along with quite a few other Caucasian prisoners. Trusty Ward [sic] now is
> very quiet in fact too quiet, after boys left on time in high and settled spirit.[17]

With dozens of prisoners to transport, authorities used train cars and treated
the group like hardened criminals. Each was shackled to a buddy and had to
stay that way through the entire journey. One man remembered when he had
to relieve himself, his shackled partner, who was much bigger than him, would
just pick him up and carry him to the latrine. The trip to Tucson was one of the
worst of their lives. The cars were hot. The trip was long. The train would pull
aside anytime another train approached, giving all other traffic on the lines preference. It was not until they arrived in Tucson that their chains were finally
removed. Some remembered that, despite the relief of having their chains off,
the final ride up the mountain in the back of trucks on steep, winding roads was
frightening at best, but once they finally arrived, they were relieved to find that
the prison environment was like summer camp, comparatively speaking.[18]

Once the men arrived in Tucson, they sent word back to the resisters still
waiting for their trials to inform them of the conditions they encountered at
this prison: They reported that they were getting "good treatment" and, surprisingly, that "there are no iron bars nor fences but rows of rocks" to mark the
boundaries of the prison grounds. The food was good, too.[19]

While waiting for their trials and eventual transfers to the Tucson prison
camp, Kubo and the remaining resisters were joined by James Omura, the same
newspaper editor who had initially written that the first resisters from Amache
were perhaps a bit rash and instead suggested that an organized resistance
might be the only way to oppose the injustice of the draft when applied to an
incarcerated population.[20] He arrived at the Denver County Jail on July 20,
1944, after being indicted on charges of sedition for his "hard-hitting edito-
rials" that increasingly supported the Heart Mountain Fair Play Committee
resisters. Specifically, he was arrested for "unlawful conspiracy to counsel, aid,
and abet violations of the draft."[21] He was placed in the trustee ward with
Kubo, Min Yenokida, and the others. As Kubo wrote in his diary:

> It seems that man of true principles cannot express his views even though
> United States boasts of her freedom of Speech & Press [sic]. He most likely
> will be arrested by those of false ideals & stooges. Imprisonment being the
> reward.[22]

Fortunately, Omura was acquitted of these charges in early November, when the court in Cheyenne, Wyoming, upheld his First Amendment right to free speech and freedom of the press.[23] "Mr. Jimmy Omura" remained with the resisters from Amache overnight.

The resisters commonly kept small autograph books, and for the rest of their lives they were able to point to the short stories, messages, and evidence of personalities they met in their journey through the prison system during the war. Before leaving them in the morning, Omura wrote a personal note in Kubo's autograph book:

> I would like to say that in the confusion of national emergency, we are somewhat confused as to our civil and constitutional rights. At least we have learned that for people of Japanese ancestry this is unpleasantly true. In such cases we can rely upon our conscience and the principles which we have been taught. I have the greatest respect and admiration for those who dare to defend their principles in the fact.[24]

Like Gordon Hirabayashi, Kubo was becoming more aware of how his own struggle intersected with the struggles of others while in jail, and in prison he would become increasingly resolute in his feelings about his relationship with the government and his ideas about his own citizenship.[25]

Kubo was among the last resisters from Amache to have his day in court and consequently was one of the last sent to Tucson. When he stood before the judge and jury, he was asked if he had anything to say. He replied that he did not care "who they were" (referring to the jury), "as long as they believed in true principles of democracy," meaning specifically "liberty, justice, equality and humanity." The judge did not like that response. He informed the jury that Kubo "was being tried on whether or not [he] went to the pre-induction physical." Attorney Samuel D. Menin objected, complaining that the judge was directing the jury. But the judge replied that "internment and evacuation [have] nothing to do with Selective Service." Kubo thought quickly and decided on the spot to change his plea from "not guilty" to "*nolo contendere.*" He wanted a chance to admit that he had committed the crime, but with good cause. He was allowed to explain the reasons he had refused to go to his physical. In his own way, like Hirabayashi, he was finally given his chance to present to the court an oral version of "why I refuse." Kubo had been born in this country. He owned a farm. He was a citizen. The judge asked him how long he had been in jail, which was nearly six months. Kubo wrote: "Bang! Bang! 6 months, Judge said." He quickly realized that he should be satisfied with this ruling. Tak Ishimoto and Frank Takamoto had been given ten months. Minoru Yenokida, Joe Norikane, and Dix Asai all got eight months. Flu Inaba, on the other hand, was given a year. As Kubo wrote, he was the biggest guy among them, but he got the shortest sentence. He began settling his affairs and prepared to leave for Tucson.[26]

"NEW FISHES" ARE WELCOMED TO PRISON

Bill Nagasaki, from Poston, Arizona, was already in prison when the first resisters from Amache arrived, and he welcomed the "new fishes" (as newly arriving inmates were called) to Tucson. He was thrilled to find that he would not be the only Nisei. It was 2:00 A.M. when Yenokida and the others finally got settled and started to fall asleep. Suddenly, Yenokida felt someone shaking him. It was Nagasaki. "Hey, I'm Bill. . . . Good to see you, good to see you!" he said. The guard came in and said, "Bill, you'd better go to sleep. You can see them in the morning." He was there again first thing in the morning, as Yenokida remembered it, very early, waiting to welcome his new friends. A family of resisters had started to form in Tucson.[27]

When Ken and Sock Yoshida got to Tucson on November 5, 1944, they found more than thirty Nisei already in the prison.[28] The resisters from Amache gave them a warm welcome, pleased to find out that some Nisei had resisted the draft at Topaz, too. Joe Norikane said, "Oh, you guys are here from Topaz? Good to see you!" By the time all the resisters had been transferred to Tucson, forty-one Nisei resided at this minimum-security prison. Thirty-one resisters came to Tucson from Amache, five from Topaz, one from Poston, and one from outside the camps. They did not know each other before going to prison, but after leaving prison, they began calling themselves "the Tucsonians." Through their prison experience, they found that their individual choices had created a common bond that for many would last their entire lives.

Conditions at the road camp in Tucson stood in sharp contrast to the resisters' experiences in the WRA camps and county jails. Some, like Ken, began wondering which had been the worse punishment: prison or the "relocation center"? "If they had left me in camp," Yoshida explained, "I would have had a more miserable life" than the time he spent in prison. "I didn't tell the government that," Yoshida concluded. "They might have sent me back to camp!"[29] The resisters enjoyed good food and good friends in a beautiful setting. They did not even have a fence to remind them of their confinement. Again, it seemed like "summer camp" to them.[30]

Nisei were not the only wartime prisoners in Tucson. Inmates at the prison matched the same basic demographic profile as the year before, when Hirabayashi had arrived. The prison housed minimum-security federal prisoners serving sentences for tax evasion, immigration violations, liquor violations, and other nonviolent federal offenses. Jehovah's Witnesses (JWs), conscientious objectors (COs), draft resisters, and Hopi were also serving sentences in Tucson for various Selective Service violations.[31]

Of the draft resisters the Tucsonians met in prison, some became best acquainted with the Hopi. Harry Yoshikawa remembered his friendship started when he asked if one of the Hopi would show him how to weave a traditional belt. The Hopi agreed, but on one condition: Yoshikawa could not show anyone else how to make the belt, because it was a sacred art. He agreed, and his

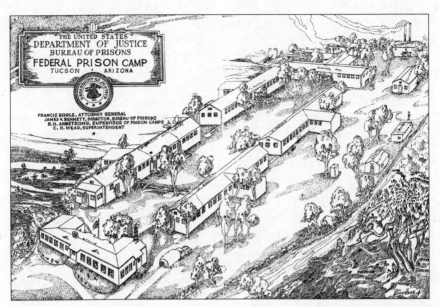

Camp illustration, by Kenneth Burress, *Roadrunner* (July–August 1944). This line drawing of the Tucson Federal Prison Camp shows the layout of the camp and identifies the individual buildings. (*Courtesy of Coronado National Forest.*)

new friend taught him how to make the belts and about the tools he would need to make more. Yoshikawa sent a letter to his sister asking her to send more thread. By the end of his prison term, Yoshikawa had made a couple dozen belts and gave most of them to family and friends.[32] This was not the first time Hopi at Tucson had welcomed Nisei as friends and fellow resisters, of course. A year earlier, a lone Nisei who came to Tucson had been ceremoniously welcomed into the Hopi family. With Hirabayashi preceding the arrival of resisters from Amache and Topaz, Hopi who were still serving time, or serving a second sentence in at least one case, welcomed the resisters openly.

The Tucsonians and Hopi lived together in the "mixed-race" barrack— Barrack "C." Prisons throughout the country segregated their inmates on the basis of race and types of crimes the inmates had committed.[33] One barrack was reserved for whites and another just for the JWs. Most Nisei shared the third barrack with Hopi, Navajo, Mexican nationals, and a couple of African Americans, but some, including Kubo and at least three others, were transferred to Barrack "B" reserved for the JWs.[34] Unlike Hirabayashi, Nisei from Topaz and Amache were not segregated with the white COs, and it does not seem from oral histories that they bonded with these COs as Hirabayashi had, for their resistance was not based on religious or moral ideals of pacifism.

The majority of prisoners at the road camp spent their days building the highway up the Catalina Mountains. As mentioned previously, Norikane thought that only prisoners in striped suits drawn into cartoon strips busted rocks with hammers until he arrived in Tucson. The road up to Mount Lemmon was able to be built through the 1930s and war years only because of the cheap labor provided by prisoners and their crude construction methods. Others recalled learning how to operate jackhammers, a more efficient method of busting rocks. Yoshida learned the most efficient method of all: dynamite. He was assigned to the blasting crew, which consisted of himself and one experienced technician and overseer. They would set up one string of explosives, blast some rock, and then do the same thing the next day. Yoshida learned a bit about explosives and engineering as he watched and assisted with this process. After some time, he suggested, why not rig two sets of explosives and blast twice as much material at once? He explained how he thought it could be done. Because his idea worked, they were then left idle for the two days it took for crews below to clear the rocks before they were ready for another set of explosions.

Kubo arrived in prison on November 13, 1944, and was introduced to road work and farm work at the prison. On his first day, he was sent to work on the prison farm that produced food for the inmates, picking and sorting tomatoes. Within two days, he was assigned to a road crew, where he hauled sand, busted rocks, and spent some time operating the jackhammer. He asked to be assigned to the sheet-metal shop, where the majority of his time would have been spent gardening and sorting food for the prison, but he remained on various road crews. He wrote in his diary that it was a lot of hard work, especially when they had to work at some distance from the main camp site and in rugged, steep terrain. They worked on the road on Thanksgiving, through rain and fog, and sometimes in the rain, sleet, and snow. Some days were harder than others. Kubo recorded that on December 1, he got a chance to do some mason work building a culvert, which he called a "Swell day." In the winter months, the road was "wet and sloppy." December seemed to be miserable, with every entry in his diary getting shorter and more to the point: "hard day," "tough day," "tough was today." But by January, things started looking up when Kubo was promoted to operating and lubing the bulldozer and operating the grader, with a few breaks to work on the farm and to run errands in Tucson with prison officials.

RECREATION IN PRISON

Work did not occupy all the inmates' time. They were required to work on the highway seven to eight hours a day, leaving a lot of free time in the evenings and on the weekends to do other things. Sometimes they filled this time with organized recreation and educational pursuits, but other times they enjoyed more informal play. Susumu Yenokida and Norikane enjoyed playing such games as mah-jongg. Sock Yoshida was well known for playing his mandolin.[35]

Sometimes they played tricks on the guards. Iwaharu Isomura, a bunk-mate of Yoshikawa, decided to play a trick on the guard one night as he was doing a head count. Isamura was on the top bunk. Everything was quiet. When the guard came around, Isomura started shouting, "*Banzai, banzai, banzai!*" The guard was so scared that he ran straight to the office. He came back with several more guards, thinking a riot might erupt. Nisei thought the joke was hilarious, but the guards did not find it so amusing. Another night, Yenokida's brother invited some Navajo inmates to join them in a little fun. It was raining, and as Yenokida remembered it, they were feeling rather confined that night. They started performing a Navajo line dance, with everyone in the barracks joining the fun. When the guard came to see what was happening, once again, he was startled by what he did not understand. He threw his hands in the air and took off running.[36]

The guards were not always so easily fooled by the inmates' antics. One night, a few of the resisters stole a couple of chickens and a turkey from the poultry pen and cooked them over a fire. They had a huge feast. Later they learned the guards had known exactly what was going on but had decided to let the men have their fun.[37]

Prison officials also encouraged the inmates to participate in structured recreational and educational opportunities as part of their rehabilitation. Every two weeks, inmates could watch a silent film on subjects ranging from agriculture to historical biographies, from American heritage to travel and personal finance. Occasionally the prison offered more entertaining films. Prisoners also organized recreational activities. Flu Inaba, Sock Yoshida, and Nagasaki were among those who helped organize sporting events, competitions, and exhibitions for the inmates. They had table-tennis tournaments, boxing matches, wrestling, and a jujitsu demonstration put on by Ken and his brother Sock. Some of the most memorable events were the softball games prisoners played against teams from the area. They played teams from local military bases, such as Marana and Davis-Monthan Air Bases, and even a team from the University of Arizona.[38] They also organized track meets for inmates and as competitions with invited teams from Tucson. Yoshi Kubo was proud to record the day when Barrack "B" won the track meet.[39]

Prisoners also produced their own newspaper, called the *Roadrunner.* Besides providing updates on the camp population, results of recent softball games, and personality profiles of guards or notable inmates, prisoners also wrote a variety of articles for the paper, some of which commented on the injustices of the war, the world, and the prison system. A secular pacifist quoted Thomas Paine on the injustices of modern society:

When it shall be said in any country in the world: "My poor are happy; neither ignorance nor distress is to be found among them; my jails are empty of prisoners; my streets of beggars; the aged are not in want; the

taxes are not oppressive. . . ." When these things can be said, then may
that country boast of its constitution and its government.[40]

Another editorial, commenting on the ineffective criminal justice system in
America, cited ways in which penologists were not only failing to curb crime
but also committing crimes of their own in unfair sentencing practices.[41] The
newspaper provided inmates with a creative outlet and became one of the only
surviving historical records of the prison.

Nagasaki wrote his article "Relocation and Its Consequences" in the *Roadrunner,* explaining to fellow inmates the difficulties Nisei families faced as the
WRA camps started to close. The restrictions against Japanese Americans
entering into the West Coast defense zones had been repealed earlier that year,
and Dillon Myer had just announced that the camps were to be closed no later
than December 15, 1945. Unlike Horace Greeley's admonition to young men
in the nineteenth century to "go west," Nagasaki wrote that, because of relocation, many Japanese Americans could no longer see their future in the West.
Instead, they were moving east, where they hoped to assimilate themselves in
"the American way of life." Yet thousands of families faced housing shortages
and still suffered the psychological and economic consequences of their evacuations and detentions.[42]

For those who remained in the camps, news that they would be forced to
leave was not always welcome. They faced an uncertain future when the camps
began closing. Although many of them welcomed the chance to "bid adieu to
camp life" once and for all, the deadline to move out by December 15 weighed
heavily on those with very few resources left to start life anew.[43] Some feared the
reception they might receive as they tried to return to their old communities
in California and along the West Coast. Some worried that it would be too difficult to rebuild their lives, having lost most of their material possessions in
the exclusion process, and many Issei were too old to start their careers over
and to amass new sources of material comfort. Many Nisei remained in the
military, unable to assist their parents and families through the process of
resettlement, and many more families were still mourning the loss of their
sons, killed in battle, never to return.

The resisters faced resettlement problems of their own, as one by one they
completed their prison sentences and had to decide where to go. Some of their
families were still being held in the WRA camps. The first Tucsonians released
from the prison early in 1945 decided to do whatever it took to reunite their
families. As ex-convicts, though, they met with painful and sometimes violent
retaliation for disobeying the draft when they returned "home."

For Kubo, prison was the last straw in a long list of wartime abuses. His
diary entries became shorter and quite matter of fact again at the end of his
term, ending March 15 with his final prison entry: "Application for expatriation, Consul General, San Francisco," and "for renunciation, Edward J. Ennis,
Justice Department, Alien Enemy Control Unit Director, Washington, D.C."[44]

COMING "HOME" A FELON

Noboru Taguma was released from the Tucson Federal Prison Camp with a new suit and $25, as was standard for all federal prisoners. He also got a one-way ticket to his final destination. Taguma requested a ticket to Amache, Colorado, where his family still resided. As he sat on the bench at the Greyhound station, he was very excited to be going home to see his parents, and he was proud of his new suit, the first suit he had ever owned. He was minding his own business when he heard someone shouting, "Hey, you! You just got out of prison, huh?" Wishing he could hide, Taguma said, "No, no, no!" The man persisted, "Hey, that's the suit I made when I was in prison!" Taguma's pride faded. He felt "very small" then. Indeed, he had just been released from prison, but he had served his time and was ready to move on with his life. The stigma of having been in prison would continue to follow Taguma and other resisters, shaping their lives in ways they never expected.[45]

When Taguma arrived at Amache, he found that he could not rejoin his family. The WRA had decided that no individuals returning from prison would be admitted to the relocation centers, not even with a day pass. In a letter to the solicitor general of the Justice Department, project attorney Donald Horn reported that one of the camp's resisters was scheduled to be paroled in the coming month and was interested in rejoining his family. Horn wrote that he was quite delighted to hear that Myer, director of the WRA, had ruled that such individuals would not be permitted to return. "It would be ironical to allow him to return," remarked Horn, "when soldiers released from the Army with honorable discharges are not allowed to return."[46] But the camp administration did grant returning soldiers permits to visit family and friends. Although they were denied government-funded room and board, furloughed soldiers could be hosted at detainee expense. Nikkei-sponsored USOs in camp provided them with food, entertainment, and even temporary places to stay. The most active USO was located in the Jerome Relocation Center near Camp Shelby in Mississippi, where nearly five thousand Nisei were stationed while they trained for combat.[47] The resisters, however, were not returning soldiers. They were returning felons, and they were not given permits to enter the camps, even for a visit.

When Norikane returned to Amache, administrators gave him a day pass by mistake. This mistake did not go unnoticed. When camp officials realized their error, they began looking for him, as Norikane said, "to throw me out of the camp, because I was blacklisted not to go in there." He was visiting his sister when internal security officers went to his mother's barracks looking for him. They never found him. "The next morning," Norikane remembered, "I walked out" the front gates of camp, "and the police chief started driving by slowly, and he said, 'Hey, you want a ride?' 'No, I'm gonna walk,'" Norikane replied. He remembered feeling like he had really gotten away with something that day.[48]

"JUST LIKE *HOGAN'S HEROES*"

Other resisters who returned to Amache to be near family did not get so lucky. When it became clear that they would not be allowed into camp through official channels, they took matters into their own hands: They sneaked under the camp fence at night. They were determined not to allow the fence to separate them from their families. Norikane said, "It was just like *Hogan's Heroes*!"[49]

Fellow resisters Susumu and Min Yenokida, Noboru Taguma, Norikane, and Kaz Kunitake rented a house together near the camp so they could be near their families. To make ends meet, they got jobs in and around the town of Granada. They would sneak into camp at night and sneak back out before they could be detected by the camp's internal security. Their midnight escapades exposed the irony of a government camp that held the families at gunpoint and let the so-called troublemakers go free. Who were the prisoners, and who were the criminals? In this case, the family members left behind, deemed loyal for all intents and purposes, remained prisoners, while the ex-convict resisters roamed free.[50]

The resisters took the risk of being arrested to check up on their families, to enjoy a little entertainment, and to get some of their mothers' "home" cooking. "My father told the children, 'Always be nice to each other,'" said Taguma, "because in time of emergency, nobody [else] will help you." So, when he sneaked into camp, his brothers and sisters would help him navigate his way and avoid being detected. If he wanted to go see a movie, they would watch outside to be sure there were no security guards. When he came out, his mother would have rice balls waiting for him to take back to the house to share with his friends, because, as Taguma said, he and his buddies didn't know how to cook.[51] But it was not just food and entertainment that drew Taguma to the camp. "We always sneaked in to make sure our Mom was okay," said Yenokida. "That's what happened." "In our day," Taguma explained, "parents were the most important things to us. You know, they suffer too much."[52] Many Nisei felt a strong obligation to keep the family together and to support their aging parents at all costs. In fact, some resisted the draft so they could sit out the war in prison and be available to support their parents through the relocation process after the war.[53]

It was not long before camp officials became aware of the comings and goings of the "blacklisted" resisters. Yenokida and his friends had been sneaking under the fence without any problems, until one night they narrowly escaped arrest. Yenokida remembered:

> One night, we were in camp, and Mom says, "you'd better go out because they're going to be looking for you." So, we went into the movie theater, which is right across the way. So, we were in the movie theater, looking at the movies, and this security officer I knew—he was a good friend of our family—he said, "Hey, you'd better get out of here, because they are looking

for you." So, we ran by the stars. It was getting dark. The desert can get awfully dark at night. And we ran and ran. We ran so hard we'd fall down and run again.

They got under the wire and out of camp without getting caught, but they knew they would never be able to sneak in that way again.[54]

The next day, vandals burned the resisters' rental house to the ground with everything in it. The four friends were left with nothing but the clothes on their backs. Although they never could prove who set the fire, Taguma and Yenokida explained that only Japanese Americans lived in the area. They were sure it was Japanese Americans who did not want resisters around and would do anything to force them to leave the area.[55]

Not long before the fire, Taguma had lost his job because fellow Japanese Americans had recognized him as a resister. They complained that they did not want to shop at a place where a resister was employed. Years after the fire, he remembered that he had been especially upset about losing his prison-issue suit, because it was the only one he owned. Susumu Yenokida and his brother Min left for Denver after the fire, where they met up with Norikane and rented an apartment together. Taguma decided to try one more time to reunite his family.[56]

RENUNCIATION OF CITIZENSHIP

With very little to lose, Taguma made one final attempt to enter the camp legitimately. He went to the front gates and asked to please be reunited with his family. The guard was sympathetic but could not let him in. He offered an alternative. "Why don't you renounce your citizenship," the guard suggested, "and then the government will send your whole family to Tule Lake?" The guard did not know that the WRA had stopped transferring renunciants to Tule Lake, and neither did Taguma. Taguma sent his request to Washington and then left for Denver to join his friends, where he would wait for a ruling on his application. When he got there, he found two FBI agents were already waiting to arrest him. Much to Taguma's surprise, they sent him to the Department of Justice internment camp in Santa Fe, New Mexico. He had expected to be sent to Tule Lake.[57]

Taguma had not been in Santa Fe long before his brother joined him. When his brother saw Taguma, he was perplexed. "What are you doing in Santa Fe?" he asked. "I thought we were going to Tule Lake!" Taguma and his brother had each tried to reunite the family by renouncing his citizenship. Each had failed.[58]

Taguma had given up his citizenship in his attempt to reunite his family, but what he got instead was indefinite internment in a Department of Justice camp. This time, he was not serving a mere nine-month sentence. The Department of Justice kept Taguma in custody for two years, transferring him to Crystal City and eventually to Sea Brooks Farm in New Jersey, while Wayne

Collins of the American Civil Liberties Union fought to restore Taguma's citizenship along with that of hundreds of other Nisei who had also renounced their citizenship under duress.[59]

Taguma was not the only Tucsonian to renounce his citizenship after leaving prison. Kubo renounced his citizenship and requested repatriation along with his parents and his siblings when he returned to Amache after his release from prison. Unlike Taguma and his friends, Kubo was able to rejoin his family in Amache. Why he was allowed to return and the others were not is not clear. But he pursued his next battle from inside Amache, living once again in Block 9E, Building 2, Apartment C-D. In a letter he addressed to the War Department, he explained:

> After serving my sentence term in Tucson Prison Camp for not reporting to Pre-Induction Physical Examination, I have applied for Repatriation to Japan and also applied for renunciation of my American Citizenship since I had dual citizen [sic]. After being treated as I have I lost faith in the government and decided to go to Japan.[60]

Even with this request, he remained on the WRA's "clear list," while his brother, who had so eloquently written to civil rights lawyer Hugh Macbeth on his behalf, had been blacklisted. Shizuma Kubo had requested repatriation to Japan before the rest of the family had, which may explain his being blacklisted. But having family members with different classifications was unsettling. This meant that, at least potentially, Shizuma could be sent to Japan without the rest of the family.

It was essential to have the entire family stay together, and one way to do that was to ensure each member of the family received the same classification. Yoshi Kubo wrote to Maj. Curtright of the Western Defense Command: "Dear Sir, Upon my return from Tucson Federal Prison on March 20, 1945, I applied for repatriation to Japan since I am dual citizen. I have also applied for a renunciation of my American citizenship," he added. Yet, as he explained, the WRA left Kubo on its clear list, while his brother was on the Army Segregation list, otherwise known as the blacklist. He wrote, "I am supposed to be on the same status as my brother," and requested, "Please send a request to the proper authorities to detain me here in Amache until your return."[61] Just as Kubo had refused to obey the draft based on complex reasons, he had complex reasons for renouncing his citizenship and requesting expatriation. He was not sent to Santa Fe, as was Taguma, but he was determined to keep the family together.

Failing to get the response he had wanted, and having time to think, Kubo changed his mind about renouncing his citizenship. Over the summer of 1945, it became clear that Japan was not going to win the war and that life would be far more difficult for those who repatriated than for those who tried to return to California. Over time, it became clearer that the family was not in imminent danger of being split up by deportation or any other means.

Finally, the family still retained its farms in California. The most rational choice was to return home.

Kubo sent a letter to Myer in the fall of 1945 explaining that he regretted his decision to renounce his citizenship and wanted to rescind this request. On November 5, 1945, Myer replied, "I am sorry to learn from your letter that you have taken action which you now regret with respect to renouncing your American citizenship." He went on to explain that whether the United States had granted his request was determined by the Department of Justice.

It was not until 1957, after resettling on his farm, that Kubo finally wrote to the Department of Justice and discovered that he had never lost his citizenship. In a letter written to Kubo on January 5, 1959, Enoch E. Ellison, chief of the Japanese Claim Section of the Office of the Assistant Attorney General, explained that because Kubo had cancelled his request for renunciation, no official action was ever taken to take his citizenship away. "In other words," Ellison wrote, "the mere filing of an application to renounce your nationality did not, in any way, effect [sic] your status."[62] Kubo had retained his farm and his citizenship, despite the trauma of his wartime experiences. He was ready to start over.

RETURNING TO CALIFORNIA

When Ken Yoshida was released from prison, he used his bus ticket to travel to California. It was no longer a restricted zone, and his parents had already relocated there from Topaz. Like other prisoners, he was sporting his new prison-issued suit and was looking forward to getting on with life and reuniting with his family.

Yoshida found his parents and siblings living in the "Hunter's Point" housing project in San Francisco. This was a temporary housing project (similar to the barracks in Topaz) built by government and charity organizations to reduce severe housing shortages. The Yoshida family moved into the project and did its best to get by on the oldest daughter's meager income from her job as a seamstress. When Yoshida got home, he went to work to support his parents and younger siblings.

For Yoshida, life after prison was not too difficult. He was used to hard work. Since he was a young teenager, his mother had looked to him as the major breadwinner in the family.[63] He got a job right away, and no one ever asked about his war record. His wife, Kay, suggested this might have been because he could pass as Chinese. He was a head taller than most Nisei and had facial features that did not immediately identify him as Japanese. The questions that bothered many resisters, such as "Where were you for the last two years?" and "Why didn't you serve in the army?" never seemed to follow Yoshida.[64]

Ken's brother Mac experienced difficulty when he returned home—not as a felon but as a veteran. Mac had joined the army, leaving his two brothers behind in jail. His father had wanted the whole family to stick together, so he

Ken Yoshida, ca. 1945. In this
picture, Yoshida is wearing his
prison-issue herringbone suit.
(*Courtesy of Ken Yoshida.*)

had been pleased when his sons decided to resist the draft. Mac worried that
he had disrespected his father, which was not an unreasonable fear. Taguma's
father told him specifically that if he decided to resist, he had better see it
through. Taguma reasoned that his father had pride, too. If his son was going
to jail to defend a principle, he did not want to see him give up his fight.[65]
When Mac was discharged from military service, he feared that he might be an
outsider in his own family. He went to live in the San Francisco YMCA instead
of going home. It did not take long for the Yoshida family to get word that Mac
was back in town. Ken and his sister went down to the YMCA to see him,
knowing that he might need an invitation to come home. With their personal
invitation and assurances that their father wanted Mac back home, the family
was once again reunited.[66]

AN UNEASY WELCOME IN CORTEZ

When the war was over and the camps closed, Susumu Yenokida finally
rejoined his family on its farm near Cortez, California. For a short time it
appeared as though life might revert to some sort of prewar normalcy. As

members of the Cortez Growers' Association, the Yenokida family was able to retain its farm during the war. The entire community returned to the area together, because they had collectively hired a white manager to oversee the farms in their absence.[67]

Yet returning home proved elusive for the Yenokidas. Animosities and rivalries that had divided the community before the war were tempered by their shared experience of evacuation and confinement. But the closer the community became, the more clearly individuals within that community defined the boundaries of inclusion and exclusion. The fact that Cortez families were able to return to California as a community is remarkable in the history of the Japanese American wartime experience and is the subject of Valerie Matsumoto's book, *Farming the Home Place*. In her research, she noted that old animosities and rivalries between the Buddhist section of town and the Christians were tempered by their shared wartime experience of exclusion and removal. This common experience made the community more close-knit and thus raised the level of intolerance for deviance or outsiders. Resisters would be among those labeled "outsiders" after the war.[68]

Japanese Americans knew they might face violent opposition when they began resettling in California, so some responded by promoting a Japanese American Citizens League (JACL) "spin" of their incarceration. They wanted reluctant white neighbors to see that they had remained loyal throughout the war and did their duty to the nation despite the injustices they faced. The JACL had dominated Cortez before the war. After the war, many residents perpetuated the JACL version of history that dismissed any resistance as the work of a small minority of Kibei agitators and instead emphasized the loyalty and quiet obedience of the vast majority of Nikkei.[69] The presence of draft resisters in their midst threatened to expose a more complicated reality.[70]

Japanese Americans' fears about returning to the West Coast were well founded. During the first few months when detainees began resettling on the West Coast, Nikkei residents of the San Joaquin Valley became victims of nearly ninety acts of violence and nineteen shootings. Some families were traumatized by night riders threatening violence and wielding Ku Klux Klan–like intimidation tactics. Those who had hoped to repair their lives and to restore a sense of normalcy were left shaken and on edge.[71]

It was in this context that the Yenokida family faced opposition to its return from an unexpected source. Susumu Yenokida recalled that his family was not welcome, because he and three of his brothers had resisted the draft. Someone from the community pulled his brother aside and said, "What are you people doing back over here? You have no right to come back over here." Susumu remembered that his brother decided it would be best to leave the area, so the family began farming in Thornton.[72] Unlike during the war years, this time the family was forced to leave and never came back.[73]

Even though the Yenokida family's experience was unique, more and more resisters experienced marginalization or became ostracized in symbolic ways.

Some Japanese Americans, particularly those closely associated with the JACL and those who volunteered for service at the first opportunity in 1943—many times, the same people—called their choices cowardly. Others seemed to try to forget. Even Kubo eventually disguised his identity as a resister. He had been central to the resisters' ability to organize in jail, and he continued to get together with other Tucsonians long after the war had ended, but when historian Matsumoto was invited by the community of Cortez, California, to write about the persistence of this community, he chose to withhold his name from her book.[74] By the 1980s, he preferred not to talk about his wartime stand with others in the community who still held strong feelings about those who had made decisions that appeared "disloyal" during the war.[75]

The resisters were marginalized often in ways that were subtle but sometimes in ways that had a much greater impact: Some, such as the Yenokida family, were forced into a second exile; others, such as Gordon Hirabayashi, faced severely restricted post-war opportunities for employment and education. Hirabayashi recalled that his resistance and associated felony record had a material impact on his ability to finish his education. Nisei who had served in the military were able to return to attend colleges and universities using the GI Bill, a government program developed to assist veterans in a variety of ways. Especially helpful for many was the GI Bill's education benefit. Hirabayashi and the rest of the Nisei resisters not only had to contend with the marginalization of having refused to serve in the military during the war—a move that led many to question their loyalty, patriotism, and courage as men—but they also failed to reap the benefits of the GI Bill. Hirabayashi had to pay for his education himself, working hard to support his wife and infant twins. Realizing the difficulty that Hirabayashi faced, the University of Washington Sociology Department chair, George Lundberg, offered him extra opportunities to teach. Admittedly, this would not make up for his lack of GI Bill benefits, but it did mean that Hirabayashi was able to give up his second job and focus more on his graduate training. Even though Hirabayashi earned the respect and support of the faculty and the department chair as an outstanding instructor, the president of the university, Raymond B. Allen, objected to Hirabayashi's appointment. He said he did not like the idea of having "a guy who's been in prison" teaching students at the University of Washington.[76] Lundberg defended Hirabayashi, asking President Allen why, if the government was satisfied that Hirabayashi had sufficiently paid the price for his crimes, the university should continue to punish him. Even though President Allen still objected to the idea of having an ex-convict teaching at the university, with Lundberg's support Hirabayashi gained valuable experience and much-needed income while he earned his doctorate in sociology.[77] Nisei draft resisters returned from prison, where they had been the subjects of citizenship rehabilitation rather than harsh forms of punishment, to communities and institutions that continued to marginalize them and, in a sense, punish them for their wartime crimes of civil disobedience.

Despite the fact that Nisei draft resisters were reminded frequently in the post-war years that there were some who could not see past the criminality of their draft resistance, the story of the Nisei draft resisters nearly fell into oblivion. When eminent historian of Japanese American history Roger Daniels returned to a community that had been torn apart over the draft, he asked why nobody bothered to mention the story of the draft and the resisters in any of the oral histories he had conducted. They responded, "Oh professor, that was so unpleasant. We didn't think that you wanted to be bothered with that." Daniels referred to the "discovery" he and historian Douglas Nelson had made of the draft-resistance movement at Heart Mountain in terms comparable to the "discovery" of America by Columbus.[78] Those who had been in the camps and personally witnessed the registration and draft crisis unfold knew all along that a draft-resistance movement had existed at more than just one camp. But in the postwar years, few were ready to talk about it. Those who chose to forget the draft did so quite deliberately, hoping to make this chapter in history vanish so that individuals, families, and communities that had been torn apart in so many ways during the war might be able to heal, even if it meant ignoring scars that refused to heal completely.

CHAPTER 7

Reunions, Redress, and Reconciliation

ᥱᥨᥩ ᥱᥩ

I N 1947, President Harry S. Truman asked an independent review board to investigate the possibility of pardoning draft resisters. The board was directed by former Supreme Court Justice Owen J. Roberts. They reviewed 15,805 cases and determined that during World War II, approximately ten thousand individuals had committed what they called "willful" and criminal violations of Selective Service regulations. They recommended that these resisters not be pardoned. By contrast, 4,300 Jehovah's Witnesses, 1,000 religious objectors, and 500 others had all resisted the draft on religious or moral grounds. It would be much easier to make a case for these resisters to receive presidential pardons. The committee took a closer look at each case to make specific recommendations to the president.[1]

When reviewing the case of Nisei resisters, former Justice Roberts commented it was clear to the committee that these resisters "deeply resented" being classified as "undesirables" during the war. The board members sympathized with Nisei. They believed that they were loyal citizens who had refused the draft as a means of protesting their wartime treatment. Full presidential pardons were recommended.[2]

On December 23, 1947, President Truman issued what he called a "Christmas pardon" for 1,523 resisters, including all 292 Nisei convicted of draft evasion, but the Nisei resisters would have to wait fifty-five years for many of their fellow Japanese Americans to recognize the moral basis for their resistance. Truman's pardon reversed their felony convictions, restored their citizenship, and freed any who remained in prison, but his pardon did not free the resisters from continued insults from Japanese Americans who found it difficult to concede the moral basis of their resistance. This chapter explains how and why the resisters were nearly forgotten but then later formally recognized between 1947, when Truman pardoned them, and 1999, when they were invited back to Tucson for the renaming of the prison site in Gordon Hirabayashi's honor. It also explains the process that led to a Japanese American Citizens League (JACL) apology to the resisters in 2002. No longer marginalizing the resisters as disloyal draft dodgers, the JACL gave them center stage as civil rights heroes.

TUCSONIAN REUNIONS

In 1947, the same year of Truman's pardon, Bill Nagasaki and Min Yenokida, Susumu Yenokida's older brother, decided to organize the first reunion of the Tucsonians. They thought it was important for this group to stay in touch with one another. Together, they would be able to remember why they took a stand against the draft, even if they were marginalized within their own communities. Nagasaki and Yenokida invited all who could come to the first annual reunion of "the Tucsonians," naming their group after the nearest city to the prison where they had been incarcerated.[3]

The idea of creating a lifelong association of resisters took hold, and for more than fifty years, the Tucsonians gathered at reunions whenever they

First anniversary of the Tucsonians, January 12, 1947, Sacramento, California. *Back row (left to right):* Minoru Yenokida, George Takamoto, Tstomu Yenokida, Ken Yoshida, Yoshi Kubo, Joe Norikane, Susumu Yenokida, James Heya. *Middle row:* Sock Yoshida, Fred Asai, Kazumi Kunitake, Terry Uyemoto, Frank Naruto, Harry Ioku, Dix Asai, George Takahashi. *Front row:* Irvine Hirabayashi, Hiroshi Yamauchi, Riyu Uyeda, Bill Nagasaki, Joe Kashiwagi, Hideo Takeuchi. *(Photograph by Kuroko Studio. Courtesy of Ken Yoshida.)*

could. In 1960, two of the Tucsonians' Hopi friends joined them. The family of resisters was growing. Wives joined the group and, later, children. The Tucsonians kept an updated list of names and addresses for each member of the group so they could always stay in contact with one another. They collected modest annual dues that allowed them to send money to the families of resisters who died. Later, the Tucsonians started attending events organized by other groups of resisters and invited some of the Heart Mountain group to their own gatherings.[4]

For decades, the Tucsonians built their friendships and gradually taught their children about the tough choices they faced during the war. Kay Yoshida, wife of Tucsonian Ken Yoshida, pointed out that few Nisei talked openly with their children about their camp experiences or the draft. She, and others, remembered harboring deep shame and guilt for having been in some kind of prison. The shame of being incarcerated in any prison, including the War Relocation Authority's (WRA's) so-called relocation centers, prevented many Nisei from talking about the war years to anyone, even their own children. The reunions made it easier for the Yoshidas to tell their kids about their father's wartime record. Kay Yoshida explained:

> We never talked to our kids about the internment camps. We were too busy trying to get our lives back together, but because of the reunions we had at Tahoe, Lake Tahoe, we finally told them. Your dad was in prison. I still remember their reaction, especially our son, "Our dad was in prison?!"[5]

Joe Norikane thought for a while when he was asked about the first time he told his son Joey about his resistance. Finally, he concluded that he had never actually told his son: Joey had simply figured it out from observing Joe's involvement with the Tucsonians over the years. It had simply become a part of their families' lives.[6]

For Ken Yoshida, reunions meant that he could identify with a larger group of resisters. In Topaz, he was one of only a handful of resisters. He and his brothers were three of the seven total, and he and Mac were two of only five who persisted despite pressures to give up and join the army. He was proud to be the first and one of the few resisters from Topaz, but being a part of a larger family of resisters was another source of pride for him later in life.

Ken Yoshida recalled being more comfortable than most in telling strangers that he was a resister. He was proud to say that he was the first resister from Topaz. But when he said this, it always stopped the conversation cold. He laughed when he said he did not know why. Kay teased him by saying, "He doesn't know why?! He stumps them." Talking about camp was usually part of a brief introduction, a way to place each other, but the conversation moved quickly to more enjoyable topics. As Kay said, "You don't talk about the camp experience because you already know," especially if someone brought up the draft.[7]

HISTORICAL MEMORY

While the resisters were busy rebuilding their lives, historians began writing about Japanese American incarceration during World War II, but few of these early publications mentioned the fact that Japanese Americans were drafted, let alone the fact that several hundred Nisei resisted the draft. Miné Okubo was the first to publish her own account of life in Tanforan and Topaz. Her graphic novel, published in 1946, contains one of the first brief accounts of the infighting and unrest caused by the registration crisis, but it makes no mention of the draft.[8]

Many books that did mention the draft minimized its importance by devoting little if any attention to the subject. Most attention was given to the volunteer enlistees, whose numbers were significantly fewer from the camps than those drafted from the camps. Even the most careful student might assume that the draft either was never applied to Nisei or came at such a late date that the majority of servicemen from inside the camps volunteered. An early example of one book that might have paid more attention to the draft, considering its focus on the law, is Frank Chuman's *The Bamboo People*, published in 1976. With a chapter devoted to the "Founding of the JACL and the 442nd Regimental Combat Team," this book could have easily discussed how the draft law applied to citizens with suspended rights. Instead, discussion of the draft itself is reduced to a single sentence. The majority of the language Chuman uses focuses on Nisei's being "accepted" into the military and a small section on dissent over "enlistment," but not the draft.[9]

Honor by Fire details the history of Nisei's serving in the military during the war and does mention the draft, but only in one paragraph. It marks a turning point in the literature from books that say nothing of the draft—including *Years of Infamy*, which skips from the registration crisis to the breakdown at Tule Lake but passes over the draft—to books that begin mentioning it as an event but offer little analysis or explanation of its impact or significance.[10]

Some authors perpetuated the War Department's claim that the draft represented a restoration of Nisei rights. For example, in JACL historian Bill Hosokawa's book, *Nisei: The Quiet Americans*, even the 2002 revised edition buries the sole reference to the draft in a chapter that details the extraordinary heroism of Nisei volunteers on the battlefield:

> Within a year after the Army opened its ranks to Nisei volunteers, full Selective Service rights were restored to them. According to a Selective Service monograph on special groups, some 33,300 Nisei—an astonishingly large figure in view of their total numbers—served in World War II. More than half were from the mainland.[11]

Although this information may be technically accurate, Hosokawa's brief description of the restoration of the draft is misleading. It sounds as though Selective Service rights were restored to the volunteers, and it is not readily apparent that additional Nisei became subject to the draft. In addition, he inflates the number of volunteers and portrays Nisei as visionary patriots, hiding the tortured reality of coercion and conflict that led many to accept military service. He writes, "Nisei had the courage and vision to see beyond the watchtowers of the American-style concentration camps."[12] The elimination of the draft from the historical narrative created a powerful and lasting form of historical amnesia that further marginalized the resisters. If no draft took place, no one could have resisted it.

Over time, the myth took hold that all those Nisei who served in the military did so on a voluntary basis. Even war memorials dedicated to the memory and sacrifice of Nisei veterans portray their service as voluntary. In a memorial at Topaz, Mac Yoshida's military service is forgotten, but other Topaz Nisei are honored as if all had been volunteers.[13] The National Japanese American Memorial is less specific but equally misleading. In its brief description of Japanese Americans in the military, it states: "Answering the call to duty, young Japanese Americans entered into military service, joining many pre-war draftees." It does not explain the circumstances of how these young Nisei "entered" the service. When contrasted with the "pre-war draftees," it is reasonable that visitors to the monument would infer that one group was drafted and the other was not.[14]

What caused narrators to misrepresent the past so blatantly? Historian Gary Okihiro explained that the JACL wanted to achieve redress for survivors of the camps. The group's political agenda drove what became a complete reinvention of history to fit the present political needs of the redress movement. In 1973, he explained that the JACL-driven narrative portrayed Japanese Americans as "downtrodden victims of a racist America gone hysterical," who rose "up from the dust of defeat to patriotic triumph when given the opportunity to prove their basic loyalty."[15] Okihiro criticized this version of history, because it whitewashed a more interesting, complex reality—it denied the fact that the majority of Nikkei resisted becoming victims in diverse and often creative ways. But for those seeking redress, admitting that detainees resisted the government, or that some even declared so-called "disloyalty" to the nation as a means of protesting their loss of rights, would have been inconvenient. Instead, a more useful narrative portrayed the camps as an unnecessary use of force against an overwhelmingly patriotic group of citizens.[16] Once redress had been achieved with passage of the Civil Liberties Act in 1988 and an official apology from President Reagan, the JACL version of history remained a part of the national consciousness.

Such scholars as Michael Kammen and Michel-Rolph Trouillot have noted aptly that history always represents choices people make regarding which portions of the story to include and which to exclude. What people forget is just as important as what they remember. Historical memory and historical amnesia work hand in hand to create a less complete but more manageable narrative.

Tetsuden Kashima applied this concept directly to the history of Japanese Americans in the immediate postwar period. Writing in terms of social amnesia, Kashima warned that so much attention had been paid to the "cataclysmic" war years and the "miraculous adjustment in the 1960s" when Japanese Americans were heralded as the "model minority," the fifteen years in between tended to be glossed over. The same sort of selective attention to certain years or to certain topics with a near absence of attention to others creates blind spots in the literature and eventually in historical memory. This absence is especially critical to the history of Japanese Americans, because the most difficult topics of loyalty, renunciation of citizenship, and the draft were still playing out in these immediate postwar years of the 1950s. Draft resisters may have been pardoned by the federal government, but communities were less willing to forgive them. Renunciants were still being threatened with deportation and would spend years without a clear resolution of their cases. Between 1944 and 1946, 5,589 Nisei renounced their citizenship; 5,461 of this total came from Tule Lake alone. Most had renounced their citizenship under duress and almost immediately began seeking ways to restore it. American Civil Liberties Union lawyer Wayne Collins fought on behalf of the renunciants, and by 1965 nearly all had successfully regained their citizenship.[17] Those sent to Tule Lake during in the wake of the registration crisis recalled the stigma of disloyalty that they carried for years.

Efforts that Japanese Americans made to forget the terrible conflicts that had divided them, the differing views over the draft and loyalty, and the entire episode of wartime incarceration and its associated guilt represented the desire to move forward and to readjust to life after confinement. Japanese Americans individually and collectively became actively engaged in the process of producing historical amnesia.[18] The resisters had not literally been forgotten, but their presence threatened a more useful historical narrative. Silencing one story (that of the draft and the resisters) to highlight the story of another (the volunteers) served the political needs of the postwar era. But political needs change over time, as would the narrative of Japanese American history.[19]

The third generation of Japanese Americans, known as Sansei, grew up during the postwar era of civil rights and race pride. Despite silences in individual families about camp life during World War II, Japanese Americans did not actually forget their lost rights during the war, and they were joined by a new generation who worked alongside the "camp generation" vigilantly to secure greater civil rights for themselves and others. Although the JACL would later be criticized heavily for cooperating with government policies during World War II, lawyers and lobbyists for the JACL worked hard to assist in overturning anti-interracial marriage, segregation, restricted citizenship rights, and race-based immigration laws. The end of race-based immigration quotas allowed immigration from Japan to be restored in 1952, yet immigration levels remained low due to a booming postwar economy in Japan. Those Japanese who did immigrate to the United States after the war often came because of family ties, such as marriage to a U.S. citizen living in Japan during the occupation, and became the first new generation of Japanese immigrants not barred from naturalization due to racial restrictions.

From the late 1960s through the 1970s, the JACL, the National Council for Japanese American Redress (NCJAR), the National Coalition for Redress/Reparations (NCRR), Japanese American politicians, lawyers, and activists worked tirelessly to achieve redress for Japanese Americans incarcerated during the war. Some, such as the NCJAR, sought redress through the courts, while others, such as the JACL, lobbied Congress. As Alice Yang Murray discovered, it was not just the strategies of the three separate redress campaigns that varied—the groups' basic understanding of the Japanese American wartime experience also varied. Murray noted that the supporters of the NCJAR promoted the history of those who resisted their wartime loss of rights, while the JACL emphasized wartime cooperation and Nisei heroism during military service. The youngest activists, many of whom were born after the end of the war, dominated the NCRR and "paid tribute to all internees, regardless of their response to military service or the loyalty questionnaire," Murray pointed out. The NCRR preferred to see common ground and linked the Japanese American experience with other groups whose rights were violated throughout U.S. history.[20] The views each group had about history shaped its strategies for redress.

The struggle for redress may have exposed competing narratives of the history of Japanese Americans during World War II, but the success of the redress movement and the process of achieving redress helped bring these divergent stories together to create a more pluralistic, complex, and inclusive history over time. Hearings held across the country by the Commission on Wartime Relocation and Internment of Civilians (CWRIC) encouraged those who had stopped talking about the war to break their silence. The CWRIC published its findings in 1983 in a report now available under the title *Personal Justice Denied,* in which the commission reported that Japanese Americans had been forcibly removed and incarcerated en masse not out of military necessity but due to racial prejudice, wartime hysteria, and a failure of leadership by politicians who allowed the policy to move forward. The commission recommended that the U.S. government officially apologize for the wrongs committed. In August 1988, Congress passed the Civil Liberties Act, and President Ronald Reagan signed it into law. Public Law 100-383 was passed to apologize to Japanese Americans for the grave injustice of wartime policies and to create an education fund to encourage research and to ensure that similar injustices would never happen again. Surviving individuals eventually each received a check for $20,000 as a token payment for the losses incurred because of their incarceration.[21] Some people returned the checks in protest, arguing that money could never repay them for all that they had lost. But for many who had lived through the war and had been incarcerated in the camps, the ultimate success of the redress movement was to free them from their own personal guilt and to encourage a new honesty in their conversations about what happened during the war.

While Congress was investigating the effects of Executive Order 9066, legal teams were fighting to overturn the convictions of Fred Korematsu, Min Yasui, and Hirabayashi based on new evidence that the Supreme Court had delivered its rulings based on partial evidence. Lawyers filed writs of *coram nobis* for all three after discovering that the government in each of these three landmark wartime cases had suppressed evidence. A writ of *coram nobis* means that the petitioner is arguing that a miscarriage of justice has been committed. Korematsu's *coram nobis* challenge was granted outright, but judges ruling in the Yasui and Hirabayashi cases were more reserved in their judgments. All three had their personal convictions vacated, and even though each *coram nobis* case turned out differently, they represented a symbolic victory for all Japanese Americans. The success the legal teams achieved in vacating the convictions of Korematsu, Hirabayashi, and Yasui not only introduced to the public the idea that Japanese Americans had been subjected to unconstitutional forced removal from their homes and inhumane incarcerations in camps but also revealed that some had stood up for their rights by refusing to comply with these unjust laws. Even though the JACL drive for redress depended on a simple narrative that emphasized loyal citizens wrongly imprisoned, legal redress made it impossible to ignore that at least three Nisei had committed acts of civil disobedience in an effort to clarify their rights during the war. Still obscured at this point was the history of the draft, draft resisters, and those who requested repatriation to Japan or renounced their U.S. citizenship, but these stories would emerge slowly as scholars and Japanese Americans started to ask new questions.

Two major questions emerged in the 1990s: To what extent did the JACL cooperate with the government during the war? Should Japanese Americans recognize the draft resisters as defenders of civil rights? To answer the first question, in 1990, the JACL hired historian Deborah K. Lim to investigate the history of JACL collaboration with the government during the war. The evidence Lim found was far more damning than the JACL had expected: The JACL had done much more than cooperate. The JACL had not defended Nisei rights as the civil rights organization that the JACL fancied itself to be in the years following the war, and JACL national leaders had suggested some of the most damaging wartime policies. In the first few months of the war, national JACL leadership had suggested placing Nikkei in relocation centers. Its members had petitioned for a restoration of the draft. Mike Masaoka had even suggested the formation of an all-Nisei suicide squad. JACL leaders had actively encouraged the government to adopt some of the most costly policies of the war.[22]

The JACL was not comfortable with this new level of criticism, especially after working hard to become a legitimate civil rights organization in the postwar years, fighting for the repeal of race-based immigration and citizenship laws, and contributing to court cases that ended segregation in schools and antimiscegenation laws. In an effort to portray its history in a more positive light, the organization suppressed Lim's report and removed her from the project. The report was trimmed down and sanitized to give a more favorable, partial admission of JACL cooperation, but in a continuing story of resistance, individuals would not allow the report to die. An informal network quickly developed among those who reproduced the original report, known as the *Lim Report,* and distributed it as widely as possible, exposing some very embarrassing segments of JACL history.[23]

RECOVERING THE MEMORY OF RESISTANCE

Along with growing criticism of the JACL's role in the wartime erosion of Japanese American civil rights emerged a growing awareness of a larger historical narrative that had been left out of mainstream Japanese American historiography. Roger Daniels and Douglas Nelson both published books in the 1970s that presented the Fair Play Committee and James Omura in a favorable light rather than as the "demented ogres" they had been treated like in JACL-favored literature. Historians trained during the explosive period of ethnic studies and subaltern studies started looking at resistance in new ways. For example, Okihiro's article "Japanese Resistance in America's Concentration Camps: A Reevaluation" looks at the ways Japanese Americans resisted their incarceration. Based on then-new literature on African anticolonialism and African American agency under slavery, Okihiro found that the myth perpetuated by the dominant JACL narratives—that Japanese Americans did not resist and that those who did represented a small minority of outside agitators—simply did not stand up against the historical evidence.[24]

Other articles followed that supported Okihiro's findings. Of particular importance among these are Arthur Hansen and David Hacker's "The Manzanar Riot: An Ethnic Perspective," published in *Amerasia Journal* out of UCLA in 1974, and James Hirabayashi's article, "Nisei: The Quiet American? A Reevaluation," published in *Amerasia Journal* in 1975. Okihiro continued writing on Japanese American resistance. His articles include "Japanese Resistance in America's Concentration Camps: A Re-evaluation," "Tule Lake under Martial Law: A Study in Japanese Resistance," and "Religion and Resistance in America's Concentration Camps."[25] Hansen went on to expand this field of study with an examination of "cultural politics" in Gila River.[26]

Even though discussions about the widespread nature of resistance were already well developed in academic literature, congressional hearings held by the CWRIC played a significant role in bringing the stories of the resisters out to the public. To gather testimony from those who had been affected directly by the wartime incarceration of "civilians," the CWRIC traveled around the country to population centers and gave Japanese Americans the chance to enter their testimony into the public record. In New York, Jack Tono, a member of the Fair Play Committee, testified before the CWRIC that the JACL, as

Hansen wrote, "had abandoned the resisters during the war and made their lives miserable thereafter, and then rebuked Ben Kuroki, 'our great war hero,' for having labeled Frank Emi and the other FPC leaders 'fascists' at their 1944 trial." In Seattle, Omura testified about his own experiences and the ways in which the JACL had ostracized him and had ruined his livelihood for years after the war for his decision to support the resisters. Frank Chin, a renowned Chinese American playwright and future supporter of the resisters, was in the audience, and he and his cohorts, including Japanese Americans, began researching the story further. They became largely responsible for, as Hansen put it, rescuing from oblivion many of the resisters' stories through oral histories and archival research. This same group of activists brought Omura, Frank Emi, and other resisters together to speak about their experiences in academic symposia and community forums.[27]

The first group of resisters to receive consistent attention in the literature was the Heart Mountain Fair Play Committee.[28] It was not only the appeal of their story as the largest single draft resistance trial in history but also the clarity of the narrative that propelled them to the forefront of the literature. Kioshi Okamoto and Emi were not only eloquent but also compelling in their constitutional appeals to reason. World War II may have been the "good war," but Japanese Americans were treated very badly, had their constitutional rights taken away, and then were compelled by law to serve in the military. Some refused, and when they did so as a group, their story became symbolic of larger historical themes. Other stories of resistance remained hidden. Where were the resisters whom Omura had criticized for being disorganized and rash in their statements of "disloyalty"? Their stories were yet to come.

A strong movement started to emerge, especially among Japanese Americans, to turn the growing awareness of the resistance into a formal recognition of their civil rights position. But as the move to recognize the resisters took hold, it became clear that a specific profile of resister would become the focus of the majority of public attention—resisters who mirrored or at least were closely related to the clear constitutional position taken by the Heart Mountain Fair Play Committee. Even though draft resisters from all camps were certainly admired, their varied and highly personal reasons for resisting the draft were never included in arguments for recognition, as they would severely complicate the process.

The same year President Reagan issued an apology to Japanese Americans and signed the Civil Liberties Act of 1988 into law, the Seattle chapter of the JACL proposed a resolution to recognize the resisters:

Now, therefore, be it resolved that the JACL recognize those Japanese American draft resisters of World War II who declared their loyalty to their country, but who were also dedicated to the principle of defending their civil rights, were willing to make significant sacrifices to uphold their beliefs of patriotism in a different form from those who sacrificed their lives on the battlefields; and that they, too, deserve a place of honor and respect in the history of Americans of Japanese ancestry. . . . The JACL regrets any pain or bitterness caused by its failure to recognize this group of patriotic Americans and further resolves to educate our own community and the public that loyalty is not necessarily demonstrated in any singular form, but can be manifested in other praiseworthy and admirable acts, and that by this recognition the JACL strives to promote and nurture the healing process of an issue that has divided our community.[29]

After two years of study and review, delegates at the 1990 San Diego JACL national convention voted unanimously to adopt the resolution.[30]

For some, the resolution went too far. One veteran wrote, "Never in my life did I ever think that a group of well dressed, well-educated Sansei and Nisei would compose a heap of 'horse manure' such as Resolution 13," meaning the resolution adopted by the JACL. He continued in disgust, "To make matters worse they had to top it off with 'hog wash' when they tried to equate the 'courage' of the draft resisters to those of the volunteers who died in battle." He called the proposal sacrilegious and suggested that a recent earthquake in the Bay area had been caused when tens of thousands of veterans buried at the National Cemetery in San Bruno rolled over in their graves.[31]

Despite resistance on the part of some veterans who balked at the idea of putting draft resisters and volunteers on the same pedestal of patriotism, support for the resisters became more common. In 1991, Clifford Uyeda, then president of the Japanese American Historical Society, commented that it took courage to stand up against the government and that those who did risked not only felony convictions but also disapproval from members of their Japanese American communities:

> Possibly the greatest stigma to a [Japanese] family was a criminal record. Yet, these resisters were willing to go to a federal penitentiary. . . . The men who resisted and those who volunteered both did what they thought was right. We should honor both groups. They made their decisions based on what they thought was right, and took the consequences. This is the American way.[32]

Again, the draft was overlooked even as the resisters were being recognized. Uyeda's call to recognize "the men who resisted and those who volunteered" demonstrated the new language that dominated discussions about the resisters. There were volunteers, who should be praised for their sacrifice and bravery, and there were resisters, who should also be praised for their commitment to civil rights and their own version of bravery. Going to prison voluntarily was not easy, after all. But where did the draftees go? It appeared that they were victims of historical amnesia, too. George Oiye, a former detainee and veteran, said that it was not that anyone had really forgotten about these stories or had refused to tell them: "It's that people weren't ready to hear them." In 1992, he said, people were not only ready but also eager to know.[33]

The younger-generation JACL members, specifically those in the Northern California–Western Nevada–Pacific (NCWNP) district, did not think the JACL resolution adopted in 1990 went far enough. They wanted to see the national JACL honor those whom they had started calling the "Resisters of Conscience" at "an appropriate public ceremony." Their renewed call for an apology baffled some who thought the issue had already been put to rest. Ken Nakano, Mas Fukuhara, and Cherry Kinoshita responded to the call for a more public ceremony of recognition by saying that a ceremony was redundant. They wrote that even the resisters seemed uninterested. Emi told them, "The Fair Play Committee never really asked for an apology. This all came internally from some members of the JACL—especially the younger members." From this, the authors concluded that these young members were well-meaning, perhaps, but were looking for "a cause célèbre" and had created an issue where none had existed. Twila Tomita rebutted this view, arguing that a public ceremony provided a rich opportunity to educate the public. Perhaps the resisters had not asked for an apology, but few historians and even fewer nonhistorians knew about the resisters, and fewer yet understood their cause. He wrote, "Wartime JACL leaders denounced them as 'cowardly' or 'deluded.'" But in 1999, Tomita said, "The resisters' stand is a model of how to deal with the infringement of civil rights." He said the JACL of the new millennium should hold up the resisters as a model for future generations. The context had changed. Japanese Americans needed new heroes for the civil rights battles they would face in the next century.[34]

THE GORDON HIRABAYASHI RECREATION SITE

While Nikkei were still debating whether the JACL should sponsor a public ceremony recognizing the resisters, the Tucsonians received recognition of their own from an unexpected source. Archaeologist Mary Farrell discovered that a former prison on the Coronado National Forest near Tucson had once housed several Japanese American draft resisters, including one very famous Nisei resister, Hirabayashi. She and her husband, Jeff Burton, archaeologist for the National Parks Department, were already working on a survey of the sites of Japanese American confinement during the war.[35] Realizing that a site of such historical significance was under her jurisdiction in the Catalina National Forest, with the support of National Forest administrators, Farrell spearheaded a massive effort to rename the site in Hirabayashi's honor.[36]

Renaming a prison in honor of one of the inmates was unusual, but the idea won instant support from a broad coalition of National Forest administrators, Japanese Americans, community activists, journalists, and scholars. Farrell knew that this site was important for many reasons. First and foremost,

Unveiling of the interpretive kiosk, Gordon Hirabayashi Recreation Site, August 2001.
Left to right: Roger Nasevema (Hopi), Ken Yoshida (Tucsonian/Topaz), Gordon Hirabayashi,
Susumu Yenokida (Tucsonian/Amache), Harry Yoshikawa (Tucsonian/Chicago-Denver),
Noboru Taguma (Tucsonian/Amache). *(Photograph by Martha Nakagawa. Courtesy of Martha
Nakagawa.)*

Hirabayashi was now quite famous for his principled stand. Peter Irons had
already compared him to such great civil rights leaders as Martin Luther King,
Jr., for his willingness to stand up for a moral commitment to a higher law. She
also knew that the resisters were important for similar reasons. In a post-Vietnam,
post–cold war context, it was easy for someone like Farrell to recognize the civil
rights bravery of their stance. Still, choosing a figure like Hirabayashi to name
the site after demonstrated that naming a public site after a draft resister on
National Forest land would not be an easy sell. Naming the former prison site
after Hirabayashi allowed the National Forest to garner impressive, broad-based
support from various levels of federal and local government, Japanese American groups, the JACL, and the community at large. In honoring the resisters
and Hirabayashi in the renaming and ribbon-cutting ceremony, she was able to
spark a discussion about those who were not formally recognized in the name
but would be featured prominently in the interpretation of the site: the Tucsonians. The research needed for the site interpretation inspired and financially
supported an oral history project. The ceremony in 1999 and the unveiling of
an interpretive kiosk in 2001 brought resisters together who had never simul-
taneously stood on the site of their own wartime confinement even though the
site was where their lives had intersected so many years before.

JACL APOLOGY

While resisters were being recognized alongside such figures as Hirabayashi in Tucson, their children, in some cases, were actively working to receive broad-based recognition and a public apology for the resisters from the JACL. In 2000, the JACL national delegation voted to recognize the resisters in a public ceremony. The younger generation of JACL leaders, the Sansei generation, and by the year 2000 the fourth generation, Yonsei, wanted to show that they acknowledged the moral basis for resisting the draft and had put old animosi-ties to rest. As Kenji Taguma, son of Tucsonian resister Noboru Taguma, said, "We Sansei and Yonsei, with our liberated spirit, would probably say that we would have fought and resisted the internment order in any way we could. This is much easier said than done." But the least they could do was honor a new group of war heroes. The younger generation voted for an apology, represent-ing the majority of the JACL national delegation, but an older minority dis-agreed and walked out of the meeting in protest.[37]

If the language of an apology still focused on the loyal resistance of the resisters, the people who worked hardest for an apology knew that more was· at stake. Their own lives crossed the boundaries of strict wartime definitions of loyalty. Kenji Taguma's father was not just a resister—his father and uncle had each renounced his citizenship in an effort to reunite the family. Others who worked to educate the public about the resisters through newspaper arti-cles and events that highlighted the constitutional basis for resistance were children of the resisters, the "no-no boys," and renunciants. But, as Farrell had chosen Hirabayashi as the figure around which the story of the resisters at Tucson would be told, an apology to the principled resisters—the loyal resist-ers of conscience—would open the door for larger discussions about wartime resistance and obsolete definitions of disloyalty.

As the momentum built toward a JACL apology for the resisters, books and documentaries became available that not only told the resister story but also, in the case of *Rabbit in the Moon* in particular, pushed the boundaries of debates over wartime resistance.[38] This film portrayed the resisters as the heroes and the JACL as the "jackals" and presented the decisions some made to renounce their citizenship as a fairly rational outcome of their wartime mis-treatment that in no way infringed on their ability to call themselves good Americans. The film and the increased attention given to the draft resisters made tensions flair within some circles of Japanese Americans.

On May 11, 2002, approximately three hundred people gathered to wit-ness a historic event: Floyd Mori, national president of the JACL, delivered a formal apology to those Japanese Americans who resisted the draft not in opposition to military service itself but out of protest against their unconstitu-tional incarceration during the war. According to Ken Yoshida, one of the last surviving members of the Tucsonians, this apology marked the final chapter in a story that had begun at least sixty years before.

The apology may have marked the beginning of a final chapter in a very long story of citizenship and civil disobedience, but it did not resolve all the conflicts between the actors. Not all JACL members agreed with the resolution. Rumors spread throughout the Bay Area that a group of veterans planned to attend the ceremony and stand with their backs to the resisters while they were being recognized. No such demonstration took place, but support for the apology never was unanimous. Even resisters disagreed with each other about the apology. Some said it was unnecessary. Norikane almost did not attend the ceremony, because he said he did not need an apology: He already knew that he had been true to his own conscience. However, he went to recognize the efforts of a new generation who needed to state publicly that they would have done things differently had they been in charge during the war. Others, such as Emi (one of the seven leaders of the Heart Mountain Fair Play Committee), argued that the apology did not go far enough:

> I wish to extend my appreciation to the JACL for sponsoring this cere-mony. As a civil rights organization, I believe it is a step in the right direc-tion. Having said that, I think it would be entirely appropriate for JACL to go one step further and hold a program directed towards the Japanese American community for the excesses committed by wartime JACL lead-ers, such as acting as informants for the government causing many inno-cent people to suffer, as recorded in the *Lim Report*. I believe such action would finally put to rest JACL's unholy ghosts of the past and would be a worthy way to start the 21st Century. The United States government apol-ogized for their wartime excesses. Can JACL do less?[39]

Emi was not the first to point out that an apology to the resisters omitted many individuals who had also made difficult, principled choices in defense of their civil rights during the war. Paul H. Ito wrote a letter in 1997 to the JACL president, pointing out that few knew anything about the veterans who refused to answer the loyalty questionnaires or the renunciants who gave up their citi-zenship under duress. He called for a full disclosure of Nikkei responses to their lack of rights during the war and a blanket JACL apology for not defend-ing Nikkei rights immediately.[40] But the JACL ceremony was more public, and the words of Emi were influential for those who heard him speak. For a short time, the resisters gained center stage. Twenty-one resisters came to the cere-mony and were recognized one at a time as "Resisters of Conscience," each of whom had taken a courageous stand to defend his beliefs in patriotism.

The ceremony, especially after Emi's bold remarks, sparked conversations about those who were not recognized. This group included not only those who were the renunciants and the "no-no boys," the expatriates and soldiers who refused to answer the loyalty questionnaires, but also all Japanese Ameri-cans who had suffered as a result of internal fighting over the limits of wartime citizenship and civil disobedience. The ceremony legitimized a group of resist-

Resisters at JACL ceremony, May 11, 2002, JCCNC, San Francisco, California. *Back row (left to right):* George Kurasaki (Heart Mountain), Bob Nagahara (Heart Mountain), Halley Minoura (Heart Mountain), son of Terry Uyemoto (Amache), Takashi Hoshizaki (Heart Mountain), Joyce Fumiko Kawasaki (daughter of Thomas Kawasaki of Amache), Gene Akutsu (Minidoka; also representing his late brother Jim Akutsu). *Middle row (left to right):* Susumu Yenokida (Amache; also representing his late brother Minoru Yenokida), James Uyeda (Heart Mountain), Noboru Taguma (Amache), Ken Yoshida (Topaz), Harry Yoshikawa (voluntary evacuee), Joe Norikane (Amache/Granada), Gloria Kubota (wife of Guntaro Kubota of Heart Mountain). *Front row (left to right):* Yoshito Kuromiya (Heart Mountain), Joe Yamakido (Jerome), George Nozawa (Heart Mountain), George Ishikawa (Heart Mountain), Frank Emi (Heart Mountain), Mitsuru Koshiyama (Heart Mountain), Toshi Kawamoto (wife of David Kawamoto of Heart Mountain), Dan Kubo (son of Yoshi Kubo of Amache). *(Photograph by Martha Nakagawa. Courtesy of Martha Nakagawa.)*

ers who had been cast aside and forgotten, and by doing so, their stories started to become part of most standard narratives of the Japanese American wartime experience. In the summer of 2008, the Japanese American National Museum organized a conference that brought together scholars, national leaders, and multiple generations of Japanese Americans to explore the topic of "Enduring Communities." The conference was held from July 3 through July 6 and offered activities for all ages, including a trip to Amache. Most impressive, though, was the fact that despite the wide-ranging audience and the historic relationship between JACL interests and the Japanese American National Museum, no topic was off limits. Finally, borrowing the language of Okihiro, the margins of Japanese American history had been integrated into the mainstream, creating a history that could not be contained in a single narrative but instead demonstrated the remarkable diversity and resiliency of the many histories of Japanese America and many Japanese American communities.[41]

CONCLUSION

The Changing Nature of Citizenship

༄༅

WHAT DO GORDON HIRABAYASHI'S and the Tucsonians' stories tell us about the changing nature of citizenship, civil disobedience, and historical memory? The aim of this book is not only to tell the stories of Hirabayashi and the Tucsonians but also to place their stories in historic and theoretical context. Making sense of their experiences brings together literature on childhood, resistance, citizenship, prisons, punishment, and historical memory.

Nisei started life with all the rights of citizenship and few of the responsibilities. Their teachers told them that their race would not prevent them from being 100 percent American, but life taught them that they might have to work harder than their white counterparts to achieve the same level of success. Nisei learned that being American also meant that when their rights were taken away, they were supposed to fight to defend those rights. But defending their rights as the country struggled to fight what some have called the "best war ever" was not always a popular decision.[1] As Joe Norikane said, he knew that during the war he was just making "a footstep in the sand of time" but that someday, someone would be curious about the resisters and would search for new meaning in his wartime civil disobedience.

The war forced Nisei to put the lessons of their childhood into practice. Would they give more than their white counterparts to prove their loyalty? Would they volunteer for service and obey the draft in the absence of their civil rights? Or would they fight, even against their own government, to defend the rights that had been theirs from birth? The war forced the issue that had been there all along. The lessons Nisei learned about their own citizenship as children were contradictory, and they chose different ways to react to these lessons. The lessons Nisei learned in school provided a moral basis for civil disobedience.

Hirabayashi and the Tucsonians fit into a long history of individuals who dared to resist the overwhelming authority of the state and in doing so more clearly defined for themselves what it meant to be citizens. The United States was shaped as a country by resisters, such as the early Quakers, abolitionists, labor activists, anarchists, suffragists, war resisters, and civil rights activists, not to mention the soldiers of the American Revolution. Hirabayashi and the Tucsonians were self-consciously aware of this history and knew that by resisting they were not alone, even if ultimately each stood alone before a judge. Hirabayashi found strength and inspiration from the writings of Jawaharlal Nehru, Mahatma Gandhi, and the independence movement in India. He was supported through fellowship by the Quakers, the Christian Student Movement, and the Fellowship of Reconciliation. The Tucsonians looked to the leaders of the American Revolution for inspiration and cited the Boston Tea Party as a very "American" example of resistance. Some Tucsonians followed Hirabayashi's story of continued resistance in the newspapers and were proud to follow in his footsteps when they arrived at the Tucson road camp not long after Hirabayashi had left.

Hirabayashi and the Tucsonians resisted based on their direct experiences with injustice and their own understandings of the nature of citizenship and civil rights. The individual natures of their resistance make it hard to put them into one category when dominant narratives of heroes and patriots tell simple stories of right and wrong, heroes and villains. But, like those of other famous resisters, their stories are more interesting and ripe for complex analysis because of their diversity.

The experiences of Hirabayashi and the Tucsonians demonstrate that citizenship is not static. Historically, the U.S. government has maintained at least two paths to citizenship: the very restrictive version based on earning citizenship and the liberal version based on mere birth in the nation.[2] Depending on the needs of the state at any given time, one version seems to gain preference over the other. In the 1920s, the nation needed the children of immigrants to see themselves as full citizens, as nonhyphenated Americans, to defend against the growing fear that immigrants and their children threatened some core essence of Americanism. Nisei who believed they were 100 percent American regardless of ancestry served the needs of the state and built up a reciprocal foundation of trust and loyalty. But war changed everything. Suddenly the state needed to defend itself against enemies, foreign and domestic.

Nisei became trapped for a time in a dynamic process in which the state tried to decide what it needed from this group of Japanese Americans. First, they were citizens in need of protection. Then, in the face of growing racial hysteria on the West Coast, the state reclassified them as non-aliens, or at times even enemy aliens, and forced them into camps with their alien parents. But how could a nation fighting racism abroad keep an entire population behind barbed wire? Would this not create a large population of citizen enemies?

The state faced an impossible dilemma, and the solution emerged only gradually: The state would restore only the obligations of Nisei citizens and call them "rights" as a means of recognizing Nisei citizenship while maintaining wartime authority over a population still treated like suspect citizens.

During the war, the state tried to control the terms of debate over the meaning of Nisei citizenship. Using euphemistic language to cloak the unconstitutional nature of the state's policies for citizen Nisei, the government called them not citizens but "non-aliens" in orders for exclusion. They were placed not in camps or prisons but in "relocation centers." Nisei could earn back their citizenship by embracing their "right" to defend their country and to serve on the "same basis" as other Americans in the military even though they clearly were not serving on the same basis at all.

Nisei fought against the endless creative realities and embraced the euphemisms for their own purposes. For leaders of the Japanese American Citizens League (JACL), this meant embracing their obligations to restore their rights. The government was not nearly as interested in reshaping public opinion as Nisei were, but it would take extraordinary means to reshape public opinion once Japanese Americans had already suffered the stigma of being forced from their homes and into prisonlike confinement under suspicion of future acts of sabotage. It would be much easier to return to the West Coast if they could be greeted as loyal Americans and not as suspicious prisoners of war. The JACL encouraged Nisei to volunteer for the military to promote the image of extraordinary loyalty, but in some camps, such as Topaz and Amache, the majority voted for some form of resistance to Nisei service in segregated combat units while their citizenship rights remained unclear.

State hegemony is never absolute. The War Department did not fully recognize this fact when it designed the plan to reintroduce military service for Japanese Americans. It did not expect broad-based resistance against registration or strong objections from Japanese Americans to their induction into racially segregated combat teams. In response to agitation from below, the War Department and the War Relocation Authority (WRA) had to design ways to encourage the desired response through the propaganda of patriotism combined with the threat of criminal prosecution. While threatening Nisei with prison, they also enticed them to give up some of their demands for equality with the promise that proving themselves loyal to the country through extraordinary sacrifices on the battlefield was in their best interest. The combined use of persuasion and criminal prosecution demonstrates the fact that the state could not dominate through absolute hegemonic rule. It had to gain the voluntary compliance and cooperation of at least some Japanese Americans.[3]

Some of the Tucsonians embraced their claims to Japanese citizenship rather than accept their partial wartime citizenship in the United States. At the root of many conflicts over the meaning and boundaries of citizenship is the question of dual citizenship. During World War II, Japanese Americans became the subject of intense debate over the meaning and limits of the Fourteenth

Amendment's guarantee of citizenship by birth regardless of race or ancestry. These debates focused in part on the theoretical dual citizenship of Nisei. The case of *Regan v. King* challenged Nisei rights to vote on the basis that the Fourteenth Amendment had been too broadly interpreted in the past. Supported by the Native Sons of the Golden West, this court case was initiated not only to strip Nisei of their voting rights; it was hoped that, by extension, the Fourteenth Amendment would be reinterpreted and the case of *Wong Kim Ark* would no longer serve as the primary legal precedent in deciding cases of contested citizenship.[4] Courts at all levels refused to reinterpret the Fourteenth Amendment and instead reaffirmed the right of all persons, regardless of race or nationality, to birthright citizenship.

The *Regan v. King* case was not the last word on Nisei citizenship. When Nisei were reclassified as IV-C, or enemy aliens, by the Selective Service, the label was a real affront to their citizenship. When the War Department determined that Nisei would be eligible for the draft, even in the absence of basic rights to due process and freedom of movement, the ruling was an affront to their citizenship. When Nisei were processed for Selective Service not on the same basis as other Americans, when they were asked to first register their loyalty with a questionnaire given only to Japanese Americans, and when they were processed only as replacement soldiers for a segregated combat unit in the army, these processes were affronts to their citizenship. In an attempt to negotiate a change, Nisei tried a variety of resistance techniques to engage the state in a dialogue about the meaning of their citizenship. This dialogue sometimes took the form of refusing to obey the draft or renouncing their U.S. citizenship.

When the war ended, another case emerged that helped answer questions that had caused so much distress during the war: Who gets to decide which citizenship the United States will recognize when individuals have legal rights to multiple citizenships? Ironically, the War Department had approached this problem in 1941 when it feared that Nisei men might be called upon to serve Japan in a time of war. This fear that a foreign nation would claim the service of dual nationals living in the United States drove many policies that stripped Nisei of their rights in the first year of the war. But by the time the War Department voted to restore Selective Service for Nisei in 1944, this fear had seemingly disappeared. Instead, Nisei could not profess their disloyalty enough to escape the obligation of military service. By the end of the war, this shift toward the nation's ability to claim citizens even in the face of deliberate attempts on the part of individuals to choose foreign citizenship over U.S.-born citizenship was upheld by the courts. In the case of *Kawakita v. United States,* Tomoya Kawakita was a Nisei with dual citizenship who was in Japan when the war began and had his name added to his family register in Japan to lay claim his Japanese citizenship. After the war, though, he tried to reclaim his U.S. citizenship to return to the United States. Recognized by U.S. servicemen as someone who had assisted in the torture of U.S. soldiers in Japan, he was arrested and tried for treason. He lost his case and was convicted of treason when the courts ruled that unless the United States accepted a citizen's application for renunciation of citizenship, that person not only was still a citizen but also was obligated to defend the United States in a time of war.

The Kawakita case is often overlooked as a major benchmark in determining the limits of citizens' rights to expatriate or to renounce their citizenship.[5] More often cited is the case of *Afroyim v. Rusk,* a case that the Supreme Court did not decide until 1967, when it declared that the United States could not involuntarily revoke the citizenship of an individual.[6] Between the Kawakita case, when the Supreme Court declared that the method an individual uses to renounce his or her citizenship must be acceptable to the United States, and the Afroyim case, which determined that the state could not involuntarily strip an individual of his or her citizenship, it became clear that citizenship is a dialectical relationship. Even though these two cases are separated by fifteen years, they have the combined effect of requiring the individual and the state to agree about when and how the relationship of citizenship is to be severed.

SIGNIFICANCE OF BROAD-BASED RESISTANCE TO SELECTIVE SERVICE

Petitions, resolutions, letters of concern, and consultations with lawyers were some of the ways that Japanese Americans demonstrated their concern over the draft early in 1944, but by the end of that year, their concern had been refocused on the high casualty rate among Nisei serving in the military. At first, Nisei men insisted that they were not being treated as other Americans were: They were still being sent into segregated units. They remained behind barbed wire, where their citizenship status was murky. Women entered the argument, too, as mothers of citizen soldiers. They had raised their sons to give service to their country, but they suggested that they would withhold their sons' service until their rights were restored. By extension, women demanded that their rights as mothers be acknowledged as well. By the end of 1944, Nisei men were honored as soldier citizens and were revered as heroes in death. Issei mothers were honored for the patriotic sacrifices that they shared with mothers throughout the country, even though they remained behind barbed wire.[7]

Early resistance to the draft enjoyed widespread support. Those resisters who eventually went to prison for civil disobedience represent only the most visible remainder of a much larger effort to resist partial restoration of Nisei citizenship. Some scholars would say that for early protests against the draft to be considered resistance, they had to effect change. By this criterion, can any of the early responses against the draft be considered resistance? Resistance in Topaz against registration certainly brought about some change, even though that change was far more favorable for Issei than for Nisei. Issei achieved success when they were allowed to respond to a revised questionnaire that, among other things, did not force them to choose between loyalty to the United States and their Japanese citizenship—the only citizenship for which they were legally eligible due to racially restrictive naturalization laws in the United States. Draft-age Nisei men in Topaz, especially the vocal Kibei, did not enjoy being threatened with prosecution under the Espionage Act when they threatened to refuse to answer the registration questions until their citizenship was fully restored. Even though their efforts to regain full citizenship did not succeed, their protest forced the state to clarify that their registration was legally part of the Selective Service process. The fact that the basis of Nisei protest against registration was its relationship to military service and to the Selective Service process makes this the first phase of resistance against the draft. The outcome was not favorable, but the resistance did effect change.

The next phase of widespread resistance to the draft came the following year in the form of petitions sent to the WRA and to the War Department. The widespread dissent at the beginning of 1944 led the WRA to stop classifying individuals as "disloyal" merely because they threatened to resist the draft. The WRA, at least at Amache, also stopped sending draft-age Nisei to Tule Lake for requesting expatriation, as doing so was seen as an attempt to avoid the draft. Furthermore, the War Department made an important fundamental shift in favor of treating all draft-age Nisei as if their birth in the country made them quite eligible for involuntary induction into the military regardless of the extremes to which individuals went to profess their "disloyalty." As we see in Hirabayashi's case, his refusal to fill out the loyalty questionnaire did not prevent the Selective Service from processing him for induction into alternative service in a Civilian Public Service camp. This attitude sharply contrasted with the universal mistrust the War Department held for Nisei in 1941. This turning point in War Department policies and WRA treatment of Nisei reinforced the fact that Nisei had become citizens once again, but only in terms of their wartime obligations to the state as soldiers. Evidence clearly shows that early resistance against this shift toward the partial restoration of Nisei rights was widely supported, although clearly not universally supported, among the incarcerated population of Nikkei.

The majority of Nikkei who protested Nisei being drafted into segregated combat units while their families were detained and their own citizenship rights remained in limbo did so through a direct process of petitioning the state for a change in policy or at least additional reassurances that service in the military would lead to a full restoration of rights. Despite the ambiguity of Japanese Americans' legal standing, they continued to act upon the political rights they did retain, especially the right to petition the state with their grievances.[8]

Citizens in a democracy are free to refuse the demands of the state and to disobey the law, but they must accept the consequences of prison. In the case of some Nisei in Amache, they refused to accept simple definitions of their citizenship. Instead, they drew on ways of defining their citizenship that defied the simple polarities of loyal soldier citizen versus disloyal draft dodger. Invoking the right of civil disobedience that repositions the ultimate source of authority over defining obligations to the state with the citizens themselves, some Nisei refused to comply with the draft when other forms of resistance failed. The majority of Nikkei reaffirmed the authority of the state to raise an army and redefined Nisei citizenship in limited terms when their resistance stopped short of civil disobedience. As John P. Diggins wrote in his analysis of civil disobedience in American political thought, the state derives its authority through the voluntary obedience of its subjects. When faced with the threat of prison terms, most complied with the draft, but this does not mean that they did not first try to resist.[9]

PRISONS, PATRIOTS, AND STORIES OF CITIZENSHIP

Prison became the place where Hirabayashi and the Tucsonians' ideas about themselves and their citizenship crystallized. The prison experience has a tremendous effect on an individual. For Hirabayashi, prison exposed him to other people's ideas about pacifism. In the early months of the war, Hirabayashi was prepared to comply with the Selective Service and even as a pacifist was ready to provide alternative service in a CPS camp. But after going to prison in Tucson and meeting pacifists who refused to cooperate in any way with the Selective Service system, he eventually came to that way of thinking as well. When he went to prison the second time for refusing the Selective Service process, he fought against the racially based, segregated way in which prisoners were moved from the initial holding tank to more permanent housing. He was prepared to go on a hunger strike if necessary to achieve his goal. In Tucson, he learned from others how inmates can shape the prison. At McNeil Island, he took that a step further and decided that every time he obeyed an order, he would do it consciously rather than blindly obeying out of habit. His prison experiences shaped Hirabayashi as a person and led him to prison one more time before the war was done.

The Tucsonians were shaped by their prison experiences, too. They emerged more convinced than ever that the decisions leading them to prison were justified. They faced insults and marginalization after prison, but they found through prison that they had become part of a larger community of resisters. They developed lifelong friendships and sustained each other for decades, not always needing to talk about prison or what led them to prison, but always knowing that they shared a common bond as resisters.

The punishment that citizens received for asserting their own definitions of citizenship represents a critical yet often underexamined aspect of citizenship theory. Michel Foucault's *Discipline and Punish: The Birth of the Prison* is helpful in this regard. As societies and the relationship between individuals and the state change, so do methods of punishment. Moving from public executions to silent isolation in prisons in the eighteenth and nineteenth centuries, states capitalized on the worst fears of the populace as a means of punishing deviant behaviors.[10] By the early twentieth century, penology had moved away from punishment toward rehabilitation.

In this climate of prison reform, where prison felt like "summer camp" compared with other forms of confinement, the state demonstrated that wartime propaganda casting resisters as disloyal and un-American, combined with threats of lengthy confinement and the loss of citizenship rights associated with felony convictions, was a more effective form of punishment and even a stronger deterrent than the prison experience itself. Following Foucault's theoretical framework, the relationship between punishment and prison shifted again. Resisters were "punished" in a variety of ways before their convictions—and for years afterward—but prison itself was supposed to be rehabilitating. The War Department and the Federal Bureau of Prisons agreed to offer felons early parole in exchange for their induction into the military. Combined with the War Department's insistence that Japanese Americans must rehabilitate their citizenship through military service, the line that separated felonious prisoners and citizen soldiers began to fade. The wartime propaganda that purported a cataclysmic divide between prisoners and patriots does not withstand close examination. The title of this book, *Prisons and Patriots*, refers to this socially constructed dichotomy, and through this study, we see that prisons created patriots in multiple ways.

Interviews conducted with Hirabayashi and the Tucsonians provide part of the narrative framework for this book; as oral historians know, memories change over time, and the stories we collect are often shaped by the narrator's present in ways that alter the specific details about the past. This does not mean that we must then question oral histories as a source any more or less than we should question the extensive errors, silences, and revisions in the historical literature on Japanese Americans. Instead, as oral historian and theorist Alessandro Portelli made clear, it is important to analyze why stories change over time and to look for errors or omissions, exploring what they tell us about that evolving nature of historical memory.[11]

The resisters' stories have changed over time. In conducting interviews, attending resister events, and researching this topic from 1999 to the present, I noticed the slight but significant ways in which the stories of some individuals changed and demanded some theoretical interpretation. In some cases, the resisters' stories became more detailed and nuanced over the years. As one Tucsonian mentioned, being asked repeatedly about stories that nobody wanted to hear for fifty-five years has had the effect of restoring his own memories of the past. But some resisters started dropping tiny details of their lives in ways that might not have been perceptible to the casual observer and may or may not have been intentional on the part of the resister. Although younger generations of Japanese Americans started looking to the resisters as civil rights heroes, these conversations were still cast in terms of loyalty and patriotism. Resisters were being described as resisters of conscience—loyal to the

United States but unwilling to participate in a system that had robbed them of their rights. Framed in this way, it became less convenient for individuals whose own lives crossed a new boundary between patriots and disloyal resisters, between draft resisters and others, such as the "no-no boys" and renunciants, to tell their complete stories. Some (but not all) of the Tucsonians who had renounced their citizenship or had requested repatriation and some who had justified their resistance by rejecting their U.S. citizenship and embracing their Japanese citizenship dropped or minimized these parts of their stories in follow-up interviews and public speaking engagements. It was easier for a contemporary audience to understand the resisters in terms of the Heart Mountain Fair Play Committee if they used the same language of pure constitutional principles. This does not mean in any way that they did not also believe in, write about, and profess the same constitutional principles as did the members of the Fair Play Committee, but some parts of the story could be left out if these details muddied the waters in an era when draft resisters were treated like patriots, but renunciants and "no-no boys" remained suspect.

When I started researching this topic, I began with stories given to me by Hirabayashi and the Tucsonians who came to Tucson for the ribbon cutting and site renaming in 1999. Like a museum that is seeking to tell a story but has no artifacts, I said goodbye to the resisters after a weekend of ceremony and oral history collection and began searching for ways to put their stories into context. I found that context in archives throughout the country and in the published works of other historians. Even though the artifacts of memory sometimes are not physical artifacts, the individuals whom I have met over the past twelve years and the individuals whom I never met but who left their words in archives and in books have contributed parts of themselves to this story and helped construct the narrative, as donors help construct the exhibits of a museum. This has been a collaborative project, and their memories have shaped the final product.[12]

Citizenship changes over time, as do personal stories and memories. Even history does not remain static. When the government itself admitted that it had made the grave error of incarcerating one hundred twenty thousand civilians without due process, Japanese American youth were inspired to stand up and to declare publicly that, if given the chance, they would have done things differently, too. But this is speculation. They did not suffer through that past. They were in the present making their own version of history useful to their needs. The contests over Nisei citizenship evolved in the form of disagreements over their wartime rights and responsibilities and over an even longer period when historians and citizens imagined, revised, and reinvented how the resisters should be remembered.

NOTES

⚜

A NOTE ON TERMINOLOGY

1. For an example of another study that does not hyphenate ethnic group names for the same reasons, see Judy Yung, *Unbound Feet: A Social History of Chinese Women in San Francisco* (Berkeley: University of California Press, 1995), ix. For an example of a scholar who disagrees with this interpretation and instead urges scholars to use the hyphenated form "Japanese-American," see William Hohri, ed., *Resistance: Challenging America's Wartime Internment of Japanese-Americans* (Lomita, CA: Epistolarian, 2001), 7–8.

2. U.S. War Relocation Authority, "A Challenge to Democracy," Washington, DC, 1944. Internet archive, Prelinger Collection, available at www.archive.org/details/Challeng 1944 (accessed September 6, 2010).

3. *A Resolution of the National Council of the Japanese American Citizens League to Support the "Power of Words" Proposal Which Relates to Euphemisms and Misnomers in Reference to the World War II Experience of Japanese Americans,* adopted by the National Council of Japanese American Citizens League, 2011, available at www.pnwjacl.org/documents/ R-2PowerofWordsresolution-Adopted.pdf (accessed June 19, 2011). See also "Resolution on Terminology," adopted by the Civil Liberties Public Education Fund, available at www .momomedia.com/CLPEF/backgrnd.html (accessed June 19, 2011); Roger Daniels, "Words Do Matter," *Discover Nikkei,* available at www.discovernikkei.org/en/journal/2008/2/1/ words-do-matter (accessed June 10, 2011); and Aiko Herzig-Yoshinaga, "Words Can Lie or Clarify: Terminology of the World War II Incarceration of Japanese Americans," *Discover Nikkei,* available at www.discovernikkei.org/en/journal/article/3246/ (accessed June 19, 2011).

INTRODUCTION

1. Joe Norikane, diary, 1943–1944.

2. Joe Norikane, interview with the author and Nicole Branton, May 11, 2002, San Francisco, California.

3. Ibid.

4. Gordon Hirabayashi Recreation Site, Coronado National Forest, Arizona.

5. Florencia Mallon, *Peasant and Nation: The Making of Postcolonial Mexico and Peru* (Berkeley: University of California Press, 1995); Mark Thurner, *From Two Republics to One*

Divided: Contradictions of Postcolonial Nationmaking in Andean Peru (Durham, NC: Duke University Press, 1997); Peter Guardino, *Peasants, Politics, and the Formation of Mexico's National State: Guerrero, 1800–1857* (Stanford, CA: Stanford University Press, 1996).

6. For an introduction to this literature, see Linda Kerber, *No Constitutional Right to Be Ladies: Women and the Obligations of Citizenship* (New York: Hill and Wang, 1998).

7. Rogers Smith, *Civic Ideals: Conflicting Visions of Citizenship in U.S. History* (New Haven, CT: Yale University Press, 1997).

8. Linda Kerber, "The Meanings of Citizenship," *Journal of American History* 84 (December 1997): 833.

9. Alice Yang Murray, *Historical Memories of the Japanese American Internment and the Struggle for Redress* (Stanford, CA: Stanford University Press, 2008).

10. Eric Muller, *Free to Die for Their Country: The Story of the Japanese American Draft Resisters in World War II* (Chicago: University of Chicago Press, 2001), 149.

11. James C. Scott, *Weapons of the Weak: Everyday Forms of Peasant Resistance* (New Haven, CT: Yale University Press, 1985).

12. Peter Irons, *Justice at War* (New York: Oxford University Press, 1983).

CHAPTER 1

1. Joe Norikane, Noboru Taguma, Hideo Takeuchi, Ken Yoshida, and Harry Yoshikawa, interview with the author and Peter Taylor, Tucson, Arizona, November 6, 1999.

2. Isami Arifuku Waugh, Alex Yamato, and Raymond Y. Okamura, "Japanese Americans in California," in *Five Views: An Ethnic Historic Site Survey for California* (Sacramento: State of California, Department of Parks and Recreation, Office of Historic Preservation, 1988), available at www.nps.gov/history/history/online_books/5views/5views4.htm (accessed June 19, 2011).

3. *Westminster School District of Orange County, et al., v. Mendez, et al.*, 161 F.2d 774 (1947); Waugh, Yamato, and Okamura, "Japanese Americans in California."

4. For a book devoted entirely to the topic of "growing up Nisei," see David K. Yoo, *Growing Up Nisei: Race, Generation, and Culture among Japanese Americans of California, 1924–49* (Urbana: University of Illinois Press, 2000). For an introduction to literature on children and adolescents as historical agents, see Eliot West and Paula Evans Petrik, eds., *Small Worlds: Children and Adolescents in America, 1850–1950* (Lawrence: University of Kansas Press, 1992); and John Modell, *Into One's Own: From Youth to Adulthood in the United States, 1920–1975* (Berkeley: University of California Press, 1989).

5. Roger Daniels, *The Politics of Prejudice: The Anti-Japanese Movement in California and the Struggle for Japanese Exclusion* (Berkeley: University of California Press, 1977); Mae Ngai, *Impossible Subjects: Illegal Aliens and the Making of Modern America* (Princeton, NJ: Princeton University Press, 2004); Aristide Zolberg, *A Nation by Design: Immigration Policy in the Fashioning of America* (Cambridge, MA: Harvard University Press, 2006).

6. Mae Ngai, "The Architecture of Race in American Immigration Law: A Reexamination of the Immigration Act of 1924," *Journal of American History* 86, no. 1 (June 1999): 67–92; House, *Hearing at Seattle, Washington, before the House Sub-Committee on Immigration and Naturalization, 27 July 1920*, as reprinted in Toyokichi Iyenaga and Kenoske Sato, *Japan and the California Problem* (New York: G. P. Putnam's Sons, 1921), 203–229.

7. Nationality Act of 1899, *Official Gazette*, Issue 66 (Japan, March 16, 1899); 1916 Amendment to the Nationality Act of 1899, *Official Gazette*, Issue 27, Articles 18–26 (Japan, March 16, 1916); Durward V. Sandifer, "A Comparative Study of Laws Relating to Nationality at Birth and to Loss of Nationality," *American Journal of International Law* 29 (1935): 248–279.

8. *Elk v. Wilkins,* 112 U.S. 94 (1884).

9. Klancy Clark de Nevers, *The Colonel and the Pacifist: Karl Bendetsen, Perry Saito and the Incarceration of Japanese Americans during World War II* (Salt Lake City: University of Utah Press, 2004); House, *Hearing at Seattle, Washington, before the House Sub-Committee on Immigration and Naturalization, 27 July 1920.*

10. "Japanese Testify at Local Hearing, American-Born Youth Tells Committee That He Does Not Recognize Any Claim Mikado May Have on Him," *Seattle Daily Times,* July 27, 1920.

11. Philip M. Glick, Memorandum to Dillon S. Myer, "Domicil: A Factor in Regard to Dual Citizenship," Manzanar, California, April 9, 1943, Record Group 210, Section 16, Box 229, Folder 31.009-1, National Archives and Records Administration, Washington, D.C. [hereafter cited as NARA RG 210]; Carey McWilliams, "Dual Citizenship," *Far Eastern Survey* 11, no. 23 (1942): 231–233.

12. Elliot Grinnell Mears, *Resident Orientals on the American Pacific Coast: The Asian Experience in North America: Chinese and Japanese* (Chicago: University of Chicago Press, 1928), 107–108, 429, quoted in *Hirabayashi v. U.S.,* 320 U.S. 81 (1943), 98, fn 8.

13. Edward K. Strong, *The Second-Generation Japanese Problem* (Stanford, CA: Stanford University Press, 1934), 142.

14. Ibid., 142–143; Glick, Memorandum to Dillon S. Myer, "Domicil"; McWilliams, "Dual Citizenship," 231–233.

15. Eileen H. Tamura, *Americanization, Acculturation, and Ethnic Identity: The Nisei Generation in Hawaii* (Urbana: University of Illinois Press, 1994), 35.

16. Yuji Ichioka, "Dai Nisei Mondai: Changing Japanese Immigrant Conceptions of the Second-Generation Problem, 1902–1941," in *Before Internment: Essays in Prewar Japanese American History,* ed. Gordon H. Chang and Eiichiro Azuma (Stanford, CA: Stanford University Press, 2006), 8; Ichioka, "A Study in Dualism: James Yoshinori Sakamoto and the *Japanese American Courier,* 1928–1942," *Amerasia Journal* 13 (1986–1987): 49–81; Tamura, *Americanization, Acculturation, and Ethnic Identity;* Yoo, *Growing Up Nisei.*

17. Ichioka, "A Study in Dualism"; Vicki Ruiz, *From Out of the Shadows: Mexican Women in Twentieth-Century America* (New York: Oxford University Press, 2008), 50.

18. Kazua Kawai, "Three Roads," *Survey Graphic* 56, no. 3 (May 1, 1926).

19. Henry Yu, *Thinking Orientals: Migration, Contact, and Exoticism in Modern America* (New York: Oxford University Press, 2001), 103–104; Paul R. Spickard, *Japanese Americans: The Formations and Transformations of an Ethnic Group* (New York: Twayne Publishers, 1996), 6.

20. *Japanese American Courier* (August 30; September 6, 13, and 20; October 4, 1930), quoted in Yuji Ichioka, "A Study in Dualism: James Yoshinori Sakamoto and the *Japanese American Courier,* 1928–1942," *Amerasia Journal* 13 (1986–1987): 54.

21. House Committee on Immigration and Naturalization, *Hearings on H.R. 5879,* 77th Cong., 1st sess., October 29, 1941.

22. Ibid., 10.

23. Ibid., 16–18.

24. Ibid., 49–58.

25. Ibid., 41–42.

26. Commander Hartwell C. Davis, speaking for a bill to amend the Nationality Act of 1940, on November 12, 1941, to the House Subcommittee of the Committee on Immigration and Naturalization, H.R. 5879, 77th Cong., 1st sess., *Congressional Record,* 9–10.

27. Ibid., 10–17.

28. John J. McCloy to Mr. E. M. Rowalt, September 1, 1943, NARA RG 210, Box 229/31.009, Folder 1; McWilliams, "Dual Citizenship," 231–233; "Dual Citizenship Status," *Rocky Shimpo* (June 2, 1944).

29. *United States v. Wong Kim Ark,* 169 U.S. 649 (1898).

30. Gordon Hirabayashi, interview with Louis Horn, Kirkland, Washington, 1990, Vertical File 574, Gordon K. Hirabayashi Papers, Special Collections, University of Washington, Seattle, Washington [hereafter cited as Hirabayashi Papers].

31. Hirabayashi, interview with Horn, 5; Gordon Hirabayashi, interview with the author, Tucson, Arizona, November 5, 1999.

32. Hirabayashi, interview with Horn, 1–5; James A. Hirabayashi, "Four Hirabayashi Cousins: A Question of Identity," in *Nikkei in the Pacific Northwest,* ed. Louis Fiset and Gail M. Nomura (Seattle: University of Washington Press, 2005), 149.

33. *State of Washington v. Taka Hirabayashi, et al., White River Gardens, Incorporated, et al.,* 133 Wash. 462 (1925).

34. Hirabayashi, "Four Hirabayashi Cousins," 146–170.

35. Frank F. Chuman, *The Bamboo People: The Law and Japanese-Americans* (Del Mar, CA: Publisher's Inc., 1976), 79.

36. Brian J. Gaines and Wendy K. Tam Cho, "On California's 1920 Alien Land Law: The Psychology and Economics of Racial Discrimination," *State Politics and Policy Quarterly* 4, no. 3 (2004): 271–293; Daniels, *Politics of Prejudice,* 66–77; Chuman, *Bamboo People,* 73–89.

37. California Board of Control, "California and the Oriental," 1920, as cited in Chuman, *Bamboo People,* 76.

38. Carey McWilliams, *Factories and the Field: The Story of Migratory Farm Labor in California* (Berkeley: University of California Press, 1939).

39. Chuman, *Bamboo People,* 76–89.

40. *The People of the State of California v. Hukichi Harada and Mine Harada, Sumi Harada and Yoshizo Harada,* Superior Court of the State of California, County of Riverside, 22 October 1918, Harada Family Collection, MS 98-108.36, Box A-15, Item 108, Riverside Metropolitan Museum, Riverside, California [hereafter cited as Harada Family Collection].

41. Chuman, *Bamboo People,* 117–119.

42. *California v. Harada.*

43. National Park Service, "National Historic Landmarks Program: Listing of National Historic Landmarks by State," available at www.nps.gov/nhl/designations/Lists/CA01.pdf (accessed September 14, 2010).

44. Attorney General Webb to F. C. Noble, Esq., December 21, 1915, Harada Family Collection, MS 98-108.36, Box A-15, Item 108; "Jap Minors May Own Land, Win in Alien Land Opinion," *Los Angeles Examiner,* January 5, 1916.

45. Chuman, *Bamboo People,* 79–80.

46. *Estate of Tetsubumi Yano,* 188 Cal. 645, 648 (206 P. 995).

47. *United States v. Wong Kim Ark,* 169 U.S. 649 (1898); *Yick Wo v. Hopkins,* 118 U.S. 356 (1886).

48. The title of the case lists the main defendant as Taka Hirabayashi, but the decision lists Taki Hirabayashi and his wife as the principal defendants. There is no explanation for the different spellings of Hirabayashi's first name. *Washington v. Hirabayashi.*

49. Ibid.

50. *State of Washington v. Chuski Kosai, et al.,* 133 Wash. 442 (1925).

51. Hirabayashi, "Four Hirabayashi Cousins," 150.

52. *Washington v. Kosai; State of Washington v. Ishikawa,* 139 Wash. 484 (1926).

53. "Deed of Reconveyance," [December 4, 1935] June 4, 1956; KK Company corporation minutes and records, Kubo Collection, Turlock, California.

54. Valerie Matsumoto, *Farming the Home Place: A Japanese American Community in California, 1919–1982* (Ithaca, NY: Cornell University Press, 1993), 25–31.

55. Ibid.

56. Ibid.

57. Susumu Yenokida, interview with Richard Potashin, Denver, Colorado, July 5, 2008, Manzanar National Historic Site Collection, Densho Digital Archive, available at http://densho.org/archive/default.asp (accessed October 12, 2010).

58. Matsumoto, *Farming the Home Place.*

59. Spickard, *Japanese Americans,* 72–73; Eiichiro Azuma, *Between Two Empires: Race, History, and Transnationalism in Japanese America* (New York: Oxford University Press, 2005).

60. Susumu Yenokida and Harry Yoshikawa, interview with the author and Nicole Branton, Tucson, Arizona, August 25, 2001.

61. Ibid.; Yoo, *Growing Up Nisei,* 108.

62. Nikkei Shimmin (July 15, 1930); as quoted in Edward K. Strong, and Reginald Bell, *Vocational Aptitudes of Second-Generation Japanese in the United States* (Stanford, CA: Stanford University Press, 1933), 13; Iyenaga and Sato, *Japan and the California Problem,* 149–150, 163–175; Yamato Ichihashi, *Japanese Immigration: Its Status in California* (San Francisco: R and E Research Associates, [1913] 1970); Yamato Ichihashi, *Japanese in the United States* (New York: Arno Press, [1932] 1969); Kiyoshi K. Kawakami, *The Real Japanese Question* (New York: Arno Press, [1921] 1978); Kiichi Kanzaki, *California and the Japanese* (San Francisco: R and E Research Associates, [1921] 1971).

63. Norikane et al., interview.

64. Ibid.

65. Him Mark Lai, "Teaching Chinese Americans to Be Chinese," in *Chinese American Transnationalism: The Flow of People, Resources, and Ideas between China and America during the Exclusion Era,* ed. Sucheng Chan (Philadelphia, PA: Temple University Press, 2006), 194–210.

66. Yuji Ichioka, "Kokugo Gakko: The Debate over the Role of Japanese-Language Schools," in *Before Internment: Essays in Prewar Japanese American History,* ed. Gordon H. Chang and Eiichiro Azuma (Stanford, CA: Stanford University Press, 2006), 92–126.

67. Yoo, *Growing Up Nisei,* 21; Frank Van Nuys, *Americanizing the West: Race, Immigrants, and Citizenship, 1890–1930* (Lawrence: University Press of Kansas, 2002); Reginald Bell, *Public School Education of Second-Generation Japanese in California* (New York: Arno Press, [1935] 1978).

68. School Code (1929), section 5.544, p. 272; *Report of the California Commission for the Study of Educational Problems* (Sacramento: California State Printing Office, 1931).

69. *Report of the California Commission for the Study of Educational Problems;* Strong, *Second-Generation Japanese Problem,* 5, 18, 20, 59, 158–159; Emory Bogardus, "Some Causes of Prejudice," *Los Angeles School Journal* 23 (December 21, 1928), 16–17, as cited in Yoo, *Growing Up Nisei,* 23–24.

70. The concept of the spread of modern racial ideologies comes from Peggy Pascoe's study of miscegenation laws and race in American history. Peggy Pascoe, "Miscegenation Law, Court Cases, and Ideologies of 'Race' in Twentieth-Century America," *Journal of American History* 83, no. 1 (1996): 44–69; and Pascoe, *What Comes Naturally: Miscegenation Law and the Making of Race in America* (New York: Oxford University Press, 2009).

71. Pascoe, "Miscegenation Law, Court Cases, and Ideologies of 'Race' in Twentieth-Century America"; Yu, *Thinking Orientals.*

72. Norikane et al., interview.

73. School Code (1929), section 5.544, p. 272; *Report of the California Commission for the Study of Educational Problems.*

74. Norikane et al., interview.

75. Ibid.

76. Gordon Hirabayashi, "Am I an American?" in *The Courage of Their Convictions: Sixteen Americans Who Fought Their Way to the Supreme Court,* ed. Peter Irons (New York: Penguin Books, 1990), 50–51.

77. Ken and Kay Yoshida, interview with the author and Nicole Branton, Tucson, Arizona, August 24, 2001.

78. Allison Varzally, *Making a Non-White America: Californians Coloring outside Ethnic Lines, 1925–1955* (Berkeley: University of California Press, 2008); Scott Kurashige, *The Shifting Grounds of Race: Black and Japanese Americans in the Making of Multiethnic Los Angeles* (Princeton, NJ: Princeton University Press, 2007).

79. Personal communications with Manzanar Oral History staff, April 2008.

80. Hirabayashi, interview with the author.

81. Ibid.

82. Norikane et al., interview.

CHAPTER 2

1. "Little Citizens Speak: 7th Graders of '43," *All Aboard* (Spring 1944): 27, Record Group 210, Field Basic Documentation, Central Utah, Publications Folder, Reel 4, National Archives and Records Administration, Washington, D.C. [hereafter cited as NARA RG 210, FBD].

2. Paul Spickard, "The Nisei Assume Power: The Japanese-American Citizens League, 1941–1942," *Pacific Historical Review* 52 (May 1983): 147–174; Donna K. Nagata, *Legacy of Injustice: Exploring the Cross-Generational Impact of the Japanese American Internment* (New York: Plenum Press, 1993).

3. Alice Yang Murray, *Historical Memories of the Japanese American Internment and the Struggle for Redress* (Stanford, CA: Stanford University Press, 2008), 30–31.

4. Joe Norikane, Noboru Taguma, Hideo Takeuchi, Ken Yoshida, and Harry Yoshikawa, interview with the author and Peter Taylor, Tucson, Arizona, November 6, 1999.

5. Ibid.; Stephen S. Fugita and Marilyn Fernandez, *Altered Lives, Enduring Community: Japanese Americans Remember Their World War II Incarceration* (Seattle: University of Washington Press, 2004), 3, 200–208; Tomi Kaizawa Knaefler, *Our House Divided: Seven Japanese American Families in World War II* (Honolulu: University of Hawaii Press, 1991), 8–9, 17; Dorothy Swaine Thomas and Richard S. Nishimoto, *The Salvage: Japanese American Relocation and Resettlement* (Berkeley: University of California Press, 1946), 330–350; John Tateishi, ed., "Mary Tsukamoto: Jerome," in *And Justice for All: An Oral History of the Japanese Detention Camps* (New York: Random House, 1984), 7.

6. *Inu* is a Japanese word for dog, which represents a pejorative accusation that one is a stool pigeon or, in this case, a spy or informer.

7. Susumu Yenokida and Harry Yoshikawa, interview with the author and Nicole Branton, Tucson, Arizona, August 25, 2001; Yosh Kuromiya, interview with Peter Taylor, Tucson, Arizona, November 8, 1999.

8. Frank S. Zelko, *Generation, Culture and Prejudice: The Japanese American Decision to Cooperate with Evacuation and Internment during World War II* (Melbourne, Australia: Monash Publications, 1992).

9. Greg Robinson, *A Tragedy of Democracy: Japanese Confinement in North America* (New York: Columbia University Press, 2009), 59–93; Klancy Clark de Nevers, *The Colonel and the Pacifist: Karl Bendetsen, Perry Saito and the Incarceration of Japanese Americans during World War II* (Salt Lake City: University of Utah Press, 2004); Peter Irons, *Justice Delayed: The Record of the Japanese American Internment Cases* (Middleton, CT: Wesleyan University Press, 1989).

10. John A. Rademaker to Edward H. Spicer, February 16, 1944, NARA RG 210, FBD, Community Analysis Reports, M 1342, Roll 15.

11. JACL loyalty oath, quoted in Frank Chin, *Born in the USA: A Story of Japanese America, 1889–1947* (Lanham, MD: Rowman and Littlefield, 2002), 308, 361.

12. Eric Muller, *Free to Die for Their Country: The Story of Japanese American Draft Resisters during World War II* (Chicago: University of Chicago Press, 2001), 20–22.

13. U.S. Congress, House, Select Committee Investigating National Defense Migration, *Hearings before the Select Committee Investigating National Defense Migration*, 77th Cong., 2d sess., 1942 (Washington, DC: Government Printing Office, 1942).

14. Tolan Committee hearings, March 7, 1942 (statement of Tokie Slocum, Togo Tanaka, Sam Minami, Fred Tayama, and Joseph Ninoda), quoted in Chin, *Born in the USA*, 278–281.

15. *Hearings before the Select Committee Investigating National Defense Migration*, pursuant to H.R. 113, a resolution to inquire further into the interstate migration of citizens, House of Representatives, 77th Cong., 2d sess., 11472–11473 (statement of James Sakamoto, JACL officer's testimony) [hereafter cited as Tolan Committee hearings].

16. Ibid.

17. Quoted in Daniels, *Concentration Camps U.S.A.*, 78.

18. Tolan Committee hearings, February 1942 (statement of James Omura), available at www.javoice.com/Omura.html (accessed September 4, 2008).

19. Daniels, *Concentration Camps, U.S.A.*; Robinson, *By Order of the President*; Weglyn, *Years of Infamy.*

20. Letter from James Y. Sakamoto to President Roosevelt (March 23, 1942), Japanese-American Evacuation and Relocation Survey Collection, Bancroft Library, Berkeley, California [hereafter cited as JERS, Bancroft Library].

21. Ibid.

22. Masaoka, "Final Report," quoted in *The Lim Report*, available at www.resisters .com/study/LimTOC.htm (accessed February 6, 2011).

23. Roger Daniels, *Prisoners without Trial: Japanese Americans in World War II*, rev. ed. (New York: Hill and Wang, 2004), 34–35.

24. House Committee on Immigration and Naturalization, *Hearings on H.R. 5879*, 77th Cong., 1st sess., November 12, 1941.

25. Lewis B. Hershey, director of Selective Service to Secretary of War Stimson, June 1, 1942. RG 389, Office of the Provost Marshal General, Box 1717, "Military Leave Clearance Jas," NARA, College Park, Maryland [hereafter cited as NARA RG 389].

26. Memorandum, Col. Alton C. Miller, director, Security and Investigations Division, Provost Marshal General's Office, to Assistant Chief of Staff, G-1, Lt. Col. E. Pasolli, July 31, 1945, RG 107, Office of the Secretary of War, Box 15, Folder "Loyalty Investigation," NARA, College Park, Maryland [hereafter cited as NARA RG 107].

27. Kubo Case Summary, 1944, Kubo Collection, Turlock, California [hereafter cited as Kubo Collection].

28. Memorandum to Mr. Dennis, RE: Gordon K. Hirabayashi, Order No. 265, Local Board No. 4, Seattle, Washington. RG 60, Classified Subject File—Correspondence, DOJ file 25-82-124, Hirabayashi, Box 1, NARA, College Park, Maryland.

29. Roger Daniels, *Concentration Camps U.S.A.: Japanese Americans and World War II* (New York: Holt, Rinehart, and Winston, 1971); Greg Robinson, *By Order of the President: FDR and the Internment of Japanese Americans* (Cambridge, MA: Harvard University Press, 2001); Michi Weglyn, *Years of Infamy: The Untold Story of America's Concentration Camps* (Seattle: University of Washington Press, 1996).

30. Linda Kerber, *No Constitutional Right to Be Ladies: Women and the Obligation of Citizenship* (New York: Hill and Wang, 1998), 221–302.

31. Peter Irons, *Justice at War* (New York: Oxford University Press, 1983), 100–101.

32. Form, "Charges, Information of Time and Manner of Answer," Wayne Miller, State Personnel Board, State of California, April 13, 1942, File A15.07, Japanese American

Evacuation and Resettlement Study, University of California Library, quoted in Irons, *Justice at War,* 101.

33. Report of the Commission on Wartime Relocation and Internment of Civilians, *Personal Justice Denied,* foreword by Tetsuden Kashima (Seattle: University of Washington Press, 1997), 36, 67–68 [hereafter cited as CWRIC].

34. Henry David Thoreau, "Resistance to Civil Government" (1849), as reprinted in *Civil Disobedience, and Other Essays* (New York: Dover Publications, 1993).

35. Gordon Hirabayashi, interview with Louis Horn, Kirkland, Washington, 1990, MS 3159, Special Collections, University of Washington, Seattle, Washington; Gordon Hirabayashi interview with the author and Nicole Branton, Tucson, Arizona, August 26, 2001.

36. Hirabayashi, interview with the author and Branton, 2001.

37. Philip G. Altbach, "The International Student Movement," *Journal of Contemporary History* 5 (1970): 156–174; Mayer N. Zald and Patricia Denton, "From Evangelism to General Service: The Transformation of the YMCA," *Administrative Science Quarterly* 8 (September 1963): 214–234.

38. Patti McGill Peterson, "Student Organizations and the Antiwar Movement in America, 1900–1960," *American Studies* (1972), available at https://journals.ku.edu/index.php/amerstud/article/viewFile/2416/2375 (accessed February 6, 2011).

39. "New York Presidents School. Training for Christian Leadership," *Intercollegian,* April 1940, 147; Hirabayashi, interview with the author and Branton, 2001; Gordon Hirabayashi, interview with Tom Ikeda and Alice Ito, Seattle, Washington, December 5, 1999, Densho Digital Archive.

40. Gordon Hirabayashi, interview with the author, Tucson, Arizona, November 5, 1999.

41. Hirabayashi, interview with Horn.

42. Hirabayashi, interview with Horn; Hirabayashi, interview with the author, 1999.

43. Hirabayashi, interview with Horn.

44. Arthur Barnett, interview with Mr. Goto [sic], n.d., Arthur G. Barnett Papers, MS 1598-4, Special Collections, University of Washington, Box 1, Folder 6.

45. Ibid.

46. Ibid.

47. Ibid.

48. Hirabayashi, interview with the author, 1999.

49. Ibid.; Irons, *Justice at War,* 91.

50. Irons, *Justice at War,* 88.

51. Gordon K. Hirabayashi, "Why I Refused to Register for Evacuation," May 13, 1943, Ring Family Papers, Box 1, Folder 17, University of Washington, Special Collections, Seattle, Washington [hereafter cited as Ring Papers].

52. Ibid.

53. Hirabayashi to Ring, May 16, 1942, Maryknoll School, Seattle, Washington, Ring Papers, Box 1, Folder 5.

54. Irons, *Justice at War,* 93.

55. Hirabayashi to Ring, May 17, 1942, King County Jail, Seattle, Washington, Ring Papers, Box 1, Folder 5.

56. Hirabayashi to Ring, May 17, 1942.

57. March Order No. 2—April 25, 1942, Headquarters Japanese Exclusion Area A, Seattle, Washington, Emergency Defense Council of the Seattle Chapter. Japanese American Citizens' League, Special Collections, University of Washington, Box 18, available at www.lib.washington.edu/exhibits/harmony/documents/march.html (accessed June 19, 2011).

58. Gordon Hirabayashi, interview with Tom Ikeda, Seattle, Washington, May 25, 1999, Densho Digital Archive.

59. Ibid.

60. Ibid.

61. Hirabayashi to Ring, July 1, 1942, Ring Papers, Box 1, Folder 5; Hirabayashi, interviews with the author, 1999 and 2001.

62. Ken Yoshida and Kay Yoshida, interview with the author and Nicole Branton, Tucson, Arizona, August 24, 2001.

63. Irons, *Justice at War,* 91–92, 117, 154.

64. Ibid.

65. Hirabayashi, interview with Ikeda and Ito.

66. Trial Brief, September 15, 1942, Criminal Case #45739, *U.S. v. Gordon K. Hirabayashi,* USDC-WDW-Tacoma, Box 181, NARA-Pacific Alaska Region, Seattle, Washington.

67. Ibid.

68. Lloyd L. Black, Ruling on Motions, September 15, 1942, Criminal Case #45739, *U.S. v. Gordon K. Hirabayashi.*

69. Hirabayashi, interview with Horn.

70. Hirabayashi to Ring, October 18, 1942, Ring Papers, Box 1, Folder 5.

71. Ibid.; Hirabayashi, interview with the author, 1999; Hirabayashi, interview with the author and Branton, 2001.

72. Carl C. Donough et al., Memorandum of Law, *U.S. v. Minoru Yasui,* Criminal Case #16056, Oregon District Court; Criminal Case #45739, *U.S. v. Gordon K. Hirabayashi.*

73. Hirabayashi to Fellowship of Reconciliation, King County Jail, October 12, 1942, Ring Papers, Box 1, Folder 5.

74. Ibid.

75. R. B. Cozzens to B. R. Stauber, War Relocation Authority, January 30, 1943; R. B. Cozzens to King County Jail, February 1, 1943; R. B. Cozzens to Frank Walters, February 1, 1943; R. B. Cozzens to Miss Evelyn Rose, Central Utah Relocation Center, Topaz, Utah, February 28, 1944; NARA RG 210, Evacuee Case Files, "Gordon Hirabayashi"; Hirabayashi, interview with Ikeda and Ito.

76. Globularius Schraubi, M.A., "Yule Greetings, Friends," *Trek* 1, no. 1 (1942): 12–16.

77. Yoshida and Yoshida, interview; Knaefler, *Our House Divided,* 19.

78. David K. Yoo, *Growing Up Nisei: Race, Generation, and Culture among Japanese Americans of California, 1924–49* (Urbana: University of Illinois Press, 2000), 108; "Nisei Problems and Behavior," October 30, 1944, NARA RG 210, FBD, Community Analysis Reports, Colorado River, Roll #10, M1342; Paul Kusuda to Mrs. Afton Nance, May 27, 1942, quoted in Yoo, *Growing Up Nisei,* 109.

79. Webb, quoted in "U.S. Court Asked to Ban Nisei Citizens, 'Fascist' Attempt Threatens Democratic Rights of Persons of Asiatic Ancestry in America," *Pacific Citizen,* July 2, 1942; *U.S. v. Wong Kim Ark* (1898).

80. *Regan v. King,* Registrar, 319 U.S. 753; 63 S. Ct. 1168; 87 L. Ed. 1706 (May 17, 1943). The Federal Appeals Court cited precedent: *U.S. v. Wong Kim Ark* (1898); in addition to cases directly related to Nisei citizenship, *In re Tetsubumi Yano's Estate,* 188 Cal. 645, 206 Pac. 995 (1922); *Morrison v. California,* 291 U.S. 82 (1943); "Nisei Citizenship Rights Upheld by Court," *Pacific Citizens* (February 25, 1943); Memorandum to the Director of the WRA from the Office of the Solicitor, Opinion No. 63, April 9, 1943, Barnhart Papers, Box 1, Binder 2, University of Arkansas, Special Collections, Fayetteville, Arkansas [hereafter cited as Barnhart Papers]; Forrest T. Hoyt to Philip Glick, "Discussion of the Doctrine of Dual Citizenship and Its Applicability to Japanese in the United States" (July 8, 1942), NARA RG 210/16, Box 229, Folder 31.009 #1.

81. "Holman Bill Challenges Nisei Citizenship, Amendment Is Proposed to Constitution," *Pacific Citizen*, September 24, 1942.

82. Hoyt to Glick, "Discussion of the Doctrine of Dual Citizenship"; War Relocation Authority, Office of the Solicitor Opinion No. 63, "Acquisition of United States Citizenship by Persons of Japanese Ancestry," April 9, 1943; DeWitt quoted in De Nevers, *Colonel and the Pacifist,* 92–93.

83. Bill Hosokawa, *Nisei: The Quiet Americans* (New York: W. Morrow, 1969), 394–399.

84. Scott Rowley to Philip Glick, September 12, 1944, NARA RG 210/16, Box 258, Folder 37.106 #8; J. Edgar Hoover to Mr. Tolson, Mr. Tamm, and Mr. Ladd, September 1942, NARA RG 65, Box 81, Folder 62-69030.

85. Memorandum to the Chief of Staff, July 22, 1942, reprinted in *American Concentration Camps*, n.p.

86. Ibid.

87. Phone conversation with Capt. Moffitt, Capt. Shepard, and Maj. Wall, July 20, 1942, and Memorandum to the Chief of Staff, July 22, 1942, reprinted in *American Concentration Camps*, n.p.

88. Letter from William A. Boekel, Lt. Col., F.A. Asst. A.C. of S., to Col. Bendetsen, July 20, 1942, reprinted in *American Concentration Camps*, n.p.

89. Theda Skocpol, *Protecting Soldiers and Mothers: The Political Origins of Social Policy in the United States* (Cambridge, MA: Harvard University Press, 1992).

90. Memorandum to the Chief of Staff, July 22, 1942, reprinted in *American Concentration Camps*, n.p.

91. Elmer Davis, October 2, 1942, quoted in CWRIC, 189.

92. Stimson to Roosevelt, October 14, 1942, quoted in Robinson, *By Order of the President,* 163–166.

93. Secretary of the Navy Knox to President Roosevelt, October 17, 1942, quoted in Robinson, *By Order of the President,* 163–164.

94. Telegram to President Roosevelt, quoted in Chin, *Born in the USA,* 304; and "Japanese American Citizens League," War Department, Military Intelligence Division, [December 17, 1942] January 2, 1943, quoted in Chin, *Born in the USA,* 307–308.

95. Telephone conversation, Col. Bendetsen and Col. Pettigrew, November 6, 1942, reprinted in *American Concentration Camps*, n.p.

96. Memo for McCloy from Col. M. S. Pettigrew, regarding progress report on Nisei statistics, November 7, 1942, RG 107, Office of the Secretary of War, College Park, Maryland, Box 860, Folder 3 [hereafter cited as RG 107]; Memo for McCloy from Col. Pettigrew, regarding formation of JA unit, November 17, 1942, RG 107, Box 860, Folder 5; Letter from E. M. Rowalt, WRA, to Col. M. W. Pettigrew, regarding JA enlistment from War Relocation Centers, December 4, 1942, RG 107, Box 970, Folder 3; Memo for McCloy from Pettigrew, regarding proposed Nisei unit, December 17, 1942, Box 980, Folder 3.

97. Art Hansen and David A. Hacker, "The Manzanar Riot: An Ethnic Perspective," *Amerasia Journal* 2, no. 2 (1974): 112–157; Brian Masaru Hayashi, *Democratizing the Enemy: The Japanese American Internment* (Princeton, NJ: Princeton University Press, 2004), 134–135; Lon Kurashige, "Resistance, Collaboration, and Manzanar Protest," *Pacific Historical Review* 70, no. 3 (2001): 387–417; Weglyn, *Years of Infamy,* 121–127.

98. Robinson, *By Order of the President,* 182; Jacobus tenBroek, Edward N. Barnhart, and Floyd W. Matson, *Prejudice, War and the Constitution* (Berkeley: University of California Press, 1954), 160–161.

99. Hirabayashi to Mr. and Mrs. Ring, October 25, 1942, King County Jail, Ring Papers, Box 1, Folder 5.

100. Arthur Hansen, "Peculiar Odyssey: Newsman Jimmie Omura's Removal from a Regeneration within Nikkei Society, History, and Memory," in *Nikkei in the Pacific Northwest: Japanese Americans and Japanese Canadians in the Twentieth Century*, ed. Louis Fiset and Gail M. Nomura (Seattle: University of Washington Press, 2005), 282.

CHAPTER 3

Epigraph: Russell A. Bankson, "Registration at Topaz," Record Group 210, Field Basic Documentation, Central Utah, Project Reports Division, Reel 6, National Archives and Records Administration, Washington, D.C. [hereafter cited as NARA RG 210, FBD].

1. Thomas Janoski, *Citizenship and Civil Society: A Framework for Rights and Obligations in Liberal, Traditional, and Social Democratic Regimes* (New York: Cambridge University Press, 1998).

2. *United States v. Schotfeldt,* 136 F. (2d) 935 (C.C.A. 7th, 1943); *United States v. Wursterbarth,* 249 Fed. 908 (D.N.J. 1918); *Johannessen v. United States,* 225 U.S. 227 (1912); *Luria v. United States,* 231 U.S. 9 (1913); *United States v. Kichin,* 276 F. 818 (1921); *In re Goldberg,* 269 F. 392 (1920); *Schurmann v. United States,* 264 F. 917 (1920).

3. *United States v. Herberger,* 272 Fed. 278, 291 (W.D. Was. 1921); see also *United States v. Wezel,* 49 F. Supp. 16, 19 (S.D. Ill. 1943); *United States v. Kuhn,* 49 F. Supp. 407, 412 (S.D.N.Y. 1943).

4. Nationality Act of October 14, 1940 (effective January 13, 1941, as 54 Statutes-at-Large 1137).

5. "Aliens. Revocation of Certificate of Citizenship for Subsequent Acts of Disloyalty Manifesting Mental Reservation at Time of Naturalization, Deprivation of Derived Citizenship," *Columbia Law Review* 4, no. 1 (1944): 80–83; *United States v. Kuhn,* 49 F. Supp. 407 (1943); *United States v. Orth,* 51 F. Supp. 682 (1943); *United States v. Jogwick,* 51 F. Supp. 2 (1943); *Meyer v. United States,* 141 F.2d 825 (1944); *United States v. Ritzen,* 50 F. Supp. 301 (1943); *United States v. Meyer,* 48 F. Supp. 926 (1943); *United States v. Mickley,* 44 F. Supp. 73 (1942); *United States ex rel. Harrington v. Schlotfeldt,* 136 F.2d 93 (1943); *Baumgartner v. United States,* 138 F.2d 2 (1943); *United States v. Kusche,* 56 F. Supp. 20 (1944); *United States v. Scheurer,* 55 F. Supp. 24 (1944); *United States v. Holtz,* 54 F. Supp. 6 (1944); *United States v. Dietz,* 52 F. Supp. 20 (1943); *United States v. Reinsch,* 50 F. Supp. 97 (1943).

6. Roosevelt to Stimson, February 1, 1943, reprinted in Roger Daniels, *American Concentration Camps, Volume 9, June 1942–May 1944, Raising Japanese American Troops* (New York: Garland, 1989), n.p.

7. Roger Daniels, *Concentration Camps, U.S.A.* (Berkeley: University of California Press, 1971); Klancy Clark de Nevers, *The Colonel and the Pacifist: Karl Bendetsen, Perry Saito and the Incarceration of Japanese Americans during World War II* (Salt Lake City: University of Utah Press, 2004); and Greg Robinson, *By Order of the President: FDR and the Internment of Japanese Americans* (Cambridge, MA: Harvard University Press, 2001).

8. Memorandum from John C. Baker, Chief from Office of Reports, WRA, to all Project Directors, February 1, 1943, NARA RG 210, FBD, Reel 6.

9. "Six Residents Give to JACL National Fund," *Topaz Times,* January 31, 1943; Bankson, "Registration at Topaz," 5.

10. Second Quarterly Report of the War Relocation Authority, July 1–September 30, 1942, available at http://home.comcast.net/~eo9066/1942/42-10/TL04.html#Community _Construction_ (accessed June 19, 2011); Paul R. Spickard, "The Nisei Assume Power: The Japanese-American Citizens League, 1941–1942," *Pacific Historical Review* 52 (May 1983): 147–174.

11. United States, Federal Bureau of Investigation, "Summary of Information: War Relocation Authority and Japanese Relocation Centers," August 2, 1945, 25, RG 65, Box 84, Folder 62-69030, College Park, Maryland [hereafter cited as RG 65]; Bankson, "Registration at Topaz," 10–11.

12. Bankson, "Registration at Topaz," 13.

13. Ibid.

14. Ibid.

15. Ibid., 14, 57.

16. "A Test," *Topaz Times*, February 6, 1943; "Army Registration," Selective Service Folder, NARA RG 210, FBD, Reel 4.

17. *Topaz Times*, February 5, 1943.

18. Bankson, "Registration at Topaz," 18; "Volunteers for Victory," NARA RG 210, FBD, Topaz, Reel 6.

19. Ibid.

20. Interview with Senator Daniel Inoye, *Time of Fear* (America Productions, PBS, 2005); "Invitation" February 6, 1943, NARA RG 210, FBD, Topaz Project Reports Division, Reel 6; Bankson, "Registration at Topaz," 9, 19–20; "President Endorses Combat Team Plans," *Topaz Times*, February 8, 1943.

21. Bankson, "Registration at Topaz," 48; *Gila News-Courier*, 1943–1944.

22. Bankson, "Registration at Topaz," 21.

23. Ibid.

24. Ibid.

25. Ibid., 22.

26. Ibid., 22–23.

27. Ibid., 23.

28. Ibid., 24.

29. "At the Shower Room" February 11, 1943, NARA RG 210, FBD, Central Utah, Project Reports Division, Reel 6.

30. FBI, "Summary of Information: War Relocation Authority and Japanese Relocation Centers," August 2, 1945, 25, RG 65, Box 84, Folder 62-69030.

31. Bankson, "Registration at Topaz," 25, and Exhibit "O."

32. Bankson, "Registration at Topaz," 26.

33. FBI, "Summary of Information."

34. Ibid.; Bankson, "Registration at Topaz," 2, and Exhibit "P."

35. Bankson, "Registration at Topaz," 29.

36. Phone conversation, Gen. Joyce, Commanding Officer, Ninth Service Command, Fort Douglas, Utah with Gen. DeWitt, February 14, 1943, reprinted in Daniels, *American Concentration Camps*, n.p.; Col. Meek and Maj. Moffitt, February 15, 1943, reprinted in Daniels, *American Concentration Camps*, n.p.

37. Col. Bendetsen and Gen. De Witt, February 13, 1943, reprinted in Daniels, *American Concentration Camps*, n.p.; De Nevers, *Colonel and the Pacifist*.

38. Lane Ryo Hirabayashi, *The Politics of Fieldwork: Research in an American Concentration Camp* (Tucson: University of Arizona Press, 1999); Edward Spicer, Asael Hansen, Katherine Luomala, and Marvin K. Opler, *Impounded People: Japanese-Americans in the Relocation Centers* (Tucson: University of Arizona Press, 1970); Yuji Ichioka, ed., *Views from Within: The Japanese American Evacuation and Resettlement Study* (Los Angeles: Asian American Studies Center, UCLA, 1989); Peter T. Suzuki, "Anthropologists in the Wartime Camps for Japanese Americans: A Documentary Study," *Dialectical Anthropology* 6 (August 1981): 23–60; Orin Starn, "Engineering Internment: Anthropologists and the War Relocation Authority," *American Ethnologist* 13 (November 1986): 700–720.

39. John F. Embree, "Registration at Central Utah, 14–17, February, 1943," War Relocation Authority, Project Analysis Series No. 1, November 1943, Leflar Papers, Box 2, Folder 4, Special Collections, University of Arkansas, Fayetteville, Arkansas [hereafter cited as Leflar Papers].

40. FBI, "Summary of Information"; Embree, "Registration at Central Utah, 14–17, February, 1943"; Bankson, "Registration at Topaz," 31.

41. Ibid., 32–33, and Exhibit "T."

42. Embree, "Registration at Central Utah, 14–17, February, 1943," 2–3; Bankson, "Registration at Topaz," 32–33.

43. FBI, "Summary of Information"; Bankson, "Registration at Topaz," 36–37.

44. Ibid., and Exhibit "V."

45. Bill Hosokawa, Nisei: The Quiet Americans (New York: W. Morrow, 1969), 91.

46. Bankson, "Registration at Topaz," and Exhibit "V."

47. Petition reprinted in the Topaz Times, February 17, 1943.

48. Bankson, "Registration at Topaz," 40–41.

49. Ibid., 43.

50. "Statement of United States Citizen of Japanese Ancestry," NARA RG 210, Evacuee Case Files, Box 7187, File 12484, Folder Ken Yoshida.

51. Ibid.

52. Eric Muller, American Inquisition: The Hunt for Japanese American Disloyalty in World War II (Chapel Hill: University of North Carolina Press, 2007).

53. "Testimony Taken before the Dies Committee," July 9, 1943, 3–4, RG 389, Box 1719, Folder "Dies," NARA, College Park, Maryland [hereafter cited as RG 389].

54. "Statement of United States Citizen of Japanese Ancestry," Evacuee Case Files, Box 7187, File 12484, Folder Ken Yoshida; Muller, American Inquisition.

55. Evacuee Case Files, Box 7187, File 12484, Folder Ken Yoshida; Ken Yoshida and Kay Yoshida, interview with the author, Tucson, Arizona, August 24, 2001.

56. Col. William P. Scobey, February 19, 1943, as quoted in Bankson, "Registration at Topaz," 45.

57. Bankson, "Registration at Topaz," 45.

58. Ibid.

59. FBI, "Summary of Information."

60. Sandra Taylor, Jewel of the Desert: Japanese American Internment at Topaz (Berkeley: University of California Press, 1993); Leonard J. Arrington, The Price of Prejudice: The Japanese-American Relocation Center in Utah during World War II, 2nd ed. (Delta, UT: Topaz Museum, 1997).

61. Michi Weglyn, Years of Infamy: The Untold Story of America's Concentration Camps (Seattle: University of Washington Press, 1996).

62. United States Commission on Wartime Relocation and Internment of Civilians, Personal Justice Denied: Report of the Commission on Wartime Relocation and Internment of Civilians (Washington, DC: Civil Liberties Public Education Fund; Seattle: University of Washington Press, 1997) [hereafter cited as CWRIC].

63. Minutes of "Meeting Held to Discuss Results of Investigation," April 9, 1943, RG 65, Box 81, Item 97; Brian Masaru Hayashi, Democratizing the Enemy: The Japanese American Internment (Princeton, NJ: Princeton University Press, 2004), 144.

64. FBI, "Summary of Information."

65. CWRIC, 208.

66. Memo, October 12, 1944, NARA RG 210/16, Box 229, "Citizenship" Folder.

67. Milton Eisenhower to President Roosevelt, April 13, 1943, quoted in Robinson, By Order of the President, 188.

68. J. Edgar Hoover, Memorandum for Mr. Edward J. Ennis, March 4, 1943, RG 65, Box 81, Folder 95.

69. Letter to Fisher (n.a.), February 10, 1943, Fisher Files, JERS, Bancroft Library, MSS 67/14, Reel 83, University of California, Berkeley, California.

CHAPTER 4

1. Gordon Hirabayashi to Eleanor Ring, King County Jail, October 27, 1942, Ring Papers; Judgment and Sentencing, *U.S. v. Hirabayashi,* October 21, 1942, Criminal Case #45739, *U.S. v. Gordon K. Hirabayashi.*

2. Sidney Fine, "Mr. Justice Murphy and the Hirabayashi Case," *Pacific Historical Review* 33 (May 1964): 195–209.

3. *Hirabayashi v. United States,* 320 U.S. 81 (June 21, 1943).

4. Peter H. Irons, *Justice at War* (New York: Oxford University Press, 1983), 250–251.

5. Blake McKelvey, "Penology in the Westward Movement," *Pacific Historical Review* 2 (December 1933): 418–438; Jane Zimmerman, "The Penal Reform Movement in the South during the Progressive Era, 1890–1917," *Journal of Southern History* 17, no. 4 (1951): 474, 485.

6. Gordon Hirabayashi, interview with Roger Daniels, University of Washington, Seattle, February 10, 1981.

7. Ibid.

8. Ibid.

9. Hirabayashi to Ring, September 15, 1943, Cedar City, Utah, Ring Papers, Box 1, Folder 6.

10. Hirabayashi, interview with Daniels.

11. Hirabayashi has described this interaction in several oral histories. In relating these stories, he does not always describe this as an encounter with a federal marshal, but this is the version that appears in the majority of his oral histories and was the one that he told to the author. Gordon Hirabayashi, interview with the author, Tucson, Arizona, November 5, 1999.

12. Ibid.

13. U.S. Department of Commerce, Bureau of Public Roads, Division Seven, *Final Construction Report: Arizona Forest Highway Project 33, Catalina Highway, Coronado National Forest, Pima County, Arizona* (unpublished report, 1951), 22–124.

14. Hirabayashi to Ring, December 23, 1943.

15. Hirabayashi, interview with the author; press release from Hopi Cultural Preservation Office (HCPO), August 2001, copy in author's possession, courtesy of HCPO. For more information on the Hopi resisters, contact the HCPO.

16. Hirabayashi, interview with Daniels.

17. Letter to Mr. James V. Bennett, Director of Bureau of Prisons, Washington, D.C., May 5, 1939; Supervisor R. H. Armstrong to Superintendent LaBrash, Tucson Prison Camp, June 8, 1939; Supervisor R. H. Armstrong to the Director of Tucson Prison Camp, June 7, 1939, RG 129, Bureau of Prison Records, College Park, Maryland, Box 97, Folder "Complaints" [hereafter cited as RG 129].

18. C. B. Mead to R. H. Armstrong, January 8, 1944, RG 129, Box 119, Folder "Resisters."

19. Ibid.

20. Ibid.

21. R. H. Armstrong to Superintendent Mead, January 11, 1944.

22. Donald Clemmer to Director of Prisons, Washington, DC, December 8, 1944, RG 129, Box 97, Folder "Complaints"; Joe Norikane, Noboru Taguma, Hideo Takeuchi, Ken

Yoshida, and Harry Yoshikawa, interview with the author and Peter Taylor, Tucson, Arizona, November 6, 1999.

23. Hirabayashi to Ring, December 23, 1943.

24. Public Law No. 71-218, 46 Stat. 325 (1930).

25. U.S. Department of Commerce, Bureau of Public Roads, *Final Construction Report.*

26. Tetsuden Kashima, *Judgment without Trial: Japanese American Imprisonment during World War II* (Seattle: University of Washington, 2003).

27. Paul W. Keve, *Prisons and the American Conscience: A History of U.S. Federal Corrections* (Carbondale: Southern Illinois University Press, 1991); Judith R. Johnson, *The Penitentiaries of Arizona, Nevada, New Mexico and Utah* (Lewiston, NY: Mellen Press, 1997); David J. Rothman, *Conscience and Convenience: The Asylum and Its Alternatives in Progressive America,* rev. ed. (New York: Aldine de Gruyter, 2002); Federal Bureau of Prisons, "Brief History of the Bureau of Prisons," available at www.bop.gov/about/history.jsp (accessed December 2, 2005).

28. Norikane et al., interview.

29. Alex Lichtenstein, "Good Roads and Chain Gangs in the Progressive South: 'The Negro Convict Is a Slave,'" *Journal of Southern History* 59 (February 1993): 85–110.

30. U.S. Department of Commerce, Bureau of Public Roads, *Final Construction Report*; Ken Yoshida and Kay Yoshida, interview with the author, Tucson, Arizona, August 24, 2001; Group interview.

31. Keve, *Prisons and the American Conscience*; Johnson, *Penitentiaries of Arizona, Nevada, New Mexico and Utah.*

32. "Camp Statistics," *Roadrunner,* July–August 1945, 33.

33. Hirabayashi to Ring, December 23, 1943.

34. Hirabayashi, interview with the author.

35. Hirabayashi to Ring, December 23, 1943.

36. Ibid.

37. Ibid.

38. Ibid.

CHAPTER 5

Epigraph: Theodore Roosevelt, Knights of Columbus speech, October 12, 1915, as quoted in Emory S. Bogardus, *Essentials of Americanization* (Los Angeles: University of California Press, 1923), 410.

1. Sandra Taylor, *Jewel of the Desert: Japanese American Internment at Topaz* (Berkeley: University of California Press, 1993), 171.

2. Copy of Confidential Report, Tab "B," n.d., Office of the Secretary of War, RG 107, College Park, Maryland, Box 15, Folder "Loyalty Investigation" [hereafter cited as RG 107].

3. Harrison A. Gerhardt to Director, Bureau of Public Relations and Assistant Chief of Staff, G-2, December 22, 1943, RG 107, Box 15, Folder "Loyalty Investigation."

4. Russell A. Bankson, "Registration at Topaz," p. 6, RG 210, Field Basic Documentation, Central Utah, Project Reports Division, Reel 6 [hereafter cited as RG 210, FBD].

5. Allen W. Gullion to Capt. C. C. Pierce, November 2, 1942, RG 107, Box 15, Folder "Loyalty Investigation."

6. Memorandum, John Lansdale to Col. Gibson, March 29, 1943, RG 107, Box 15, Folder "Loyalty Investigation."

7. Ibid.

8. Gullion to Pierce, November 2, 1942.

9. Ibid.

10. Ibid.

11. Ibid.

12. John A. Rademaker to Edward H. Spicer, February 16, 1944, Community Analysis Reports, RG 210, FBD, M 1342, Roll 15.

13. Ibid.

14. Rademaker to Spicer, February 16, 1944.

15. Ibid.

16. Ibid.; United States, Commission on Wartime Relocation and Internment of Civilians, *Personal Justice Denied* (Washington, DC: Civil Liberties Public Education Fund, 1997), 253–257 [hereafter cited as CWRIC].

17. Ibid.

18. Art Hansen, "The 1944 Nisei Draft at Heart Mountain, Wyoming: Its Relationship to Historical Representation of the World War II Japanese American Evacuation," *Magazine of History* 10, no. 4 (1996): 48–60.

19. Kiyoshi Okamoto, "We Should Know," February 25, 1944, available at www.resisters.com/images/WeShdKnow2.jpg (accessed November 14, 2010).

20. Hansen, "The 1944 Nisei Draft at Heart Mountain, Wyoming," 49.

21. "Topaz," *Rocky Shimpo,* February 19, 1944.

22. Frank Yamasaki and Seiko Yakahi, "Recommendations of Topaz Citizens for the Principles of American Democracy (Non-Segregated Units)," February 26, 1944, RG 210, FBD, Central Utah, Reel 4, Selective Service Folder; Frank Yamasaki, Chairman of the Citizens Committee of Topaz, "Our Fight for Equal Rights," February 26, 1944, RG 210, FBD, Central Utah, Reel 4, Internal Security, Reports Publications Folder. For reactions to the draft in other camps, see Community Analysis Reports, Colorado River, M 1342, Roll 10, Item 145; Community Analysis Report, "Chronology of the Draft," February 17, 1944, Granada 53, M 1342, Roll 15.

23. "Statement from Mothers of Topaz, W.R.A. Center," March 11, 1944, RG 210, FBD, Central Utah, Internal Security Report, Reel 4; Leland Barrows to Mrs. Wakako Adachi, March 22, 1944, reprinted in "Mothers' Petition Answered," *Topaz Times,* April 12, 1944.

24. "Amache Women to File Petition," *Rocky Shimpo,* March 13, 1944.

25. Robert H. Dunlop to Adachi, March 24, 1944, reprinted in "Mothers' Petition Answered," *Topaz Times,* April 12, 1944; Leland Barrows to Mrs. Wakako Adachi, March 22, 1944, reprinted in "Mothers' Petition Answered," *Topaz Times,* April 12, 1944; "Three Answers to Mothers' Petition Here," *Topaz Times,* April 18, 1944.

26. Dillon Myer to Adachi, March 27, 1944, reprinted in "Mothers' Petition Answered," *Topaz Times,* April 12, 1944.

27. "Amache to Petition Draft Grievances," *Rocky Shimpo,* February 21, 1944.

28. Donald Horn to Philip Glick, February 19, 1944, Leflar Papers, Special Collections, University of Arkansas, Fayetteville, Arkansas, Box 3, Folder 16.

29. Teletype from D. Myer to all project attorneys, February 21, 1944, RG 210, FBD, Community Analysis Reports, M 1342, Roll 15.

30. Ibid.

31. James G. Lindley, "Open letter to all Block Managers," n.d., RG 210, FBD, Community Analysis Reports, M 1342, Roll 15.

32. Speech of Paul Terry, Superintendent of Education, Amache, Colorado, February 20, RG 210, FBD, "Attitudes" Folder 37, Reel 47.

33. Rademaker to Spicer, February 22, 1944.

34. Ibid.

35. *Topaz Times*; Rademaker to Spicer, February 22, 1944.

36. Jimmie Omura, "Let Us Not Be Rash," *Rocky Shimpo,* February 28, 1944.

37. Ibid.

38. Rademaker to Harbison, April 1, 1944, RG 210, FBD, Community Analysis Reports, Roll 15.

39. Ibid.

40. Horn to Glick, February 26, 1944, NARA RG 210/16, Box 266, Folder 37.111, No. 4.

41. *Yasui v. U.S.*, 320 U.S. 115 (1943).

42. Rademaker to Harbison, April 1, 1944; "Two Granada Draft Resisters Are Inducted," *Rocky Shimpo*, n.d. (copy courtesy of Joe Norikane).

43. Noboru Taguma, interview with the author, Tucson, Arizona, August 26, 2001; Frank Chin, "Min Yasui: Resister or Turncoat?" in *Born in the USA: A Story of Japanese America, 1889–1947* (Lanham, MD: Rowman and Littlefield, 2002), 438.

44. Horn to Glick, June 16, 1944.

45. John A. Rademaker to James O. Lindley, March 30, 1944.

46. Ibid.

47. Rademaker to Donald E. Harbison, April 1, 1944.

48. Ibid. The vast majority of resisters were from Blocks 7, 8, 9, 10, and 11. The only reported resister from 6H was Yoshitatsu Nakaguma. Selective Service Violations—Internal Security indexes, 1942–1946, RG 210.

49. Rademaker to Harbison, April 1, 1944.

50. Ibid.

51. Ibid.

52. Myer to Omura, March 10, 1944, Leflar Papers, Box 3, Folder 16.

53. Ibid.

54. Saburo Kido, *JACL Bulletin* 10, April 19, 1944, MSS 67/14, JACL Reels 83–84, JERS, Bancroft Library.

55. Selective Service Bulletin no. 49, April 14, 1944, RG 210, FBD, Central Utah, Reel 4, Selective Service Folder.

56. "Jap Convicted as Evader in Denver Court," *Denver Post*, June 28, 1944; Susumu Yenokida and Harry Yoshikawa, interview with the author and Nicole Branton, Tucson, Arizona, August 25, 2001.

57. "Guilty," *Rocky Shimpo*, June 28, 1944; "Jap Convicted as Evader in Denver Court," *Denver Post*, June 28, 1944; "Eleven Granada Nisei Convicted in Draft Cases: Sentenced to Terms of 10 to 18 Months in Denver Court," *Pacific Citizen*, July 8, 1944.

58. Greg Robinson, "The Great Unknown and the Unknown Great: African American Attorney Was Defender of Japanese Americans during WWII," *Nichi Bei Times Weekly*, June 7, 2007.

59. Shizuma Kubo, Tsugime Heya, and Michitaka Nakaguma to Hugh E. Macbeth, June 2, 1944, Kubo Collection.

60. Samuel David Menin Papers, 1931–1984, MS 29, Auraria Library Archives and Special Collections, Denver, Colorado.

61. List of expenses; notebook of resisters' names, addresses, contributions to defense fund, and miscellaneous expenditures, Kubo Collection.

62. Criminal Case Files 10347–10360, District of Colorado, Records of the District Courts of the United States, RG 21, NARA, Denver, Colorado.

63. Eric Muller, *Free to Die for Their Country: The Story of Japanese American Draft Resisters during World War II* (Chicago: University of Chicago Press, 2001).

64. Selective Service Board #115 to Yoshi Kubo, March 14, 1944, Kubo Collection.

65. "Four More Granada Japs Are Convicted of Evading the Draft," *Denver Post*, July 1, 1944.

66. Motion to Quash, *United States v. Harry Shuichi Ioka*, September 18, 1944, RG 295, Entry 32, Box 298, Criminal Case File 10454, NARA, Denver, Colorado.

67. Muller, *Free to Die for Their Country,* 131–160.

68. The term "evacuation" was used in the original source. "Four More Granada Japs Are Convicted of Evading the Draft," *Denver Post,* July 1, 1944; *Fred Korematsu v United States,* 323 US 214, 65 S. Ct. 193, 89 L. Ed.

69. Criminal Case Files, RG 295, Entry 32, Boxes 295–298, NARA, Denver, Colorado; "Seven Sentenced in Draft Law Case: Crime Never Pays," *Denver Post,* November 30, 1944; "Eleven Granada Nisei Convicted in Draft Cases: Sentenced to Terms of 10 to 18 Months in Denver Court," *Pacific Citizen,* July 8, 1944; "Eight Amache Men Receive Sentences from Federal Judge," *Rocky Shimpo,* November 6, 1944.

70. "Eleven Granada Nisei Convicted in Draft Cases: Sentenced to Terms of 10 to 18 Months in Denver Court," *Pacific Citizen* July 8, 1944.

71. Horn to Glick, July 15, 1944, Leflar Papers, Box 3, Folder 16.

72. "Army Service Forces Transmittal Sheet," Archibald King, Colonel, JAGD, Chief, International Law Division to the PMG, April 9, 1945, Comment no. 2, RG 107, Box 15, Folder "Loyalty Investigation."

73. John J. McCloy to Gen. McNarney, October 2, 1943, RG 107, Box 15, Folder "Loyalty Investigation."

74. Gordon K. Hirabayashi to Local Board 4, Seattle, Washington, February 12, 1944, Barnett Papers, Box 1, Folder 9.

75. F. Cleveland Hendrick, Selective Service, to Tom C. Clark, Assistant Attorney General, Department of Justice, October 13, 1944, RG 60, Classified Subject File—Correspondence, Department of Justice file 25-82-124, Hirabayashi, Box 1 of 1.

76. J. A. Ulio, Maj. Gen., Adjutant General's Office to the Commanding Generals of the Army Air Forces, Army Ground Forces, and Army Service Forces, August 20, 1944, RG 389, Box 1719, Folder "Disaffected Military Personnel."

77. Shirley Castelnuovo, *Soldiers of Conscience: Japanese American Military Resisters in World War II* (Lincoln: University of Nebraska Press, 2010); Cedrick Shimo, interview with Sojin Kim and Erick Molinar, Japanese American National Museum, Los Angeles, California, March 19, 2001.

78. Hirabayashi to Ring, February 18, 1944, Spokane, Washington.

79. Gordon Hirabayashi, interview with Roger Daniels, Seattle, February 10, 1981; Heather T. Frazer and John O'Sullivan, "From CPS to Prison: Bent Anderson," in *"We Have Just Begun to Not Fight": An Oral History of Conscientious Objectors in Civilian Public Service during World War II* (New York: Twayne Publishers, 1996), 117–118.

80. Hirabayashi to Ring, February 18, 1944; Hirabayashi, interview with Daniels.

81. Hirabayashi to Ring, February 18, 1944.

82. Philip Glick, Solicitor to A. L. Wirin, April 29, 1944, ACLU Files, University of Washington, Special Collections, Seattle, Washington.

83. Ibid.

84. A. L. Wirin to Philip M. Glick, Solicitor, May 8, 1944.

85. A. L. Wirin to Roger Baldwin, May 8, 1944; Baldwin to Glick, May 11, 1944.

86. Harrison A. Gerhardt, Lt. Col. Staff Corps, Executive Assistant to Secretary of War, to Melvin H. Harter, Director of the Japanese American Unit, United Service Organization (USO), May 25, 1944, RG 210/16, Box 325, Folder 61.116—USO.

87. Art Hansen, "Sergeant Ben Kuroki's Perilous 'Home Mission': Contested Loyalty and Patriotism in the Japanese American Detention Camps, 1944," in *Remembering Heart Mountain: Essays on Japanese American Internment in Wyoming,* ed. Mike Mackey (Powell, WY: Western History Publications, 1998): 153–175.

88. Community Analysis Newsletter, No. 6, May 24, 1944, RG 210, BFD, Community Analysis Reports, Trend Report, No. 6, Roll 8.

89. Ibid.

90. Ibid.

91. Ibid. Other war heroes followed Kuroki's visit to Topaz. See Oscar Hoffman, "Supplementary Newsletter, July 15, 1944," RG 210, BFD, Topaz Community Analysis Reports, Trend Report 9, Reel 8.

92. "Seattle Nisei Saves Platoon of Marauders," *Times,* Seattle, WA, March 4, 1945.

93. "Jap-American Volunteer from Tule Lake WRA Center Fights Nips in India," *Herald and News,* Klamath Falls, OR, n.d.

94. "Seven Nisei Brothers Serving Uncle Sam," a title given the article by the WRA, reprinted from "Luzon Victories Gladden Nisei," *Los Angeles Times,* February 10, 1945.

95. "Nisei in the War against Japan," Department of the Interior, WRA (Washington, DC, April 1945), Spicer Collection, MS 042, University of Arizona, Special Collections, Tucson, Arizona.

96. Horn to Glick, July 29, 1944, Leflar Papers, MC 206, Box 3, Folder 16.

97. Community Analysis Trend Report, No. 25, December 15, 1944, Community Analysis Section, Topaz, Roll 8.

98. Ken Yoshida and Kay Yoshida, interview with the author and Nicole Branton, San Mateo, California, May 10, 2002.

99. Saburo Kido to all Community Councils and Block Managers in the camps, August 16, 1944, and JACL press release, "Wrote to Home Town Papers Suggests JACL National Headquarters," August 21, 1944, JERS, MSS 67/14, Reels 83–84.

100. Saburo Kido to Chaplain Masao Yamada, March 30, 1944, RG 210/16, Box 471, Folder 71.505.

101. Merle Eugene Curti, *Roots of American Loyalty* (New York: Columbia University Press, 1946), 191.

102. Horn to Glick, August 19, 1944.

CHAPTER 6

1. Transcript of Proceedings in Criminal Cases, *United States v. Kenchiro Mike Yoshida,* District of Utah Central Division, No. 722, RG 21, Entry 7, Box 87, File 14640, Denver, Colorado; Joe Norikane, Noboru Taguma, Hideo Takeuchi, Ken Yoshida, and Harry Yoshikawa, interview with the author and Peter Taylor, Tucson, Arizona, November 6, 1999.

2. Norikane et al., interview.

3. Ibid.; documents of the Tucsonian reunions, courtesy of Ken Yoshida.

4. Norikane et al., interview; Yosh Kuromiya, interview with Peter Taylor, Tucson, Arizona, November 6, 1999; Takashi Hoshizaki, interview with the author and Peter Taylor, Tucson, Arizona, November 7, 1999.

5. Transcript of Proceedings in Criminal Cases, *United States v. Kenchiro Mike Yoshida,* District of Utah Central Division, No. 722, RG 21, Entry 7, Box 87, File 14640, Denver, Colorado; Norikane et al., interview.

6. Project Attorney's Reports, Poston, Arizona, 1944–1945, Field Basic Documentation; and Leflar Papers, Arkansas; Eric Muller, "A Penny for Their Thoughts: Draft Resistance at the Poston Relocation Center," *Law and Contemporary Problems* 68 (Winter 2004), available at http://ssrn.com/abstract=631183 (accessed February 6, 2011).

7. Muller, "The Minidoka Draft Resisters in a Federal Kangaroo Court," in *Nikkei in the Pacific Northwest,* ed. Louis Fiset and Gail M. Nomura (Seattle: University of Washington Press, 2005), 171–189.

8. Rademaker to Harbison, April 1, 1944, Field Basic Documentation, Community Analysis Reports, Roll 15; Horn to Glick, February 26, 1944, RG 210/16, Box 266, Folder 37.111, No. 4; Rademaker to Harbison, April 1, 1944; "Two Granada Draft Resisters Are Inducted," *Rocky Shimpo,* n.d. (copy courtesy of Joe Norikane); Norikane et al., interview.

9. Ken Yoshida and Kay Yoshida, interview with the author and Nicole Branton, Tucson, Arizona, August 24, 2001; Norikane et al., interview; Kuromiya, interview; Hoshizaki, interview.

10. Dan B. Shields to Attorney General Frances Biddle, December 2, 1944, Criminal Case Files, RG 21, Entry 7, Box 87, File 14641.

11. Rademaker to Spicer, February 22, 1944; Ken Yoshida and Kay Yoshida, interview with the author and Nicole Branton, San Mateo, California, May 10, 2002.

12. Yoshida and Yoshida, interview, 2002.

13. Gordon Hirabayashi, interview with the author, Tucson, Arizona, November 5, 1999; Norikane et al., interview; Frank Emi, personal conversation with the author, Boston, Massachusetts, March 2003; William Hohri, ed., *Resistance: Challenging America's Wartime Internment of Japanese-Americans* (Lomita, CA: Epistolarian, 2001).

14. Nisei, anonymous, July 19, 1944, RG 210/16, Community Analysis Reports, Colorado River, M 1342, Roll 10, Item 145.

15. Rademaker to Spicer, February 22, 1944; Tetsuden Kashima, *Judgment without Trial: Japanese American Imprisonment during World War II* (Seattle: University of Washington, 2003).

16. Yoshida and Yoshida, interview, 2001.

17. Kubo Diary, July 12, 1942, Kubo Collection.

18. Norikane et al., interview.

19. Kubo Diary, July 24, 1944, Kubo Collection.

20. James Omura, "Nisei America: Know the Facts, Let Us Not Be Rash," *Rafu Shimpo*, February 28, 1944.

21. Art Hansen, "The 1944 Nisei Draft at Heart Mountain, Wyoming: Its Relationship to Historical Representation of the World War II Japanese American Evacuation," *Magazine of History* 10, no. 4 (1996), 50.

22. Kubo Diary, July 20, 1944.

23. Hansen, "Peculiar Odyssey: Newsman Jimmie Omura's Removal from and Regeneration within Nikkei Society, History, and Memory," in *Nikkei in the Pacific Northwest*, 286–287.

24. James Omura to Yoshi Kubo, July 21, 1944, Kubo Autograph Book, Kubo Collection.

25. Kubo Diary, 1944–1945.

26. Yoshi Kubo to Shig [*sic*], Trustee Ward, Denver County Jail, November 1, 1944, Kubo Collection.

27. Yenokida and Yoshikawa, interview, 2001.

28. Kubo Diary, November 5, 1944.

29. Yoshida, interview with the author, 2001.

30. Norikane et al., interview; Yenokida and Yoshikawa, interview, 2001.

31. U.S. Department of Commerce, Bureau of Public Roads, *Final Construction Report, Arizona Forest Highway Project 33, Catalina Highway, Coronado National Forest* (Washington, DC: G.P.O., 1951).

32. Susumu Yenokida and Harry Yoshikawa, interview with the author and Nicole Branton, Tucson, Arizona, August 25, 2001.

33. Paul W. Keve, *Prisons and the American Conscience: A History of U.S. Federal Corrections* (Carbondale: Southern Illinois University Press, 1991), 205–208.

34. Kubo Diary, November 16, 1944.

35. "Personality Portraits: 'Sock' Yoshida," *Roadrunner* (November–December 1945): 37; Yenokida and Yoshikawa, interview.

36. Yenokida and Yoshikawa, interview.

37. Ibid.

38. Jack Howard, "Big Gym Show," *Roadrunner* (July–August 1945): 15, 32; Jack Howard, "Sports Review," *Roadrunner* (July–August 1945): 12–14; "Personality Portraits: 'Sock' Yoshida," *Roadrunner* (November–December 1945): 40; Jack Howard, "Sports Review," *Roadrunner* (November–December 1945): 16–19; Norikane et al., interview.

39. Kubo Diary, January 7, 1945.

40. "Philosophical Tidbits," *Roadrunner* (July–August 1945): 34.

41. James Harley, "Editorial," *Roadrunner* (November–December 1945): 4–5.

42. Bill Nagasaki, "Relocation and Its Consequences," *Roadrunner* (November–December 1945), 20–23.

43. Ibid.

44. Kubo Diary, January–March 1945.

45. Yenokida and Yoshikawa, interview.

46. Horn to Ferguson, January 27, 1945, Leflar Papers, MC 206, Box 3, Folder 17.

47. Edward B. Marks to W. Noel Hudson, USO Regional Executive, October 13, 1943, RG 210/16, Box 325, "USO" Folder 61.116.

48. Norikane et al., interview.

49. Ibid.

50. Yenokida and Yoshikawa, interview.

51. Ibid.

52. Ibid.

53. Takashi Fujitani, "Cultures of Resistance: Japanese American Draft Resisters in Transnational Perspective," in *A Matter of Conscience: Essays on the World War II Heart Mountain Draft Resistance Movement,* ed. Mike Mackey (Powell, WY: Western History Publications, 2002), 21–38.

54. Yenokida and Yoshikawa, interview.

55. Ibid.

56. Ibid.; Noboru Taguma, interview with the author and Nicole Branton, Tucson, Arizona, August 26, 2001; Norikane et al., interview.

57. Taguma, interview.

58. Ibid.

59. Ibid.

60. Yoshi Kubo to War Department, n.d., Amache, Colorado, Kubo Collection.

61. Yoshi Kubo to Major Curtright, Western Defense Command, March 22, 1945, Kubo Collection.

62. Enoch E. Ellison to Yoshi Kubo, Turlock, California, January 5, 1959, Kubo Collection.

63. Yoshida and Yoshida, interview, 2001.

64. Ibid.

65. Taguma, interview

66. Yoshida and Yoshida, interview, 2002.

67. Yenokida and Yoshikawa, interview; Valerie Matsumoto, *Farming the Home Place: A Japanese American Community in California, 1919–1982* (Ithaca, NY: Cornell University Press, 1993), 161–168.

68. Matsumoto, *Farming the Home Place.*

69. Bill Hosokawa, *Nisei: The Quiet Americans* (New York: W. Morrow, 1969); Leonard J. Arrington, *The Price of Prejudice: The Japanese-American Relocation Center in Utah during World War II,* 2nd ed. (Delta, UT: Topaz Museum, 1997).

70. Yenokida and Yoshikawa, interview.

71. Matsumoto, *Farming the Home Place,* 161–168.

72. Yenokida and Yoshikawa, interview.

73. Ibid.

74. Matsumoto, *Farming the Home Place,* 135.

75. Dan Kubo, personal conversation with the author, June 20, 2009.

76. Hirabayashi, interview with the author and Nicole Branton, Tucson, Arizona, August 26, 2001.

77. Ibid.

78. Roger Daniels, "Preface," in *A Matter of Conscience: Essays on the World War II Heart Mountain Draft Resistance Movement,* ed. Mike Mackey (Powell, WY: Western History Publications, 2002), 3.

CHAPTER 7

1. "1,523 Draft Evaders Get Truman Pardons," Associated Press, December 23, 1947; "Truman Christmas Pardon Given to Nisei Objectors," *Nichi Bei Times,* December 24, 1947; Executive Order 9814; Presidential Proclamation 2762, December 23, 1947; Amnesty Board's report to the President, Tom C. Clark Papers, Box 66, Truman Presidential Library, Independence, Missouri.

2. "1,523 Draft Evaders Get Truman Pardons."

3. Susumu Yenokida and Harry Yoshikawa, interview with the author and Nicole Branton, Tucson, Arizona, August 25, 2001; Joe Norikane, Noboru Taguma, Hideo Takeuchi, Ken Yoshida, and Harry Yoshikawa, interview with the author and Peter Taylor, Tucson, Arizona, November 6, 1999; miscellaneous documents of the Tucsonians, courtesy of Ken Yoshida.

4. Miscellaneous documents of the Tucsonians, including list of dues collected, courtesy of Ken Yoshida; Ken Yoshida and Kay Yoshida, interview with the author and Nicole Branton, San Mateo, California, May 10, 2002.

5. Ken Yoshida and Kay Yoshida, interview with the author and Nicole Branton, Tucson, Arizona, August 24, 2001.

6. Yoshida and Yoshida, interview, 2002; Joe Norikane, interview with the author and Nicole Branton, San Francisco, California, May 11, 2002.

7. Yoshida and Yoshida, interview, 2001.

8. Miné Okubo, *Citizen 13660* (Seattle: University of Washington Press, 1983 [1946]).

9. Frank F. Chuman, *The Bamboo People: The Law and Japanese-Americans* (Del Mar, CA: Publisher's, Inc., 1976), 174–178.

10. Lyn Crost, *Honor by Fire: Japanese Americans at War in Europe and the Pacific* (Novato, CA: Presidio, 1994); and Michi Weglyn, *Years of Infamy: The Untold Story of America's Concentration Camps* (Seattle: University of Washington Press), 1996.

11. Bill Hosokawa, *Nisei: The Quiet Americans* (New York: W. Morrow, 1969), 417–418.

12. Ibid., 403.

13. Veterans Memorial, Topaz, Utah.

14. National Japanese American Memorial Foundation, Memorial Inscriptions, available at www.njamf.com (accessed December 10, 2005).

15. Gary Y. Okihiro, "Japanese Resistance in America's Concentration Camps: A Reevaluation," *Amerasia Journal* 2 (Fall 1973): 20.

16. Okihiro, "Japanese Resistance in America's Concentration Camps," 20–34.

17. John Christgau, "Collins Versus the World: The Fight to Restore Citizenship to Japanese American Renunciants of World War II," *Pacific Historical Review* 54, no. 1 (1985): 1–31.

18. Tetsuden Kashima, "Japanese American Internees Return, 1945–1955: Readjustment and Social Amnesia," *Phylon* 41, no. 2 (1980): 107–115; Alice Yang Murray, *Histori-*

cal Memories of the Japanese American Internment and the Struggle for Redress (Stanford, CA: Stanford University Press, 2008).

19. Michael Kammen, *Mystic Chords of Memory: The Transformation of Tradition in American Culture* (New York: Knopf, 1991); and Michel-Rolph Trouillot, *Silencing the Past: Power and the Production of History* (Boston: Beacon Press, 1995).

20. Murray, *Historical Memories of the Japanese American Internment and the Struggle for Redress*, 2–4.

21. Japanese Latin Americans were not included in the 1988 Civil Liberties Act, because they did not fall under the categories of U.S.-born citizens and resident aliens of Japanese ancestry. In 1998, Japanese Latin Americans received an official apology and $5,000 payments from the U.S. government for losses incurred due to their internment in the United States. The Campaign for Justice is still working to achieve the same level of redress for Japanese Latin Americans as was given to Japanese Americans.

22. *Lim Report*, available at www.resisters.com (accessed December 10, 2005).

23. *Lim Report*.

24. Okihiro, "Japanese Resistance in America's Concentration Camps."

25. Arthur A. Hansen and David A. Hacker, "The Manzanar Riot: An Ethnic Perspective," *Amerasia Journal* 2, no. 2 (1974): 112–157; and James Hirabayashi, "Nisei: The Quiet American? A Re-evaluation," *Amerasia Journal* 3 (Summer 1975): 114–129. Gary Okihiro continued writing on Japanese American resistance. His subsequent articles include "Tule Lake under Martial Law: A Study in Japanese Resistance," *Journal of Ethnic Studies* 5, no. 3 (1977): 71–85; and "Religion and Resistance in America's Concentration Camps," *Phylon* 45, no. 3 (1984): 220–233.

26. Art Hansen, "Cultural Politics in the Gila River Relocation Center, 1942–1943," *Journal of the Southwest* 27, no. 4 (1985): 327–362.

27. Art Hansen, "The 1944 Nisei Draft at Heart Mountain, Wyoming: Its Relationship to Historical Representation of the World War II Japanese American Evacuation," *Magazine of History* 10, no. 4 (1996): 52.

28. Douglas W. Nelson, *Heart Mountain: The Story of an American Concentration Camp* (Madison: State Historical Society of Wisconsin, 1976); Frank Emi, "Draft Resistance at the Heart Mountain Concentration Camp and the Fair Play Committee," in *Frontiers of Asian American Studies: Writing, Research, Commentary,* ed. Gail M. Nomura et al. (Pullman: Washington State University Press, 1989), 41–69; Frank Emi, "Resistance: The Heart Mountain Fair Play Committee's Fight for Justice," *Amerasia Journal* 17, no. 1 (1991): 47–51; Hansen, "The 1944 Nisei Draft at Heart Mountain, Wyoming"; Mike Mackey, ed., *Remembering Heart Mountain: Essays on Japanese American Internment in Wyoming* (Powell, WY: Western History Publications, 1998); Roger Daniels, "Relocation of Japanese Americans during World War II: The Heart Mountain Experience," *Peace and Change* 23, no. 2 (1998): 117–134; Frank T. Inouye, "Immediate Origins of the Heart Mountain Experience," *Peace and Change* 23, no. 2 (1998): 148–166; William Minoru Hohri, ed., *Resistance: Challenging America's Wartime Internment of Japanese-Americans* (Lomita, CA: Epistolarian, 2000); Frank Chin, *Born in the USA: A Story of Japanese America, 1889–1947* (Lanham, MD: Rowman and Littlefield, 2002); Mike Mackey, ed., *A Matter of Conscience: Essays on the World War II Heart Mountain Draft Resistance Movement* (Powell, WY: Western History Publications, 2002).

29. Ken Nakano, "Draft Resisters Recognized by National JACL in 1990," *Pacific Citizen*, July 2–8, 1999.

30. Ibid.

31. Jim Izumizaki, "A Sacrilegious Comparison," *Pacific Citizen,* February 8, 1991.

32. Clifford Uyeda, as quoted in Thelma Chang, *"I Can Never Forget": Men of the 100th/442nd* (Honolulu, HI: Sigi Productions, 1991), 104.

33. Harry K. Honda, "50 Years Later: Tales of Poignancy," *Pacific Citizen,* February 28, 1992.

34. Nakano, et al., "Draft Resisters Recognized by National JACL in 1990"; Twila Tomita, "Reexamining the Resisters' Resolution," *Pacific Citizen,* July 2–8, 1999.

35. Jeffrey F. Burton, Mary M. Farrell, and Florence B. Lord, *Confinement and Ethnicity: An Overview of World War II Japanese American Relocation Sites* (Tucson: Western Archeological and Conservation Center, U.S. Department of the Interior, 1999).

36. Gordon Hirabayashi Recreation Site, Coronado National Forest, Tucson, Arizona.

37. Kenji Taguma, "The Resister," *National Japanese American Historical Society* (n.d.—copy courtesy of Ken Yoshida).

38. Emiko Omori, *Rabbit in the Moon,* Wabi-Sabi Production (Hohokus, NJ: New Day Films, 1999).

39. Frank Emi, remarks, May 11, 2002, available at www.resisters.com/study/jacl_apology.htm (accessed December 12, 2005).

40. Paul H. Ito to Helen Kawagoe, February 24, 1997, courtesy of Ken Yoshida.

41. Gary Okihiro, *Margins and Mainstreams: Asians in American History and Culture* (Seattle: University of Washington Press, 1994); Japanese American National Museum, "Whose America? Who's American? Diversity, Civil Liberties, and Social Justice," Hyatt Regency, Denver, Colorado, July 3–6, 2008, available at www.janm.org/projects/ec/conference (accessed January 23, 2011); Japanese American National Museum, "Enduring Communities: The Japanese American Experience in Arizona, Colorado, New Mexico, Texas, and Utah," available at www.janm.org/projects/ec (accessed January 23, 2011).

CONCLUSION

1. Michael C. C. Adams, *The Best War Ever: America and World War II* (Baltimore, MD: Johns Hopkins University Press, 1993).

2. Rogers Smith, *Civic Ideals: Conflicting Visions of Citizenship in U.S. History* (New Haven, CT: Yale University Press, 1997).

3. T. J. Jackson Lears, "The Concept of Cultural Hegemony: Problems and Possibilities," *American Historical Review* 90, no. 3 (1985): 567–593.

4. *Regan v. King, Registrar,* 319 U.S. 753 (May 17, 1943); *U.S. v. Wong Kim Ark* (1898); *In re Tetsubumi Yano's Estate,* 188 Cal. 645 (1922); *Morrison v. California,* 291 U.S. 82 (1943); "Nisei Citizenship Rights Upheld by Court," *Pacific Citizens,* February 25, 1943.

5. *Kawakita v. United States,* 343 U.S. 717 (1952).

6. *Afroyim v. Rusk,* 387 U.S. 253 (1967).

7. Theda Skocpol, *Protecting Soldiers and Mothers: The Political Origins of Social Policy in the United States* (Cambridge, MA: Harvard University Press, 1992).

8. James C. Scott, *Weapons of the Weak: Everyday Forms of Peasant Resistance* (New Haven, CT: Yale University Press, 1985).

9. John P. Diggins, "Civil Disobedience in American Political Thought," in *Making America: The Society and Culture of the United States,* ed. Luther S. Luedtke (Chapel Hill: University of North Carolina Press, 1992), 453–454.

10. Michel Foucault, *Discipline and Punish: The Birth of the Prison* (New York: Vintage Books, 1979).

11. Alessandro Portelli, *The Order Has Been Carried Out: History, Memory, and Meaning of a Nazi Massacre in Rome* (New York: Palgrave Macmillan, 2003).

12. Karen L. Ishizuka, *Lost and Found: Reclaiming the Japanese American Incarceration* (Chicago: University of Illinois Press, 2006); Michael Frisch, *A Shared Authority: Essays on the Craft and Meaning of Oral and Public History* (New York: State University of New York, 1990).

BIBLIOGRAPHY

❦

ORAL HISTORY INTERVIEWS

Barnett, Arthur. Interview with Mr. Goto [sic], n.d., Arthur G. Barnett Papers, MS 1598-4, Special Collections, University of Washington, Box 1, Folder 6.

Hirabayashi, Gordon. Interview with the author. Tucson, Arizona, November 5, 1999.

———. Interview with the author and Nicole Branton. Tucson, Arizona, August 26, 2001.

———. Interview with Roger Daniels, Seattle, Washington, February 10, 1981; and interview with Louis Horn, Kirkland, Washington, 1990, 1981–1990, MS 3159, Special Collections, University of Washington, Seattle, Washington.

Hoshizaki, Takashi. Interview with the author and Peter Taylor. Tucson, Arizona, November 7, 1999.

Kuromiya, Yosh. Interview with Peter Taylor. Tucson, Arizona, November 8, 1999.

Norikane, Joe. Interview with the author and Nicole Branton. San Francisco, California, May 11, 2002.

Norikane, Joe, Noboru Taguma, Hideo Takeuchi, Ken Yoshida, and Harry Yoshikawa. Interview with the author and Peter Taylor. Tucson, Arizona, November 6, 1999.

Taguma, Noboru. Interview with the author and Nicole Branton. Tucson, Arizona, August 26, 2001.

Yenokida, Susumu, and Harry Yoshikawa. Interview with the author and Nicole Branton. Tucson, Arizona, August 25, 2001.

Yoshida, Ken, and Kay Yoshida. Interview with the author and Nicole Branton. Tucson, Arizona, August 24, 2001.

———. Interview with the author and Nicole Branton. San Mateo, California, May 10, 2002.

ARCHIVAL COLLECTIONS

American Civil Liberties Union. Special Collections, University of Washington, Seattle, Washington.

American Civil Liberties Union Collection. Princeton University. Access provided by Special Collections, University of Washington, Seattle, Washington.

Barnett, Arthur G. Papers, MS 1598. Special Collections, University of Washington, Seattle, Washington.

Barnhart Papers. Special Collections, University of Arkansas, Fayetteville, Arkansas.
Clark, Tom C. Papers. Truman Presidential Library, Independence, Missouri.
Densho Digital Archives. *Densho: The Japanese American Legacy Project,* http://densho.org.
Fisher Files. Bancroft Library, University of California, Berkeley, California.
Harada Family Collection. Riverside Metropolitan Museum, Riverside, California.
Hirabayashi, Gordon K. Papers. Special Collections, University of Washington, Seattle, Washington.
Japanese American Citizens League. Bancroft Library, University of California, Berkeley, California.
Kautz Family YMCA Archives. University of Minnesota Libraries, Minneapolis, Minnesota.
Kubo Collection, Turlock, California.
Leflar Papers. Special Collections, University of Arkansas, Fayetteville, Arkansas.
Menin, Samuel David. Papers. Auraria Library Archives and Special Collections, Denver, Colorado.
Ring Family Papers. Special Collections, University of Washington, Seattle, Washington.
Spicer, Edward. War Relocation Authority Collection. Special Collections, University of Arizona, Tucson, Arizona.
Walters, Frank L. Papers. Special Collections, University of Washington, Seattle, Washington.
War Relocation Authority Collection. Bancroft Library, University of California, Berkeley, California.
Yoshida Collection, San Mateo, California.

NATIONAL ARCHIVES AND RECORDS ADMINISTRATION RECORD GROUPS

RG 21, Records of the District Courts of the United States, Denver, Colorado, and Seattle, Washington.
RG 60, General Records of the Department of Justice, College Park, Maryland.
RG 65, Records of the Federal Bureau of Investigation, College Park, Maryland.
RG 107, Office of the Secretary of War, College Park, Maryland.
RG 129, Bureau of Prisons Records, College Park, Maryland.
RG 210, Records of the War Relocation Authority, Washington, D.C.
RG 389, Office of the Provost Marshal General, College Park, Maryland.

OTHER PRIMARY DOCUMENTS

Roadrunner (July–August 1945 and November–December 1945), courtesy of Ken Yoshida.
Trek and *All Aboard* (1942–1944), available at http://digital.lib.usu.edu/cdm/landingpage/collection/Topaz (accessed June 19, 2011).
U.S. Department of Commerce, Bureau of Public Roads, *Final Construction Report, Arizona Forest Highway Project 33, Catalina Highway, Coronado National Forest* (Washington, DC: GPO, 1951).

SECONDARY SOURCES

Abe, Frank. *Conscience and the Constitution.* Hohokus, NJ: Transit Media, 2000.
Adams, Michael C. C. *The Best War Ever: America and World War II.* Baltimore, MD: Johns Hopkins University Press, 1993.
Altbach, Philip G. "The International Student Movement." *Journal of Contemporary History* 5 (1970): 156–174.

Arrington, Leonard J. *The Price of Prejudice: The Japanese-American Relocation Center in Utah during World War II*, second edition. Delta, UT: Topaz Museum, 1997.

Azuma, Eiichiro. *Between Two Empires: Race, History, and Transnationalism in Japanese America*. New York: Oxford University Press, 2005.

Bell, Reginald. *Public School Education of Second-Generation Japanese in California*. New York: Arno Press, [1935] 1978.

Boris, Eileen. "The Racialized Gendered State: Constructions of Citizenship in the United States." *Social Politics* 2 (Summer 1995): 160–180.

Burton, Jeffrey F., Mary M. Farrell, and Florence B. Lord. *Confinement and Ethnicity: An Overview of World War II Japanese American Relocation Sites*. Tucson, AZ: Western Archeological and Conservation Center, U.S. Department of the Interior, 1999.

Castelnuovo, Shirley. *Soldiers of Conscience: Japanese American Military Resisters in World War II*. Lincoln: University of Nebraska Press, 2010.

Chin, Frank. *Born in the USA: A Story of Japanese America, 1889–1947*. Lanham, MD: Rowman and Littlefield, 2002.

Christgau, John. "Collins Versus the World: The Fight to Restore Citizenship to Japanese American Renunciants of World War II." *Pacific Historical Review* 54, no. 1 (1985): 1–31.

Chuman, Frank F. *The Bamboo People: The Law and Japanese-Americans*. Del Mar, CA: Publisher's, Inc., 1976.

Collins, Donald E. *Native American Aliens: Disloyalty and the Renunciation of Citizenship by Japanese Americans during World War II*. Westport, CT: Greenwood Press, 1985.

Commission on Wartime Relocation and Internment of Civilians (CWRIC), *Personal Justice Denied*, foreword by Tetsuden Kashima. Seattle: University of Washington Press, 1997.

Crost, Lyn. *Honor by Fire: Japanese Americans at War in Europe and the Pacific*. Novato, CA: Presidio, 1994.

Daniels, Roger, ed. *American Concentration Camps, Volume 9, June 1942–May 1944, Raising Japanese American Troops*. New York: Garland, 1989.

———. *Concentration Camps USA: Japanese Americans and World War II*. New York: Holt, Rinehart and Winston, 1971.

———. *The Politics of Prejudice: The Anti-Japanese Movement in California and the Struggle for Japanese Exclusion*. Berkeley: University of California Press, 1977.

———. *Prisoners without Trial: Japanese Americans in World War II*, revised edition. New York: Hill and Wang, 2004.

———. "Relocation of Japanese Americans during World War II: The Heart Mountain Experience." *Peace and Change* 23, no. 2 (1998): 117–134.

———. "Words Do Matter," *Discover Nikkei*, February 1, 2008, available at www.discover nikkei.org/en/journal/2008/2/1/words-do-matter (accessed June 10, 2011).

De Nevers, Klancy Clark. *The Colonel and the Pacifist: Karl Bendetsen, Perry Saito and the Incarceration of Japanese Americans during World War II*. Salt Lake City: University of Utah Press, 2004.

Diggins, John P. "Civil Disobedience in American Political Thought." In *Making America: The Society and Culture of the United States*. Edited by Luther S. Luedtke, 453–454. Chapel Hill: University of North Carolina Press, 1992.

Eller, Cynthia. *Conscientious Objectors and the Second World War: Moral and Religious Arguments in Support of Pacifism*. New York: Greenwood Publishers, 1991.

Emi, Frank. "Draft Resistance at the Heart Mountain Concentration Camp and the Fair Play Committee." In *Frontiers of Asian American Studies: Writing, Research, Commentary*. Edited by Gail M. Nomura, Russell Endo, Stephen H. Sumida, and Russell Leong, 41–69. Pullman: Washington State University Press, 1989.

———. "Resistance: The Heart Mountain Fair Play Committee's Fight for Justice." *Amerasia Journal* 17, no. 1 (1991): 47–51.

Fine, Sidney. "Mr. Justice Murphy and the Hirabayashi Case." *Pacific Historical Review* 33 (May 1964): 195–209.

Fiset, Louis, and Gail M. Nomura, eds. *Nikkei in the Pacific Northwest: Japanese Americans and Japanese Canadians in the Twentieth Century.* Seattle: University of Washington Press, 2005.

Foucault, Michel. *Discipline and Punish: The Birth of the Prison.* New York: Vintage Books, 1979.

Frazer, Heather T., and John O'Sullivan. *"We Have Just Begun to Not Fight": An Oral History of Conscientious Objectors in Civilian Public Service during World War II.* New York: Twayne Publishers, 1996.

Frisch, Michael. *A Shared Authority: Essays on the Craft and Meaning of Oral and Public History.* New York: State University of New York Press, 1990.

Fugita, Stephen S., and Marilyn Fernandez. *Altered Lives, Enduring Community: Japanese Americans Remember Their World War II Incarceration.* Seattle: University of Washington Press, 2004.

Fujitani, Takashi. "Cultures of Resistance: Japanese American Draft Resisters in Transnational Perspective." In *A Matter of Conscience: Essays on the World War II Heart Mountain Draft Resistance Movement.* Edited by Mike Mackey, 21–38. Powell, WY: Western History Publications, 2002.

Gaines, Brian J., and Wendy K. Tam Cho. "On California's 1920 Alien Land Law: The Psychology and Economics of Racial Discrimination." *State Politics and Policy Quarterly* 4, no. 3 (2004): 271–293.

Gara, Larry, and Lenna Mae Gara, eds. *A Few Small Candles: War Resisters of World War II Tell Their Stories.* Kent, OH: Kent State University Press, 1999.

Goosen, Rachel Waltner. *Women against the Good War: Conscientious Objection and Gender on the American Homefront, 1941–1947.* Chapel Hill: University of North Carolina Press, 1997.

Guardino, Peter. *Peasants, Politics, and the Formation of Mexico's National State: Guerrero, 1800–1857.* Stanford: Stanford University Press, 1996.

Haney López, Ian F. *White by Law: The Legal Construction of Race.* New York: New York University Press, 1996.

Hansen, Art. "Cultural Politics in the Gila River Relocation Center, 1942–1943." *Journal of the Southwest* 27, no. 4 (1985): 327–362.

———. "The 1944 Nisei Draft at Heart Mountain, Wyoming: Its Relationship to Historical Representation of the World War II Japanese American Evacuation." *Magazine of History* 10, no. 4 (1996): 48–60.

———. "Peculiar Odyssey: Newsman Jimmie Omura's Removal from a Regeneration within Nikkei Society, History, and Memory." In *Nikkei in the Pacific Northwest: Japanese Americans and Japanese Canadians in the Twentieth Century.* Edited by Louis Fiset and Gail M. Nomura, 278–307. Seattle: University of Washington Press, 2005.

Hansen, Arthur A., and David A. Hacker. "The Manzanar Riot: An Ethnic Perspective." *Amerasia Journal* 2, no. 2 (1974): 112–157.

Hatamiya, Leslie T. *Righting a Wrong: Japanese Americans and the Passage of the Civil Liberties Act of 1988.* Stanford: Stanford University Press, 1993.

Hayashi, Brian Masaru. *Democratizing the Enemy: The Japanese American Internment.* Princeton, NJ: Princeton University Press, 2004.

Hershberger, G. L. *The Development of the Federal Prison System.* Washington, DC: U.S. Government Printing Office, 1979.

Herzig-Yoshinaga, Aiko. "Words Can Lie or Clarify: Terminology of the World War II

Incarceration of Japanese Americans," *Discover Nikkei*, February 2, 2010, available at www.discovernikkei.org/en/journal/article/3246 (accessed June 19, 2011).

Hirabayashi, Gordon. "Am I an American?" In *The Courage of Their Convictions: Sixteen Americans Who Fought Their Way to the Supreme Court*. Edited by Peter Irons, 50–51. New York: Penguin Books, 1990.

Hirabayashi, James. "Four Hirabayashi Cousins: A Question of Identity." In *Nikkei in the Pacific Northwest*. Edited by Louis Fiset and Gail M. Nomura, 146–170. Seattle: University of Washington Press, 2005.

———. "Nisei: The Quiet American? A Re-evaluation." *Amerasia Journal* 3 (Summer 1975): 114–129.

Hirabayashi, Lane Ryo. *The Politics of Fieldwork: Research in an American Concentration Camp*. Tucson: University of Arizona Press, 1999.

Hohri, William Minoru. *Repairing American: An Account of the Movement for Japanese-American Redress*. Pullman: Washington State University Press, 1987.

———, ed. *Resistance: Challenging America's Wartime Internment of Japanese-Americans*. Lomita, CA: Epistolarian, 2001.

Hosokawa, Bill. *Nisei: The Quiet Americans*. New York: W. Morrow, 1969.

Ichihashi, Yamato. *Japanese Immigration: Its Status in California*. San Francisco: R and E Research Associates, [1913] 1970.

———. *Japanese in the United States*. New York: Arno Press, [1932] 1969.

Ichioka, Yuji. *Before Internment: Essays in Prewar Japanese American History*. Edited by Gordon H. Chang and Eiichiro Azuma. Stanford, CA: Stanford University Press, 2006.

———. "A Study in Dualism: James Yoshinori Sakamoto and the *Japanese American Courier*, 1928–1942." *Amerasia Journal* 13 (1986–1987): 49–81.

———, ed. *Views from Within: The Japanese American Evacuation and Resettlement Study*. Los Angeles: Asian American Studies Center, UCLA, 1989.

Inouye, Frank T. "Immediate Origins of the Heart Mountain Experience." *Peace and Change* 23, no. 2 (1998): 148–166.

Irons, Peter. *Justice at War*. New York: Oxford University Press, 1983.

———. *Justice Delayed: The Record of the Japanese American Internment Cases*. Middleton, CT: Wesleyan University Press, 1989.

Ishizuka, Karen L. *Lost and Found: Reclaiming the Japanese American Incarceration*. Chicago: University of Illinois Press, 2006.

Iyenaga, Toyokichi, and Kenoske Sato. *Japan and the California Problem*. New York: G. P. Putnam's Sons, 1921.

Jacobs, J. B. *New Perspectives on Prisons and Imprisonment*. Ithaca, NY: Cornell University Press, 1983.

Janoski, Thomas. *Citizenship and Civil Society: A Framework for Rights and Obligations in Liberal, Traditional, and Social Democratic Regimes*. New York: Cambridge University Press, 1998.

Johnson, Judith R. *The Penitentiaries of Arizona, Nevada, New Mexico and Utah*. Lewiston, NY: Mellen Press, 1997.

Kammen, Michael. *Mystic Chords of Memory: The Transformation of Tradition in American Culture*. New York: Knopf, 1991.

Kanzaki, Kiichi. *California and the Japanese*. San Francisco: R and E Research Associates, [1921] 1971.

Kashima, Tetsuden. "Japanese American Internees Return, 1945–1955: Readjustment and Social Amnesia." *Phylon* 41, no. 2 (1980): 107–115.

———. *Judgment without Trial: Japanese American Imprisonment during World War II*. Seattle: University of Washington, 2003.

Kawai, Kazua. "Three Roads." *Survey Graphic* 56, no. 3 (May 1, 1926).

Kawakami, Kiyoshi K. *The Real Japanese Question*. New York: Arno Press, [1921] 1978.

Kerber, Linda. "The Meanings of Citizenship." *Journal of American History* 84 (December 1997): 833–854.

———. *No Constitutional Right to Be Ladies: Women and the Obligation of Citizenship*. New York: Hill and Wang, 1998.

Keve, Paul W. *Prisons and the American Conscience: A History of U.S. Federal Corrections*. Carbondale: Southern Illinois University Press, 1991.

Knaefler, Tomi Kaizawa. *Our House Divided: Seven Japanese American Families in World War II*. Honolulu: University of Hawaii Press, 1991.

Kurashige, Lon. "Resistance, Collaboration, and Manzanar Protest." *Pacific Historical Review* 70, no. 3 (2001): 387–417.

Kurashige, Scott. *The Shifting Grounds of Race: Black and Japanese Americans in the Making of Multiethnic Los Angeles*. Princeton, NJ: Princeton University Press, 2007.

Lai, Him Mark. "Teaching Chinese Americans to Be Chinese." In *Chinese American Transnationalism: The Flow of People, Resources, and Ideas between China and America during the Exclusion Era*. Edited by Sucheng Chan, 194–210. Philadelphia, PA: Temple University Press, 2006.

Lears, T. J. Jackson. "The Concept of Cultural Hegemony: Problems and Possibilities." *American Historical Review* 90, no. 3 (1985): 567–593.

Lichtenstein, Alex. "Good Roads and Chain Gangs in the Progressive South: 'The Negro Convict is a Slave.'" *Journal of Southern History* 59 (February 1993): 85–110.

Lyman, Stanford M. *Militarism, Imperialism, and Racial Accommodation: An Analysis and Interpretation of the Early Writings of Robert E. Park*. Fayetteville: University of Arkansas Press, 1992.

Mackey, Mike, ed. *A Matter of Conscience: Essays on the World War II Heart Mountain Draft Resistance Movement*. Powell, WY: Western History Publications, 2002.

———, ed. *Remembering Heart Mountain: Essays on Japanese American Internment in Wyoming*. Powell, WY: Western History Publications, 1998.

Maki, Mitchell, Harry H. L. Kitano, and S. Megan Berthold. *Achieving the Impossible Dream: How Japanese Americans Obtained Redress*. Urbana: University of Illinois Press, 1999.

Mallon, Florencia. *Peasant and Nation: The Making of Postcolonial Mexico and Peru*. Berkeley: University of California Press, 1995.

Marshall, T. H. *Citizenship and Social Class*. Cambridge, UK: Cambridge University Press, 1952.

Matsumoto, Valerie. *Farming the Home Place: A Japanese American Community in California, 1919–1982*. Ithaca, NY: Cornell University Press, 1993.

McClain, Charles, ed. *Chinese Immigrants and American Law*. New York: Garland Publishing, 1994.

———. *The Mass Internment of Japanese Americans and the Quest for Legal Redress*. New York: Garland Publishing, 1994.

McKelvey, Blake. "Penology in the Westward Movement." *Pacific Historical Review* 2 (December 1933): 418–438.

McWilliams, Carey. "Dual Citizenship," *Far Eastern Survey* 11, no. 23 (1942): 231–233.

———. *Factories and the Field: The Story of Migratory Farm Labor in California*. Berkeley: University of California Press, 1939.

Modell, John. *Into One's Own: From Youth to Adulthood in the United States, 1920–1975*. Berkeley: University of California Press, 1989.

Muller, Eric. *American Inquisition: The Hunt for Japanese American Disloyalty in World War II*. Chapel Hill: University of North Carolina Press, 2007.

———. *Free to Die for Their Country: The Story of Japanese American Draft Resisters during World War II*. Chicago: University of Chicago Press, 2001.

———. "The Minidoka Draft Resisters in a Federal Kangaroo Court." In *Nikkei in the Pacific Northwest*. Edited by Louis Fiset and Gail M. Nomura, 171–189. Seattle: University of Washington Press, 2005.

———. "A Penny for Their Thoughts: Draft Resistance at the Poston Relocation Center." *Law and Contemporary Problems* 68 (Winter 2004), available at http://ssrn.com/abstract=631183 (accessed February 6, 2011).

Murray, Alice Yang. *Historical Memories of the Japanese American Internment and the Struggle for Redress*. Stanford: Stanford University Press, 2008.

Nagata, Donna K. *Legacy of Injustice: Exploring the Cross-Generational Impact of the Japanese American Internment*. New York: Plenum Press, 1993.

Nelson, Douglas W. *Heart Mountain: The Story of an American Concentration Camp*. Madison: State Historical Society of Wisconsin, 1976.

Ngai, Mae. "The Architecture of Race in American Immigration Law: A Reexamination of the Immigration Act of 1924." *Journal of American History* 86, no. 1 (June 1999): 67–92.

———. *Impossible Subjects: Illegal Aliens and the Making of Modern America*. Princeton, NJ: Princeton University Press, 2004.

Okihiro, Gary Y. "Japanese Resistance in America's Concentration Camps: A Re-evaluation." *Amerasia Journal* 2 (Fall 1973): 20–34.

———. *Margins and Mainstreams: Asians in American History and Culture*. Seattle: University of Washington Press, 1994.

———. "Religion and Resistance in America's Concentration Camps." *Phylon* 45, no. 3 (1984): 220–233.

———. "Tule Lake under Martial Law: A Study in Japanese Resistance." *Journal of Ethnic Studies* 5, no. 3 (1977): 71–85.

Okubo, Miné. *Citizen 13660*. Seattle: University of Washington Press, 1983 [1946].

Park, Robert. "Our Racial Frontier on the Pacific." *Survey Graphic* 56 (May 1926): 192–196.

Pascoe, Peggy. "Miscegenation Law, Court Cases, and Ideologies of 'Race' in Twentieth-Century America." *Journal of American History* 83, no. 1 (1996): 44–69.

———. *What Comes Naturally: Miscegenation Law and the Making of Race in America*. New York: Oxford University Press, 2009.

Peterson, Patti McGill. "Student Organizations and the Antiwar Movement in America, 1900–1960." *American Studies* (1972), available at https://journals.ku.edu/index.php/amerstud/article/viewFile/2416/2375 (accessed February 6, 2011).

Portelli, Alessandro. *The Order Has Been Carried Out: History, Memory, and Meaning of a Nazi Massacre in Rome*. New York: Palgrave Macmillan, 2003.

Robinson, Greg. *By Order of the President: FDR and the Internment of Japanese Americans*. Cambridge, MA: Harvard University Press, 2001.

———. *A Tragedy of Democracy: Japanese American Confinement in North America*. New York: Columbia University Press, 2009.

Rothman, David J. *Conscience and Convenience: The Asylum and Its Alternatives in Progressive America*, revised edition. New York: Aldine de Gruyter, 2002.

Ruiz, Vicki. *From Out of the Shadows: Mexican Women in Twentieth-Century America*. New York: Oxford University Press, 2008.

Sandifer, Durward V. "A Comparative Study of Laws Relating to Nationality at Birth and to Loss of Nationality." *American Journal of International Law* 29 (1935): 248–279.

Schonberger, Howard. "Dilemmas of Loyalty: Japanese Americans and the Psychological Warfare Campaigns of the Office of Strategic Services, 1943–45." *Amerasia Journal* 16, no. 1 (1990): 21–39.

Scott, James C. *Weapons of the Weak: Everyday Forms of Peasant Resistance*. New Haven, CT: Yale University Press, 1985.

Skocpol, Theda. *Protecting Soldiers and Mothers: The Political Origins of Social Policy in the United States.* Cambridge, MA: Harvard University Press, 1992.

Smith, Page. *Democracy on Trial: The Japanese-American Evacuation and Relocation in World War II.* New York: Simon and Schuster, 1995.

Smith, Rogers. *Civic Ideals: Conflicting Visions of Citizenship in U.S. History.* New Haven, CT: Yale University Press, 1997.

Spicer, Edward, Asael Hansen, Katherine Luomala, and Marvin K. Opler. *Impounded People: Japanese-Americans in the Relocation Centers.* Tucson: University of Arizona Press, 1970.

Spickard, Paul R. *Japanese Americans: The Formations and Transformations of an Ethnic Group.* New York: Twayne Publishers, 1996.

———. "The Nisei Assume Power: The Japanese-American Citizens League, 1941–1942." *Pacific Historical Review* 52 (May 1983): 147–174.

Starn, Orin. "Engineering Internment: Anthropologists and the War Relocation Authority." *American Ethnologist* 13 (November 1986): 700–720.

Strong, Edward K. *The Second-Generation Japanese Problem.* Stanford, CA: Stanford University Press, 1934.

Strong, Edward K., and Reginald Bell. *Vocational Aptitudes of Second-Generation Japanese in the United States.* Stanford, CA: Stanford University Press, 1933.

Suzuki, Peter T. "Anthropologists in the Wartime Camps for Japanese Americans: A Documentary Study." *Dialectical Anthropology* 6 (August 1981): 23–60.

Tamura, Eileen. *Americanization, Acculturation, and Ethnic Identity: The Nisei Generation in Hawaii.* Urbana: University of Illinois Press, 1994.

Tateishi, John, ed. *And Justice for All: An Oral History of the Japanese Detention Camps.* New York: Random House, 1984.

Taylor, Sandra. *Jewel of the Desert: Japanese American Internment at Topaz.* Berkeley: University of California Press, 1993.

tenBroek, Jacobus, Edward N. Barnhart, and Floyd W. Matson. *Prejudice, War and the Constitution.* Berkeley: University of California Press, 1954.

Thomas, Dorothy Swaine, and Richard S. Nishimoto. *The Salvage: Japanese American Relocation and Resettlement.* Berkeley: University of California Press, 1946.

Thurner, Mark. *From Two Republics to One Divided: Contradictions of Postcolonial Nationmaking in Andean Peru.* Durham, NC: Duke University Press, 1997.

Trouillot, Michel-Rolph. *Silencing the Past: Power and the Production of History.* Boston, MA: Beacon Press, 1995.

Van Nuys, Frank. *Americanizing the West: Race, Immigrants, and Citizenship, 1890–1930.* Lawrence: University Press of Kansas, 2002.

Varzally, Allison. *Making a Non-white America: Californians Coloring outside Ethnic Lines, 1925–1955.* Berkeley: University of California Press, 2008.

Waugh, Isami Arifuku, Alex Yamato, and Raymond Y. Okamura. "Japanese Americans in California." In *Five Views: An Ethnic Historic Site Survey for California* (Sacramento: State of California, Department of Parks and Recreation, Office of Historic Preservation, 1988), available at www.nps.gov/history/history/online_books/5views/5views4.htm (accessed June 19, 2011).

Weglyn, Michi. *Years of Infamy: The Untold Story of America's Concentration Camps.* Seattle: University of Washington Press, 1996.

West, Eliot, and Paula Evans Petrik, eds. *Small Worlds: Children and Adolescents in America, 1850–1950.* Lawrence: University of Kansas Press, 1992.

Yoo, David K. *Growing Up Nisei: Race, Generation, and Culture among Japanese Americans of California, 1924–49.* Urbana: University of Illinois Press, 2000.

Yu, Henry. *Thinking Orientals: Migration, Contact, and Exoticism in Modern America.* New York: Oxford University Press, 2001.

Yung, Judy. *Unbound Feet: A Social History of Chinese Women in San Francisco*. Berkeley: University of California Press, 1995.

Zald, Mayer N., and Patricia Denton. "From Evangelism to General Service: The Transformation of the YMCA." *Administrative Science Quarterly* 8 (September 1963): 214–234.

Zelko, Frank S. *Generation, Culture and Prejudice: The Japanese American Decision to Cooperate with Evacuation and Internment during World War II*. Melbourne, Australia: Monash University Publications in History, 1992.

Zimmerman, Jane. "The Penal Reform Movement in the South During the Progressive Era, 1890–1917." *Journal of Southern History* 17, no. 4 (1951): 462–492.

Zolberg, Aristide. *A Nation by Design: Immigration Policy in the Fashioning of America*. Cambridge, MA: Harvard University Press, 2006.

INDEX

CHERSTIN M. LYON is Assistant Professor of History, California State University, San Bernardino.